PIERO

EDMOND BAUDOIN was born in Nice in 1942. As a
young man he was an accountant and he didn't start
drawing comics professionally until his late thirties.
After having some short work published in magazines he
had his first book published in 1981. He has gone on to be
a prolific author and a guiding light of contemporary
comics, having won prizes at the Angoulême Comics
Festival for his books *Couma acò* (best album, 1992) and
Le Voyage (best script, 1997). In addition to his output of
autobiographical albums he has also branched out into
children's books, illustrated editions of classic works of
world fiction, and live drawing performances in collaboration with dancers and musicians. Most recently he
published a science fiction graphic novel co-written with
the celebrated French mathematician Cedric Villani.
When he is not traveling for book fairs and residencies,
Baudoin divides his time between Paris and Villars-sur-
Vars, the town outside Nice where he grew up.

MATT MADDEN is a translator and cartoonist. He is the
author of *99 Ways to Tell a Story: Exercises in Style*, which is
a comics adaptation of Raymond Queneau's *Exercises in
Style*, and of two textbooks co-written with his wife, Jessica
Abel, *Drawing Words & Writing Pictures* and *Mastering
Comics*. Madden and Abel were series editors of *The Best
American Comics* for six years. He lives in Philadelphia.

THIS IS A NEW YORK REVIEW COMIC
PUBLISHED BY THE NEW YORK REVIEW OF BOOKS
435 Hudson Street, New York, NY 10014
www.nyrb.com

First published by Éditions du Seuil, 1998.
Cover image by Piero.

Cet ouvrage a bénéficié du soutien des Programmes d'aide à la publication de l'Institut français.

A catalog record for this book is available from the Library of Congress

ISBN 978-1-68137-296-9
Available as an electronic book; 978-1-68137-297-6

Printed in China
10 9 8 7 6 5 4 3 2 1

BAUDOIN

Piero

TRANSLATED AND WITH
AN INTRODUCTION BY

MATT MADDEN

ENGLISH LETTERING BY

DEAN SUDARSKY

NEW YORK REVIEW COMICS · *New York*

INTRODUCTION

EDMOND BAUDOIN is a force of nature who holds a singular position in the French comics scene. An ink-stained Proust, his drawings and his memory keep bringing him back to the small, southern French village of his youth as well as the nearby city of Nice, on the Mediterranean coast. In many of his books you see the same woodland paths, the same barren views of Nice harbor, the same faces: his own adolescent self, his parents, his brother...

He came to cartooning relatively late in life—his first "album" (as the French call their bound comic books) wasn't published until he was forty years old, in the early 1980s. From his earliest works, Baudoin focused on autobiography, making him one of the first French cartoonists to explore this domain, which has gone on to become one of the most prominent features of European literary comics. At the same time, his art—already confident, with an inky expressionist manner reminiscent of his contemporaries Jacques Tardi or José Muñoz— evolved quickly into a daringly loose, calligraphic brush style which has made him one of the most respected and recognizable cartoonists in Europe.

After his first few albums, Étienne Robial—the legendary graphic designer and co-founder, along with Florence Cestac, of Futuropolis, one of France's most influential independent publishers—prodded Baudoin to break with traditional narrative structure. Shortly thereafter, an epiphanic Miles Davis concert gave the cartoonist the courage to start improvising in his work by introducing digressions, elements of collage, and post-modern authorial interruptions. Books like *Un flip Coca!* and *Un rubis sur les lèvres* are full of jarring juxtapositions and shifts in style. A few years later, *Couma acò* harnessed this jazzy improvised style to the form of a more classical family memoir, a template he has returned to numerous times, notably in the book you are now reading. *Couma acò* was also his first big critical breakthrough, winning him the prize for best album of the year at the Angoulême Comics Festival in 1992. He would go on to win two scriptwriting awards: for *Le Voyage* in 1997 and for *Les Quatres Fleuves* (in collaboration with the mystery writer Fred Vargas) in 2002.

Baudoin's focus on everyday life, his unconventional drawing, and his philosophical, self-questioning approach to memoir set him apart from better-known contemporaries like Tardi or Jacques Loustal. He had to wait another decade or so before a new generation of artists and publishers, centering around the Parisian publishing collective L'Association, would claim him as one of their own, making of him a crucial bridge between their punk, DIY new comics wave and the more classicist auteurs Baudoin came up with. He remains much admired and respected by both camps to this day.

At age seventy-six he continues producing books and drawings at a furious rate, giving lie to the maxim that comics is "a young man's game," as R. Crumb has said (himself another septuagenarian who still cranks out a two-hundred-page book when he feels like it). Speaking of Crumb, it was he and Aline Kominsky who gave Americans their first taste of Baudoin's work some twenty years ago in the last issue of their anthology *Weirdo*—an issue put together from the Crumb's new home in southern France, with the English title of the issue, "weirdo," replaced by the phonetically Frenchified *Verre d'eau*.

To some extent, *Piero* stands apart in Baudoin's œuvre. It was commissioned by a short-lived comics imprint of Seuil Jeunesse, the young-adult wing of a major French publisher, in an attempt (alongside many other mainstream publishers at the time) to repeat the success L'Association was having then with its simple-yet-elegant paperback comic books. In that period, L'Association managed to retain their artistic credibility while also publishing the occasional bestseller like Emmanuel Guibert's *La Guerre d'Alan* and, most notably, Marjane Satrapi's blockbuster hit *Persepolis*. Inspired by this model, Seuil put out a series of trade paperback–sized comics, nominally destined for young adult readers, made by authors poached from this burgeoning French indie scene. Baudoin created *Piero* and one other book for them, a fable about a young boy living in Nice called *Mat*, before the imprint shut down. (The books have since been reissued in France by the publisher Gallimard.)

To readers familiar with Baudoin's work, what's most unusual about *Piero* is that it does not feature his trademark virtuosic brush art. Instead, he opts for the busy, scratching and scribbling lines of a Rotring ArtPen, presumably in order to emulate the ballpoint pens and pencils with which the young protagonists are constantly drawing. Perhaps he also aims to create a sense of intimacy in this smaller-than-usual format (a typical French album is about 8" by 12"), much the way Art Spiegelman chose to draw the art for his book Maus at the actual size it would be printed, instead of drawing the original art half again or twice as large—a common technique cartoonists use to make their art look better when printed. Personally, I love the pen drawing in this book, and if it's not as flashy as Baudoin's brush work it just goes to show that he doesn't need flashy virtuosity to create an indelible image. Just look at the forlorn Martian on page 20 or admire the graceful simplicity of the two boys floating in the outer space of their dream world on page 91. Furthermore, the choice of pen underscores an important quality of Baudoin as an artist: that, above all, he is interested in using drawing to tell stories and to examine life and the nature of art.

The scene we enter in Piero is the modest world of Momo (as Baudoin was called as a child) and his older brother Pierre, nicknamed Piero, living out their childhood between an apartment in Nice, where their father worked as an accountant, and, more importantly, a tiny rural hamlet called Villars-sur-Vars, where he and his brother would spend their summers (and where Baudoin still spends part of the year, alternating with his cozy studio in Paris). This sun-bleached, woody terrain, full of creeks and valleys, is a recurring setting in Baudoin's work. He has drawn it countless times and from countless angles, never tiring of exploring its rich forms and emotional resonances.

A particular charm of Piero resides in Baudoin's ability to evoke the creativity of children at play. When I read the scenes showing the two siblings drawing together it puts me immediately back in my own childhood fantasies, my younger brother and I devising invisible city blocks along the apartment hallway where we and our stuffed animals (we dubbed them the "Sweeties") could drive around in miniature cars. Similarly, I observe my own eight- and ten-year-old children hunched over a piece of paper, punctuating long stretches of silent concentration with giggles, and I think of Edmond and his brother drawing their epic battle scenes. It's clear that Baudoin has captured something elemental in these sequences that he presents so matter-of-factly and unsentimentally (which is not to say they are not also suffused with nostalgia).

In a sense, Piero contains the distillation of all the themes of Baudoin's work, from the places where he grew up to the people he knew and, especially, his family. Curiously, although Baudoin's mother and father show up regularly in his other books, his brother rarely appears except in the occasional passing mention. It's as if this is the sum of what Baudoin feels he has to say about his brother and the influence he had on him. It is in many ways akin, though with much less tragic contours, to Crumb's idolization of his older brother Charles, who similarly rejected art, leaving the task—perceived as an almost holy duty—to his younger brother. *Piero* is in this sense an "origin story" which ends with Baudoin in the position of James Joyce's Stephen Dedalus at the end of *A Portrait of the Artist as a Young Man*, about to go forth and encounter the reality of experience and to forge in the smithy of his soul the uncreated conscience of his race.

—MATT MADDEN

Piero

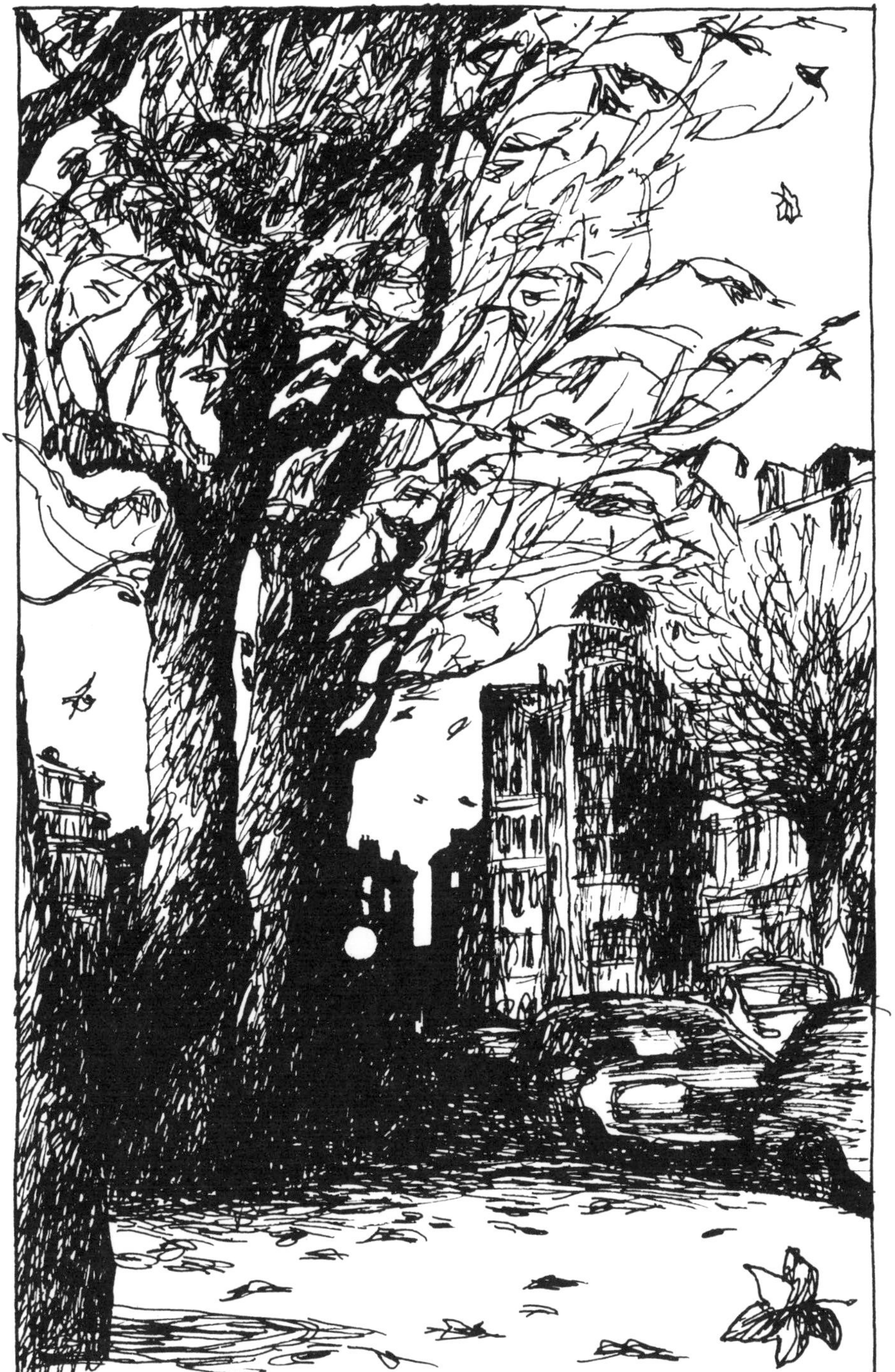

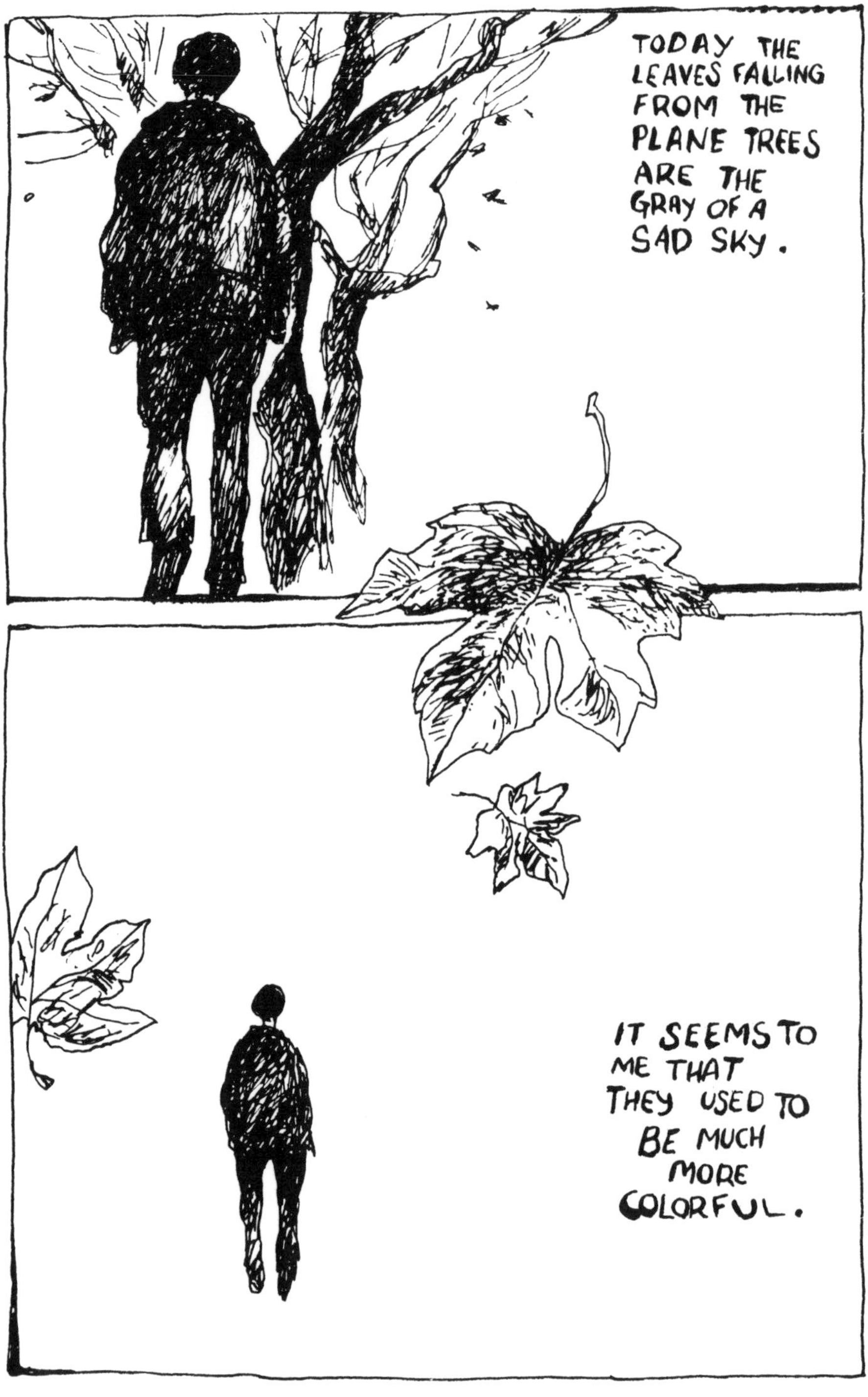
TODAY THE LEAVES FALLING FROM THE PLANE TREES ARE THE GRAY OF A SAD SKY.
IT SEEMS TO ME THAT THEY USED TO BE MUCH MORE COLORFUL.

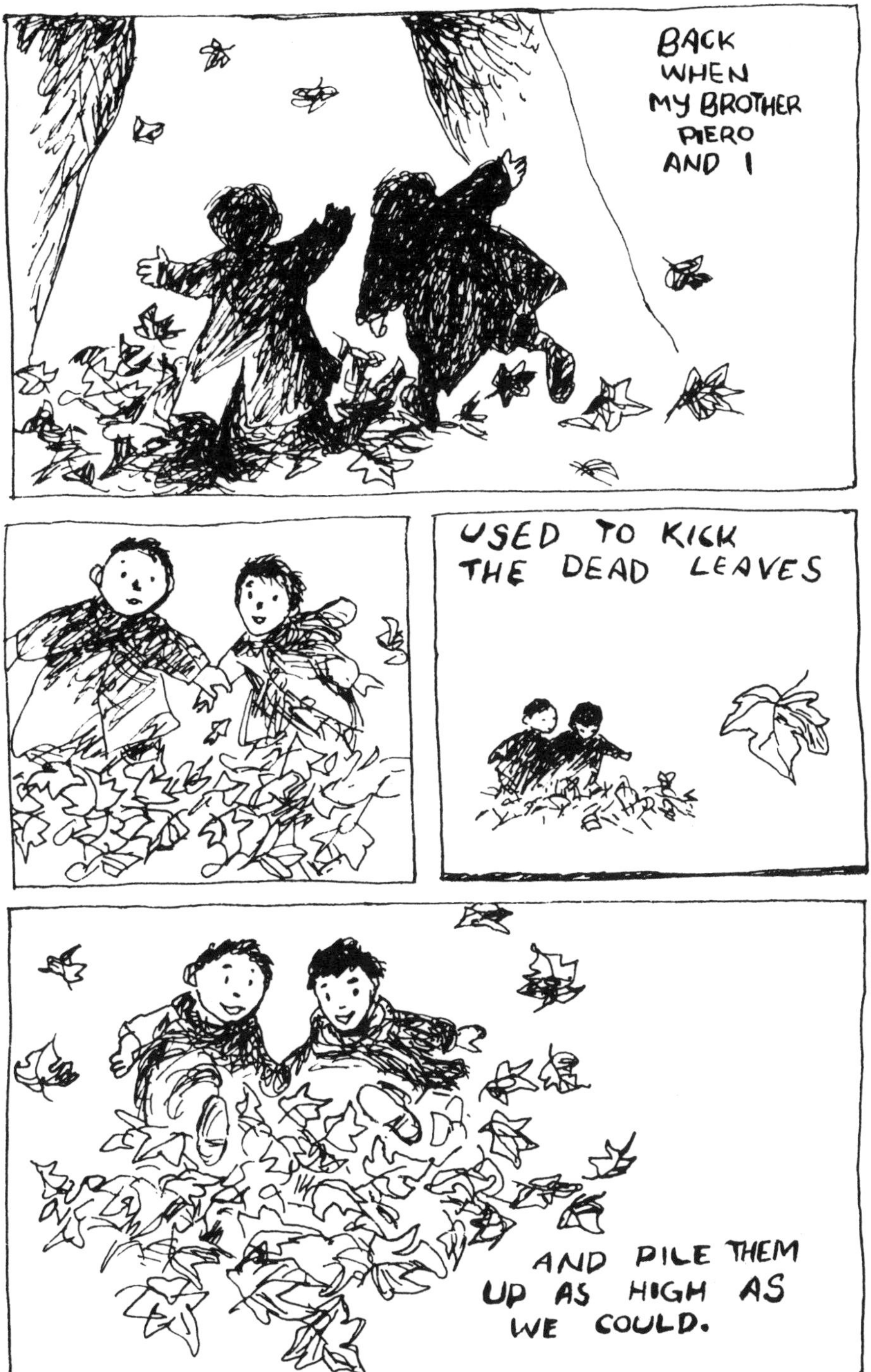
BACK WHEN MY BROTHER PIERO AND I
USED TO KICK THE DEAD LEAVES
AND PILE THEM UP AS HIGH AS WE COULD.

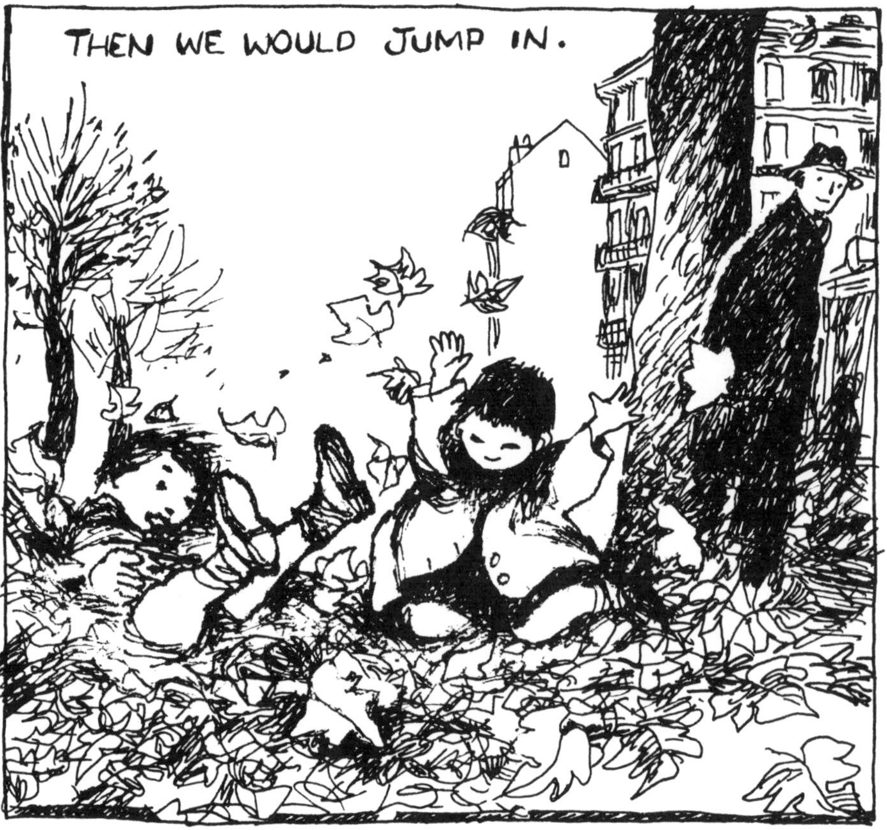
THEN WE WOULD JUMP IN.

THEN WE WOULD CHOOSE THE TWO PRETTIEST LEAVES.

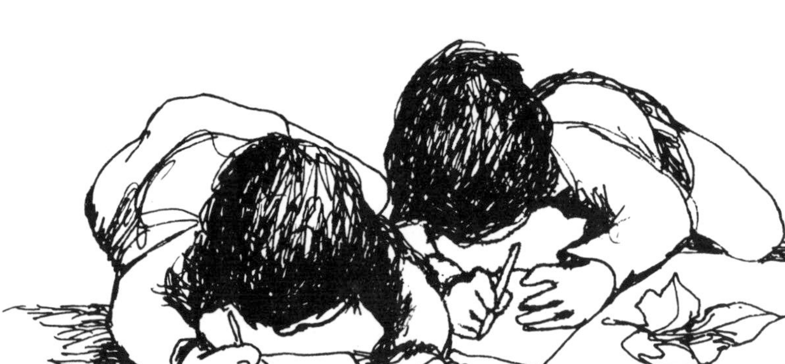

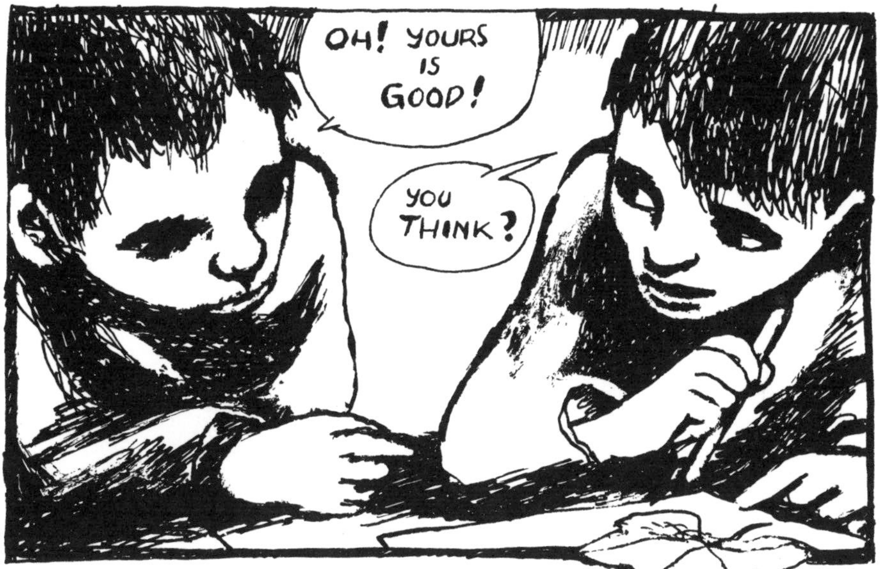
OH! YOURS IS GOOD!
YOU THINK?

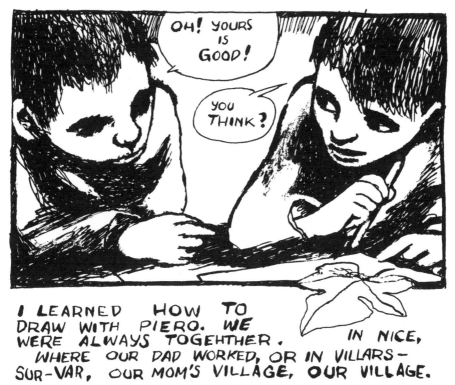

I LEARNED HOW TO DRAW WITH PIERO. WE WERE ALWAYS TOGEHTHER. IN NICE, WHERE OUR DAD WORKED, OR IN VILLARS-SUR-VAR, OUR MOM'S VILLAGE, OUR VILLAGE.

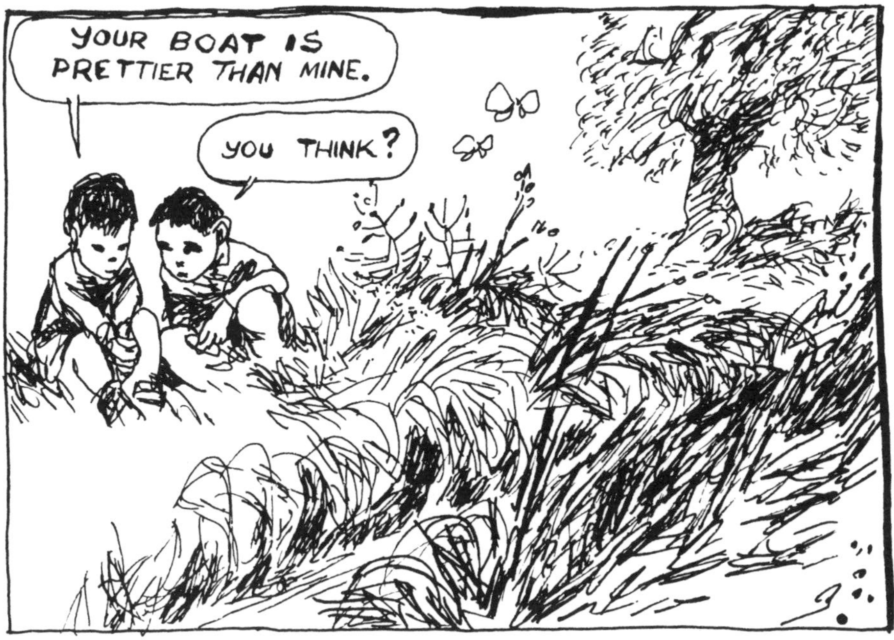
YOUR BOAT IS PRETTIER THAN MINE.
YOU THINK?

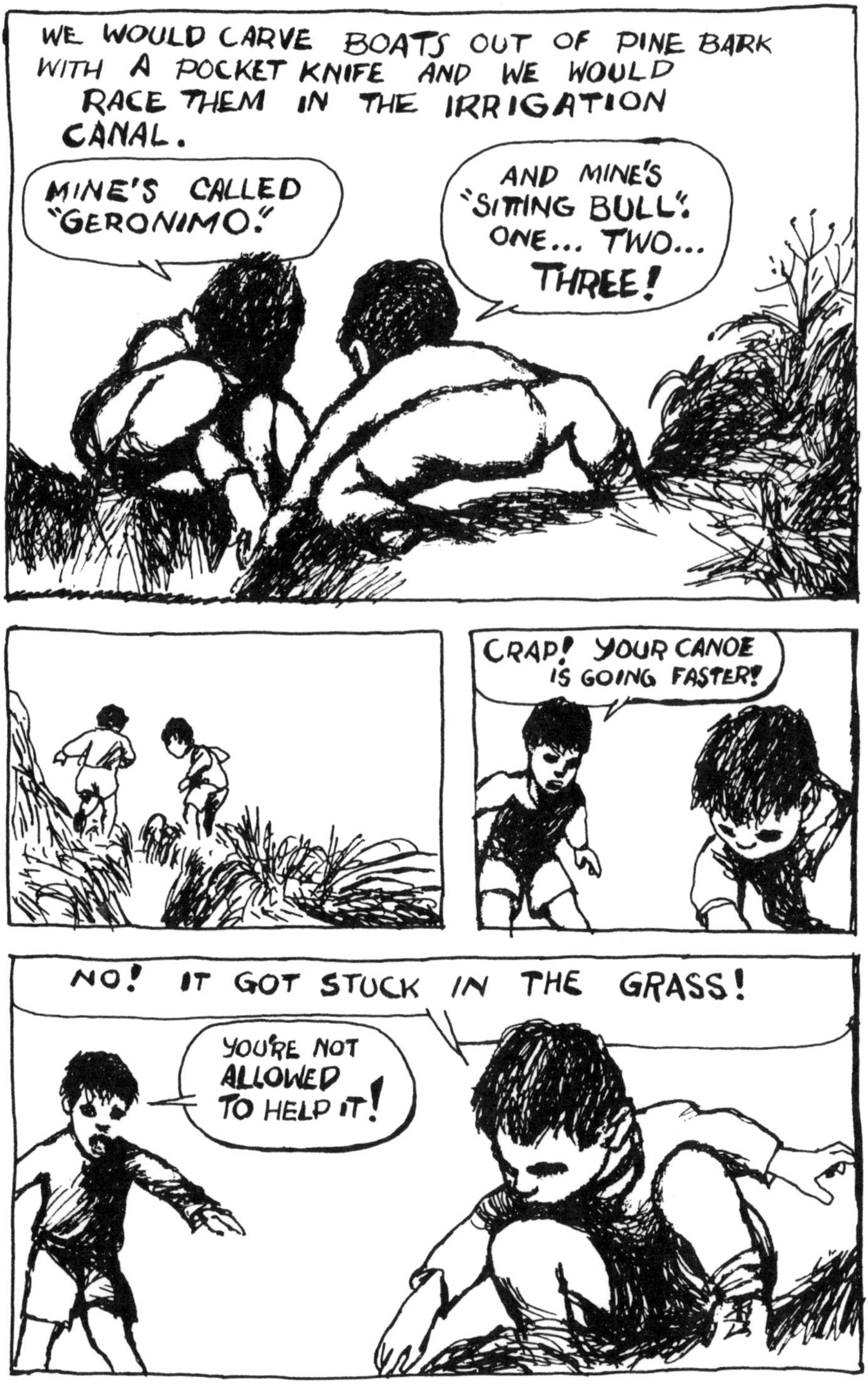
WE WOULD CARVE BOATS OUT OF PINE BARK WITH A POCKET KNIFE AND WE WOULD RACE THEM IN THE IRRIGATION CANAL.
MINE'S CALLED "GERONIMO."
AND MINE'S "SITTING BULL". ONE... TWO... THREE!
CRAP! YOUR CANOE IS GOING FASTER!
NO! IT GOT STUCK IN THE GRASS!
YOU'RE NOT ALLOWED TO HELP IT!

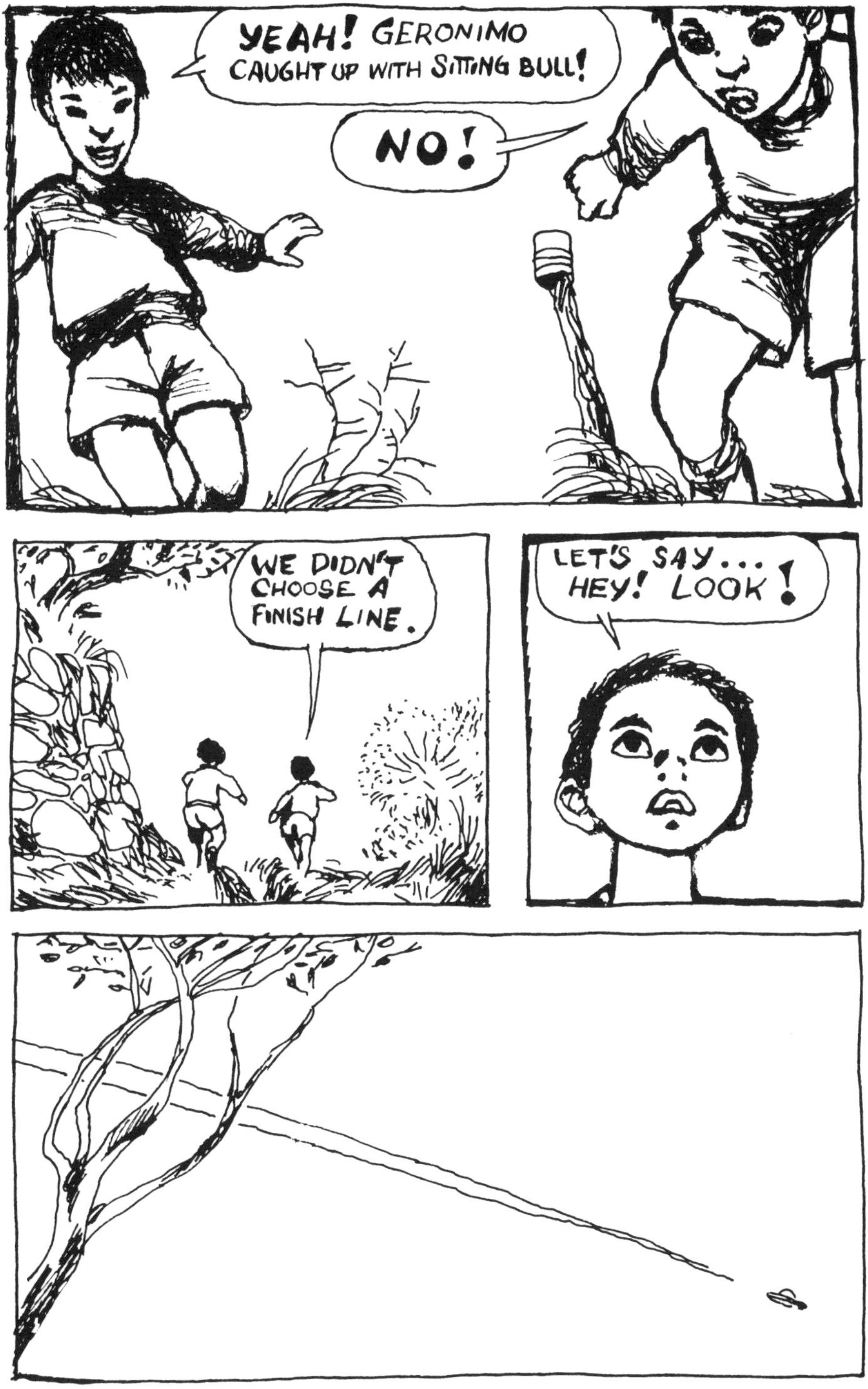
YEAH! GERONIMO CAUGHT UP WITH SITTING BULL!
NO!
WE DIDN'T CHOOSE A FINISH LINE.
LET'S SAY... HEY! LOOK!

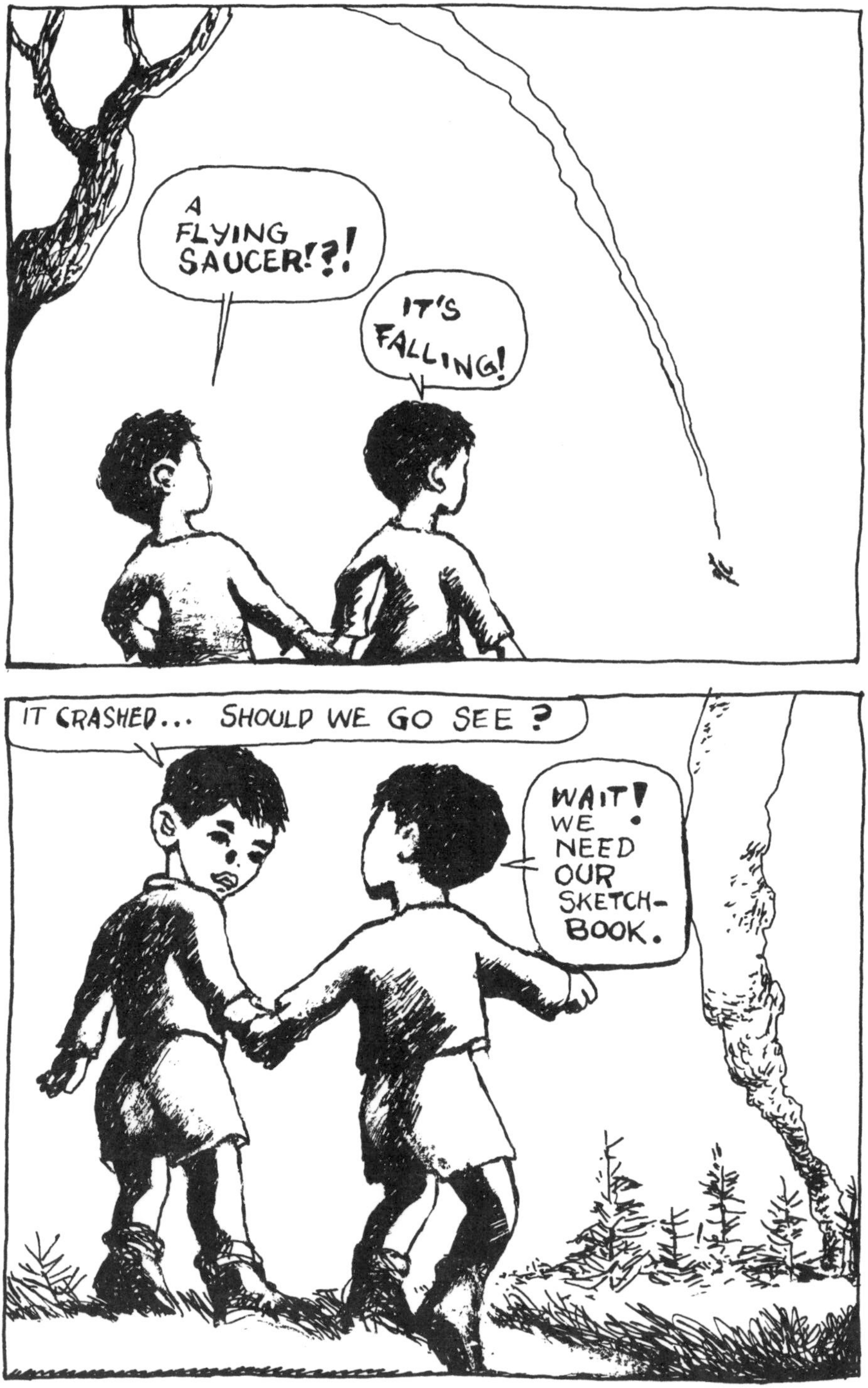
A FLYING SAUCER!?!
IT'S FALLING!
IT CRASHED... SHOULD WE GO SEE?
WAIT! WE NEED OUR SKETCH-BOOK.

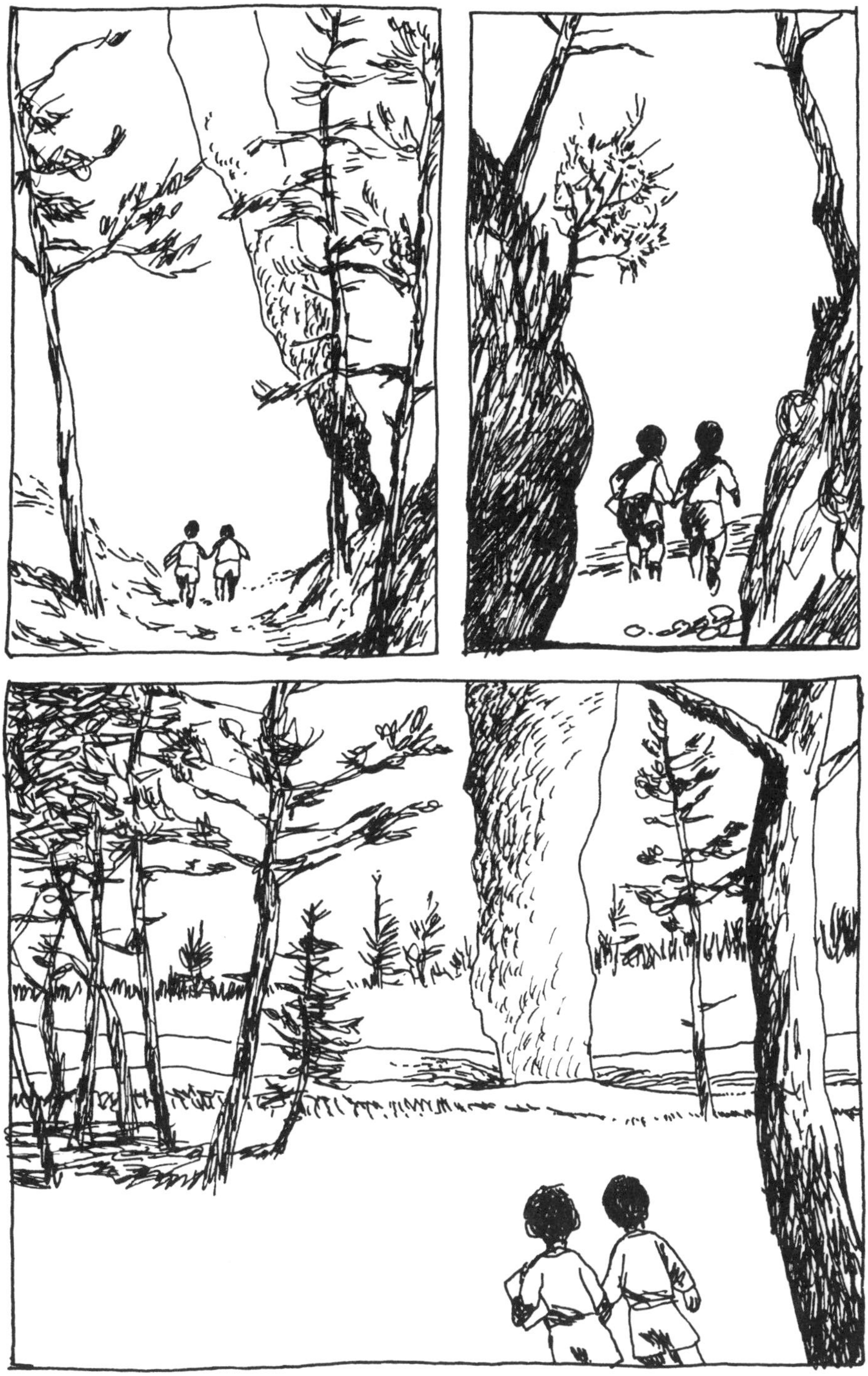

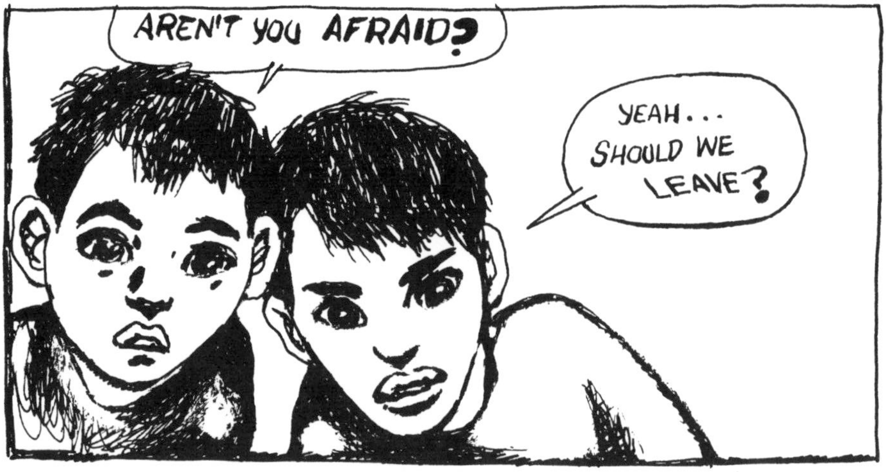
ARE'NT YOU AFRAID?
YEAH... SHOULD WE LEAVE?

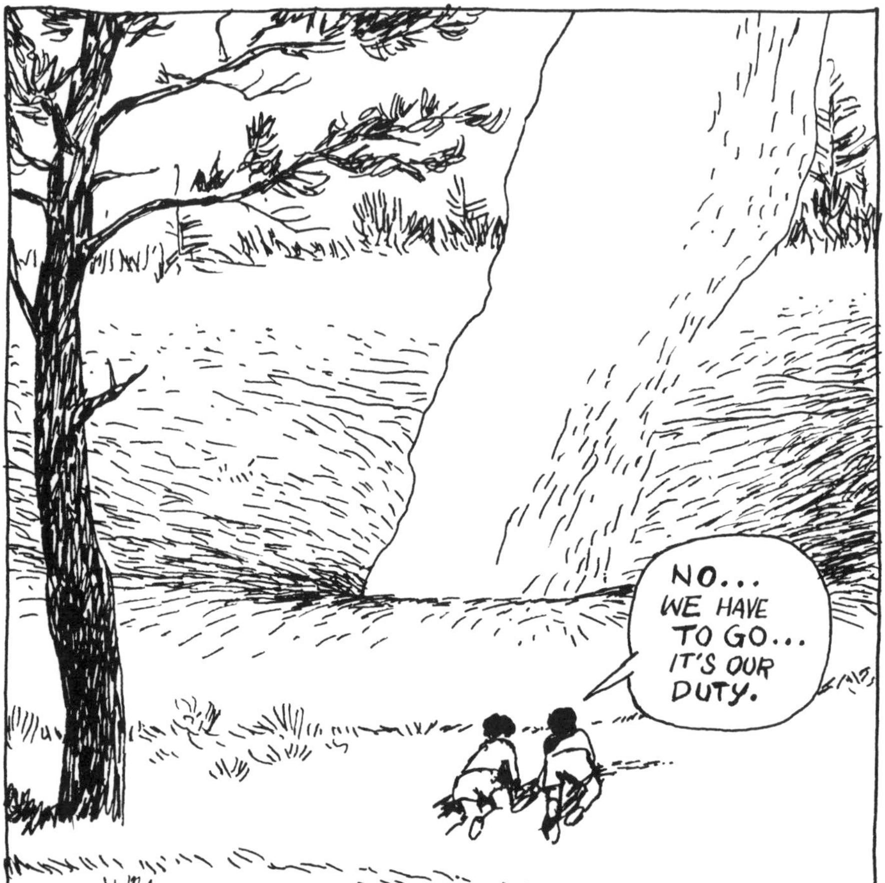
NO... WE HAVE TO GO... IT'S OUR DUTY.

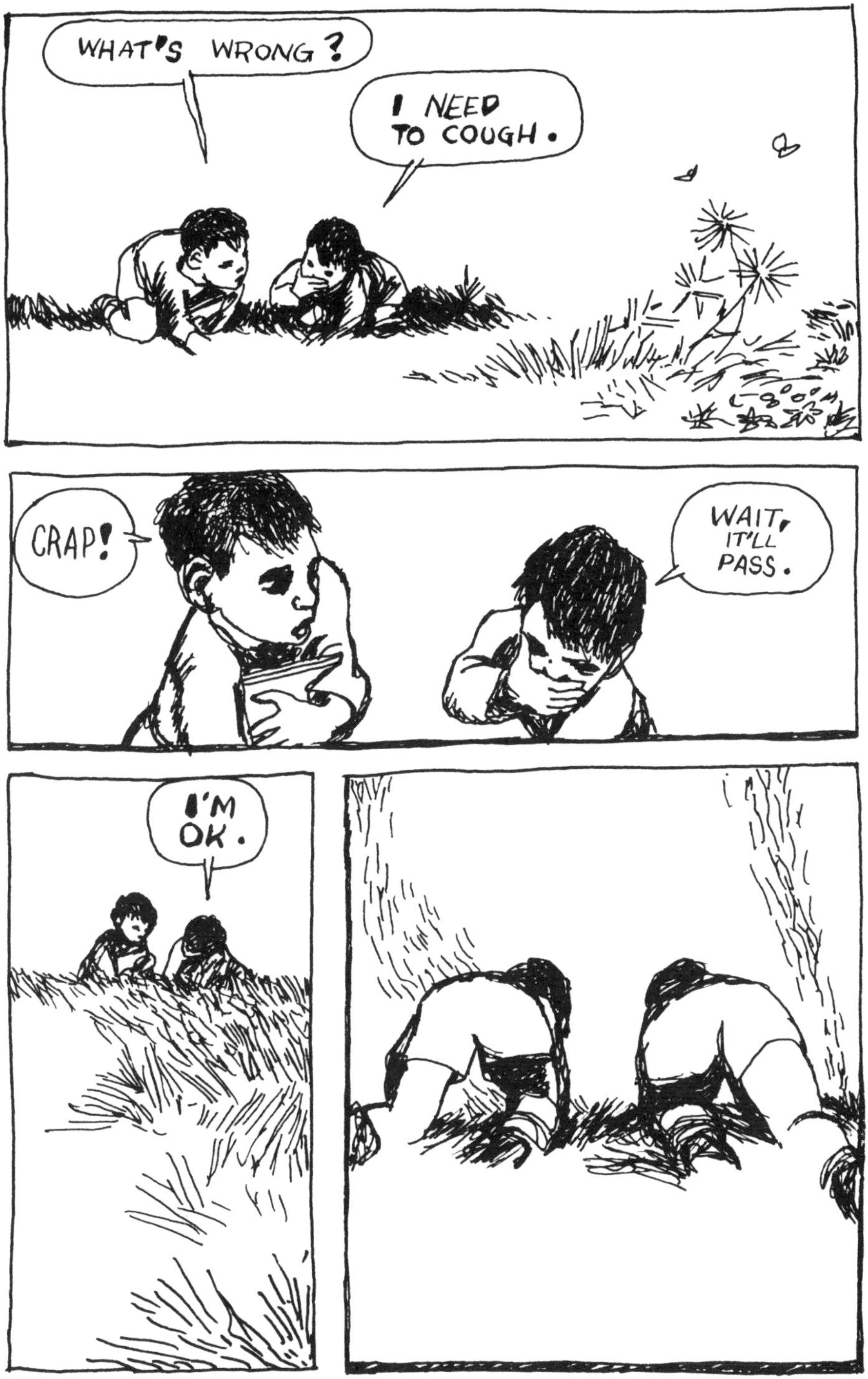
WHAT'S WRONG?
I NEED TO COUGH.
CRAP!
WAIT, IT'LL PASS.
I'M OK.

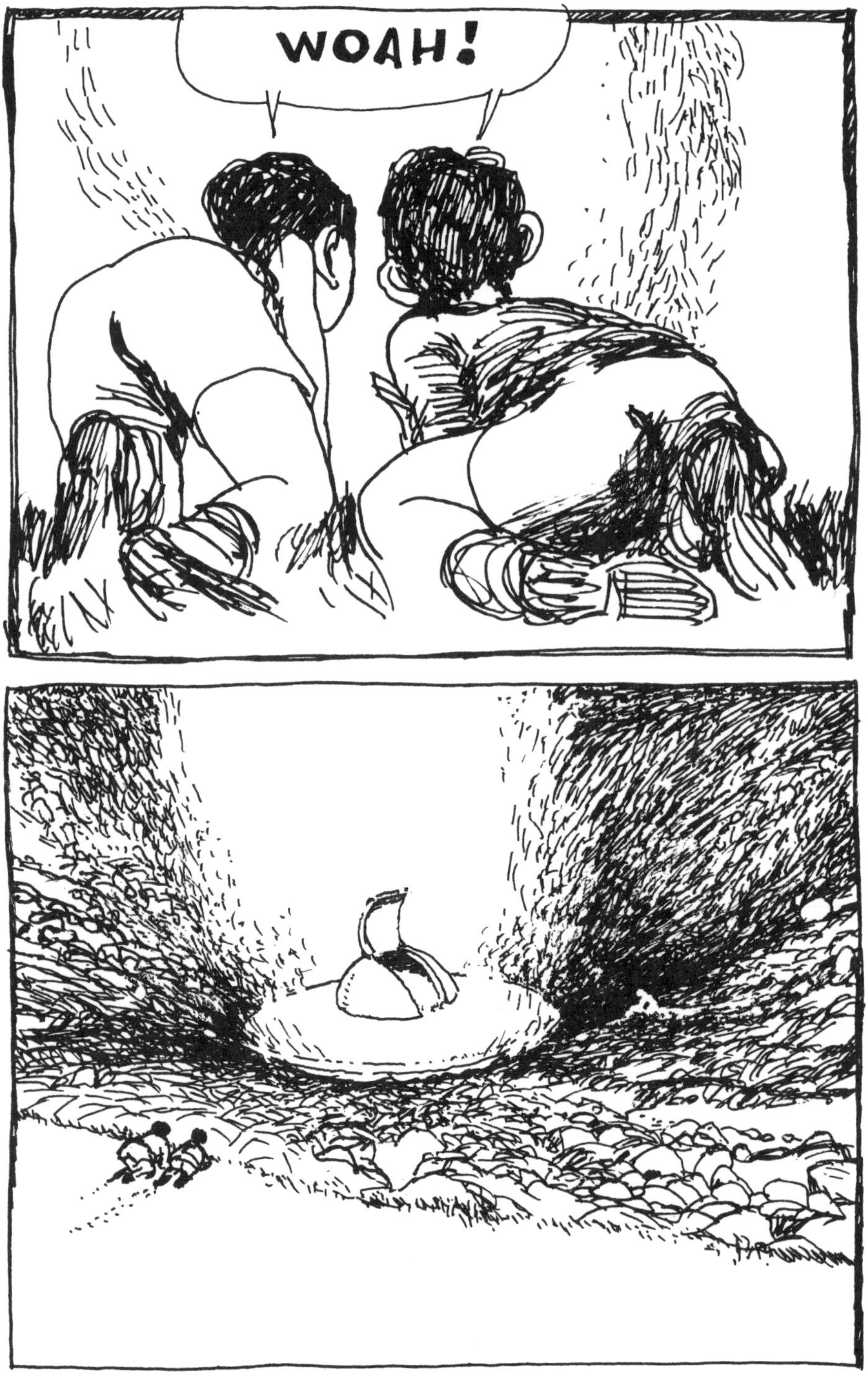
WOAH!

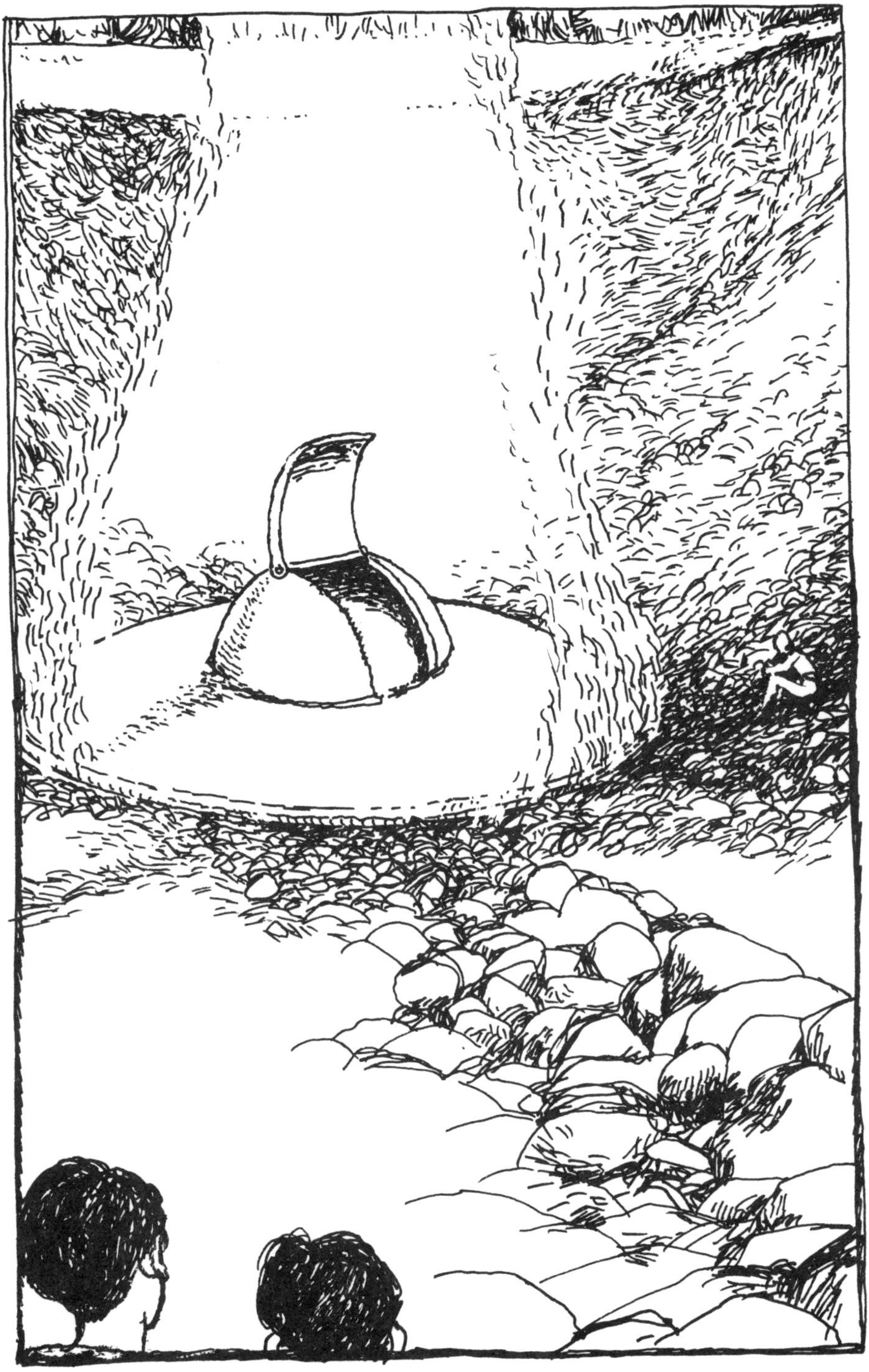

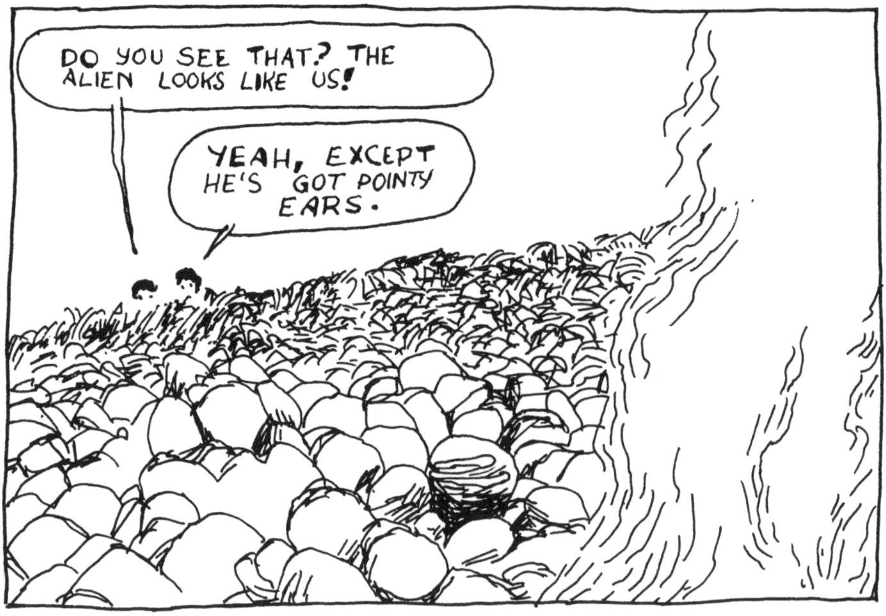
DO YOU SEE THAT? THE ALIEN LOOKS LIKE US!
YEAH, EXCEPT HE'S GOT POINTY EARS.

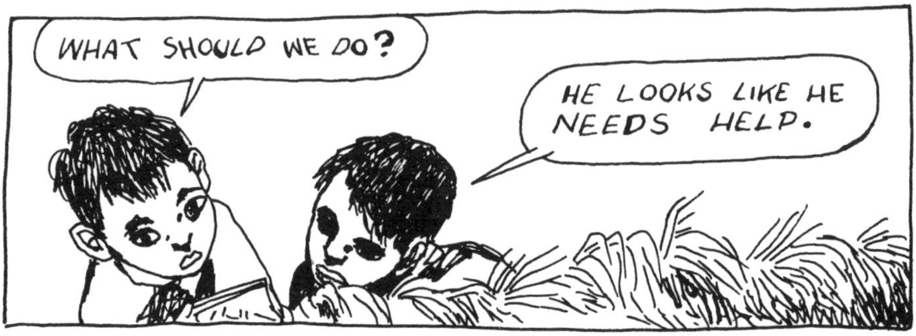
WHAT SHOULD WE DO?
HE LOOKS LIKE HE NEEDS HELP.

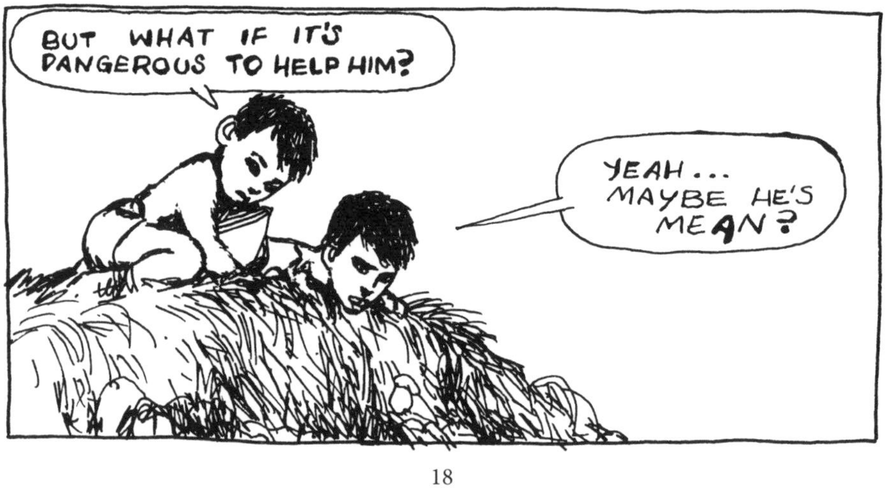
BUT WHAT IF IT'S DANGEROUS TO HELP HIM?
YEAH... MAYBE HE'S MEAN?

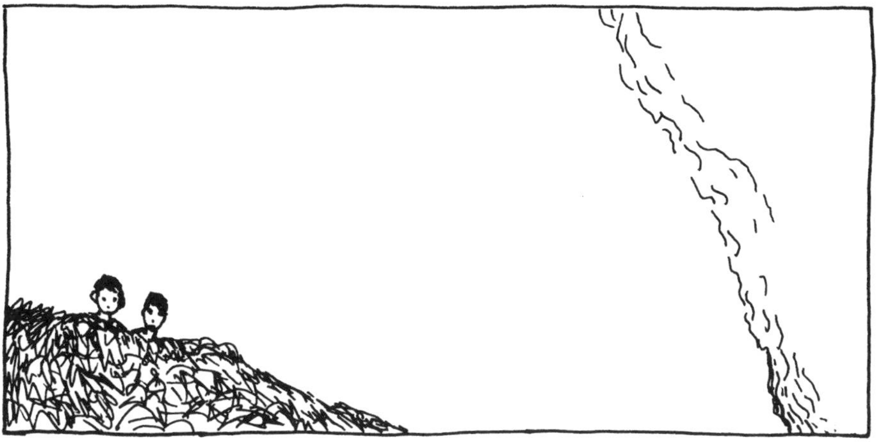

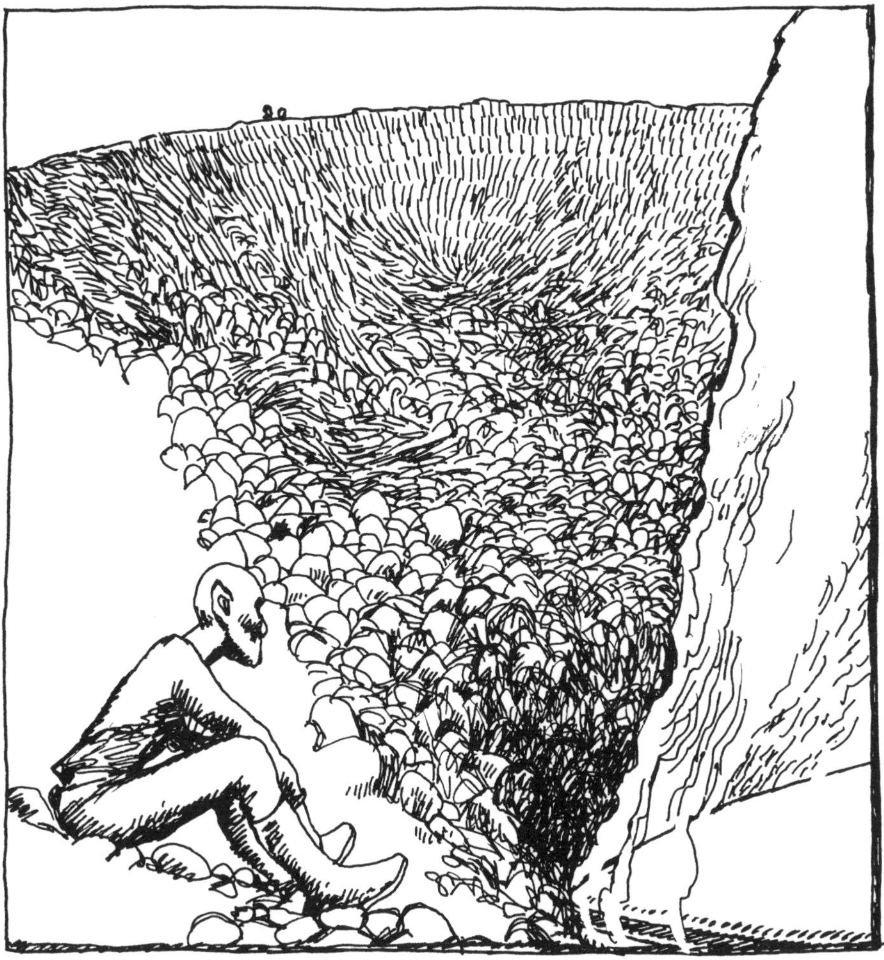

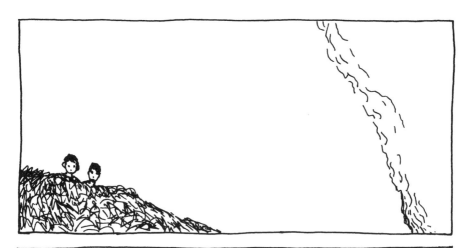

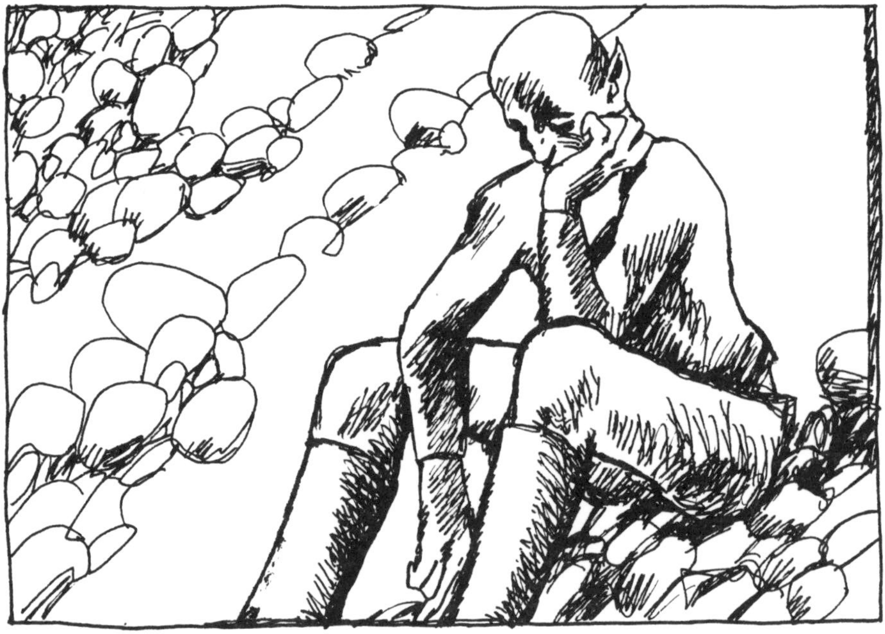

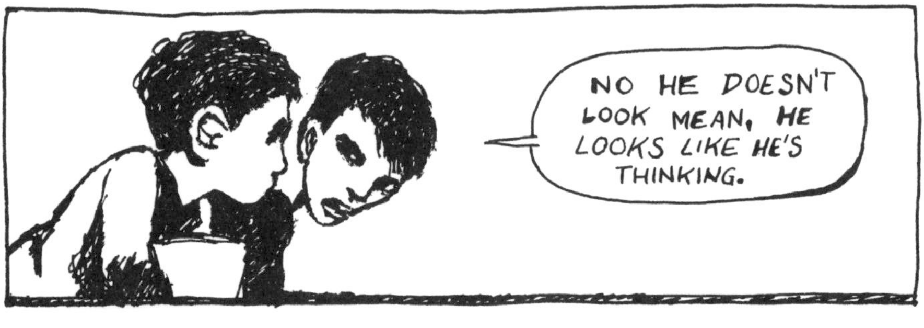
NO HE DOESN'T LOOK MEAN, HE LOOKS LIKE HE'S THINKING.

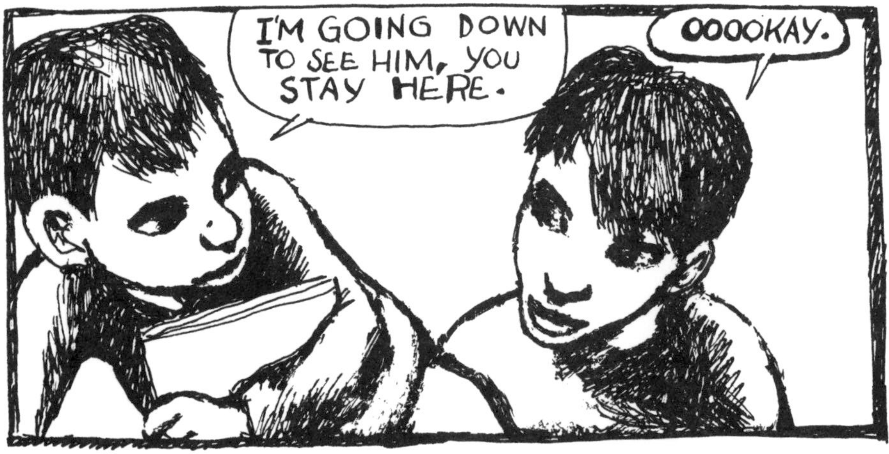
I'M GOING DOWN TO SEE HIM, YOU STAY HERE.
OOOOKAY.

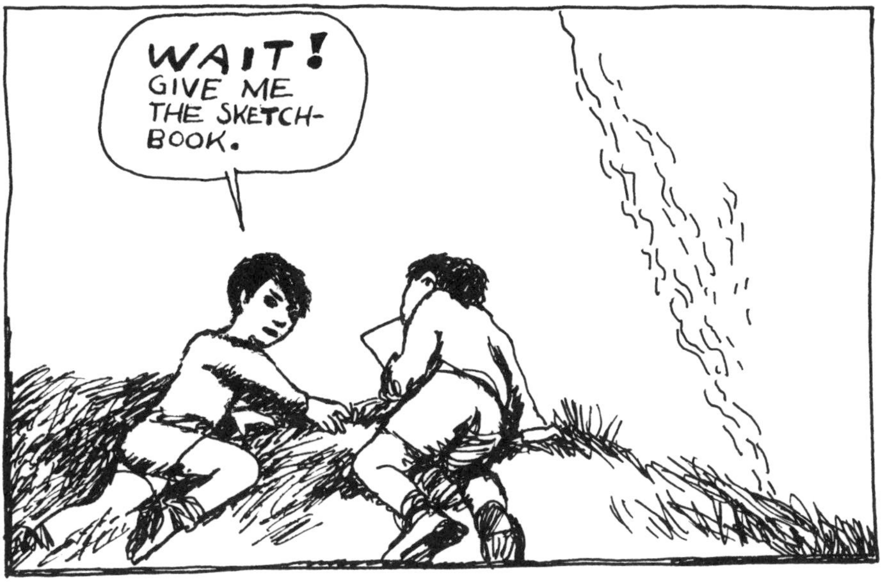
WAIT! GIVE ME THE SKETCH-BOOK.

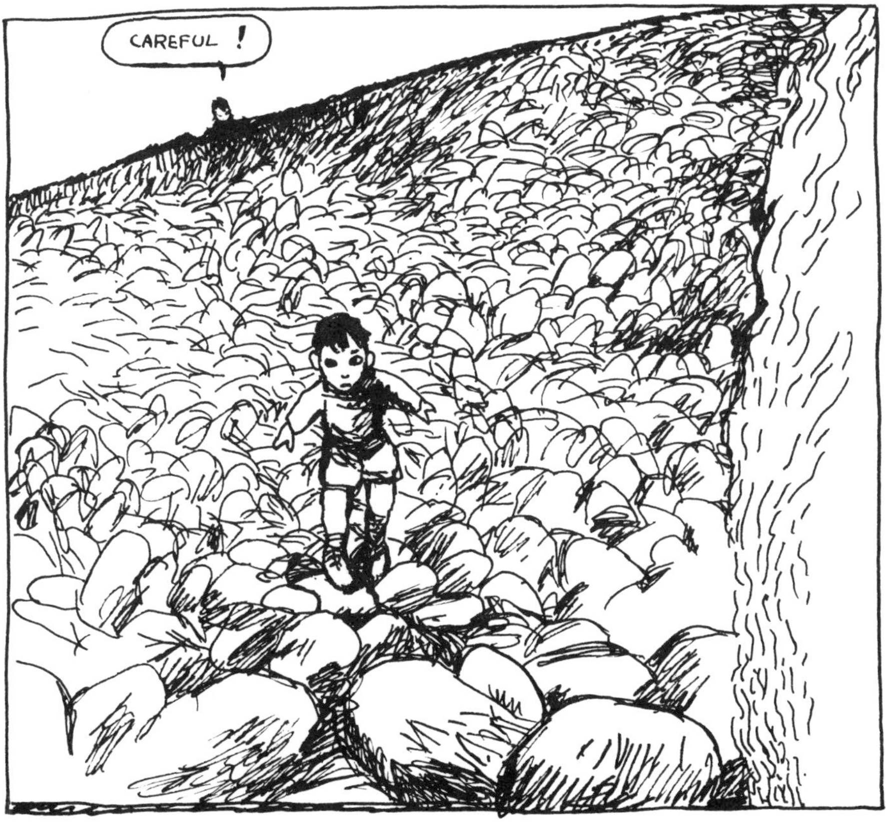
CAREFUL!

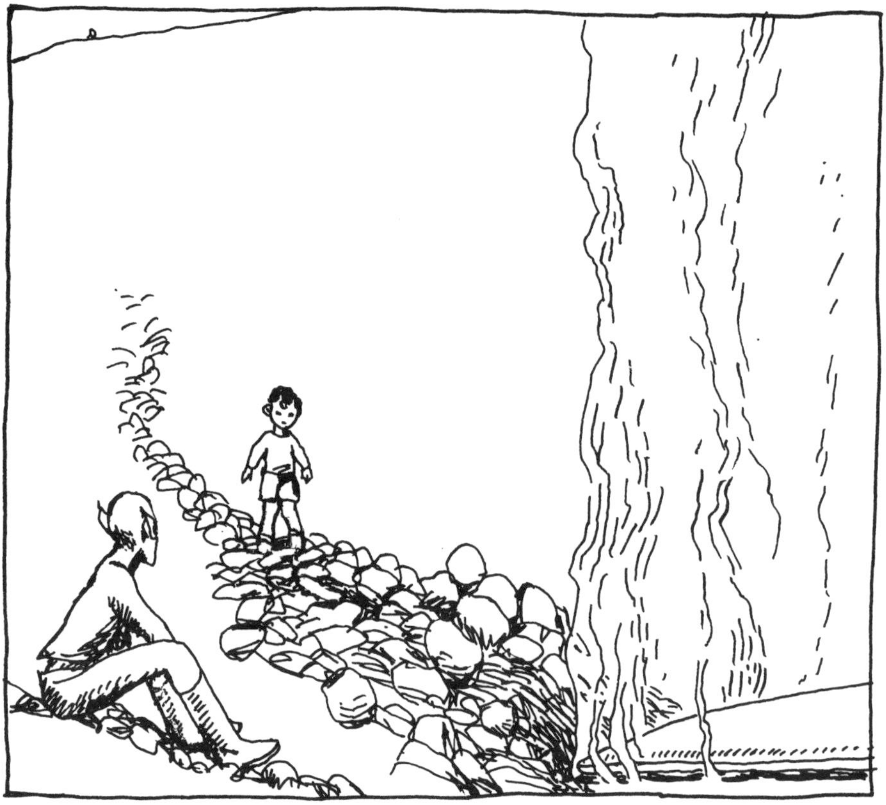

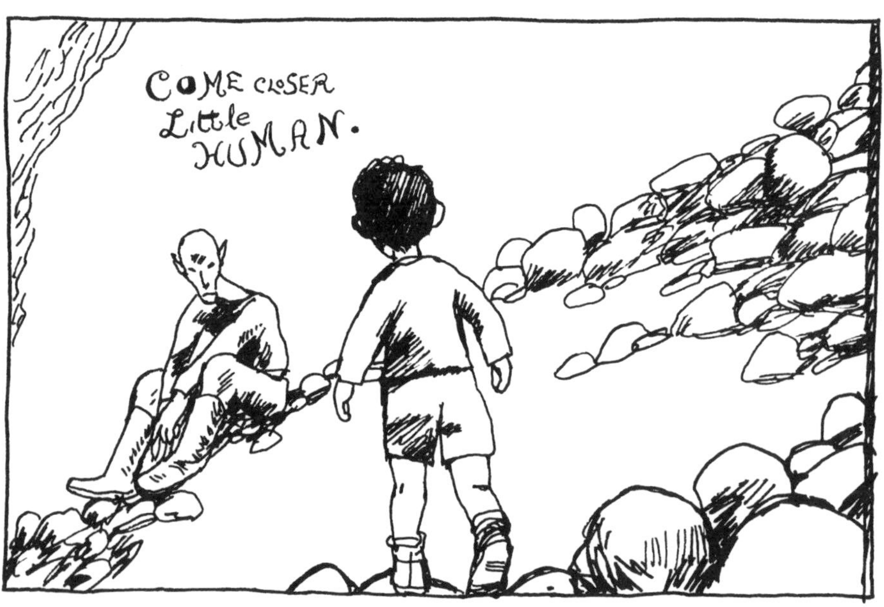
COME CLOSER
Little
HUMAN.

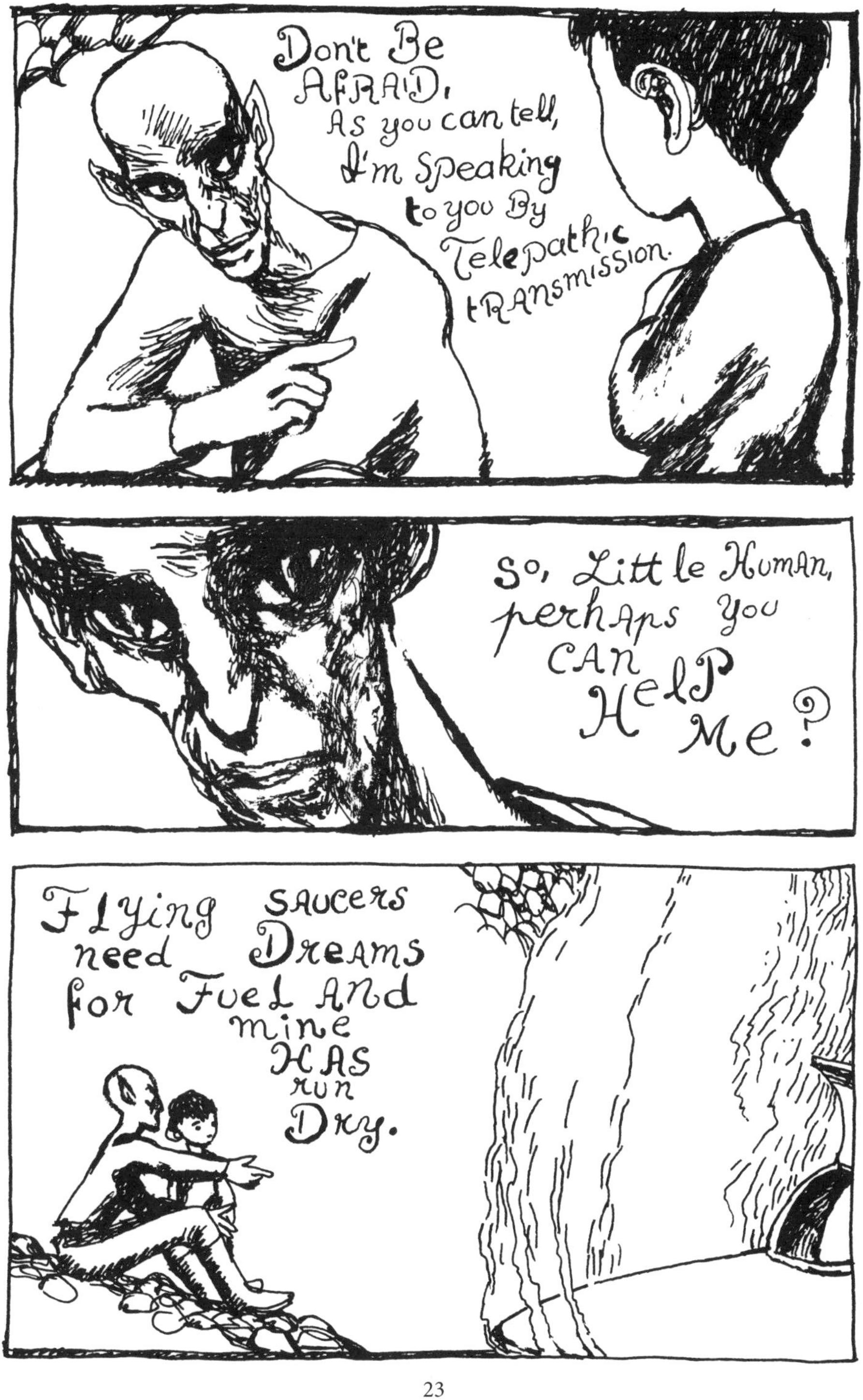
Don't Be AFRAID, As you can tell, I'm Speaking to you By Telepathic TRANSMISSION.
So, Little Human, perhAps You CAN HelP Me?
Flying SAUCERS need DREAMS for Fuel And mine HAS run Dry.

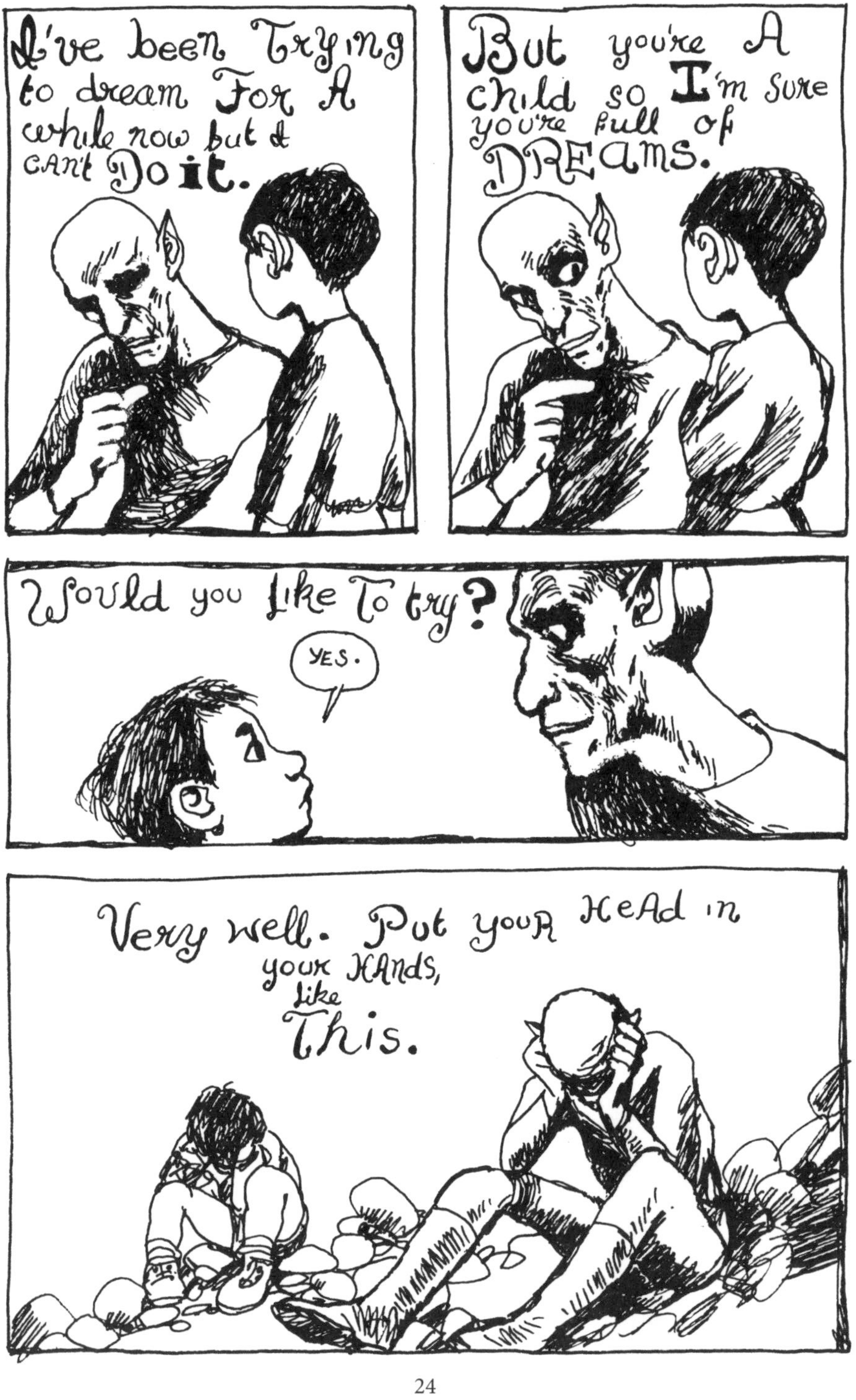
I've been Trying to dream For A while now but I can't Do it.
But you're A child so I'm sure you're full of DREAMS.
Would you like To try?
YES.
Very well. Put your Head in your HAnds, like This.

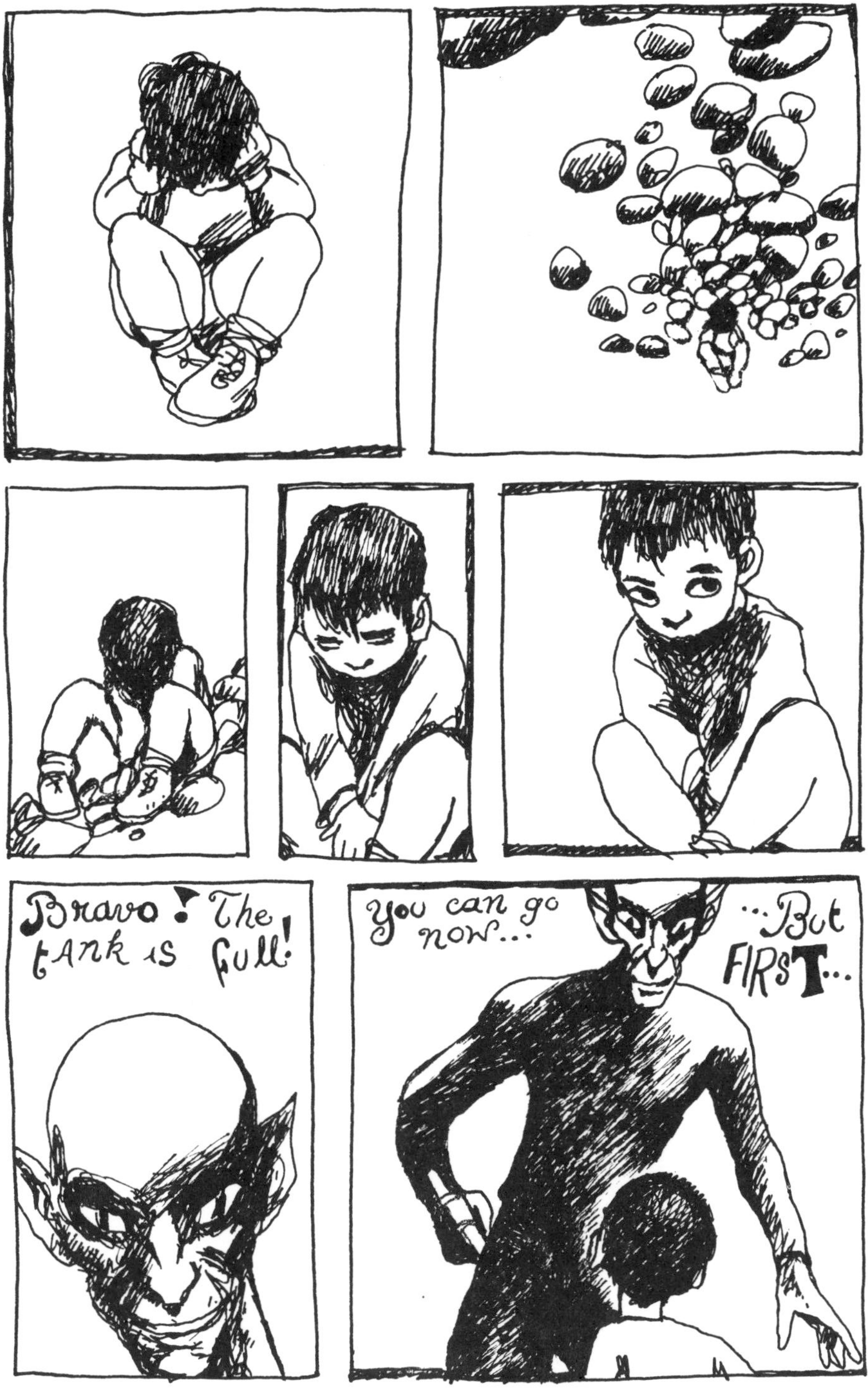
Bravo! The tank is full!
You can go now...
...But FIRST...

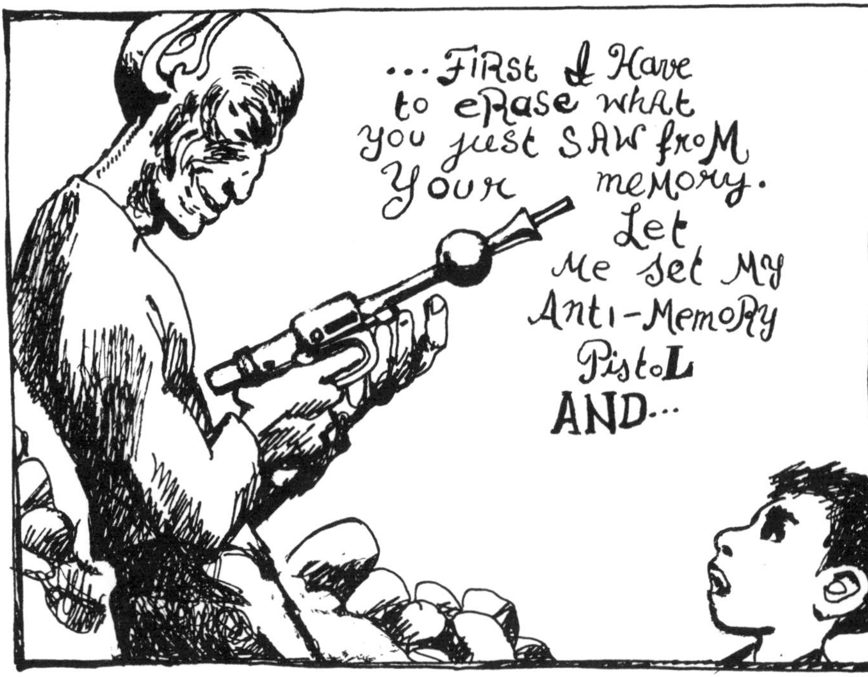
...FIRST I HAVE TO ERASE WHAT YOU JUST SAW FROM YOUR MEMORY. LET ME SET MY ANTI-MEMORY PISTOL AND...

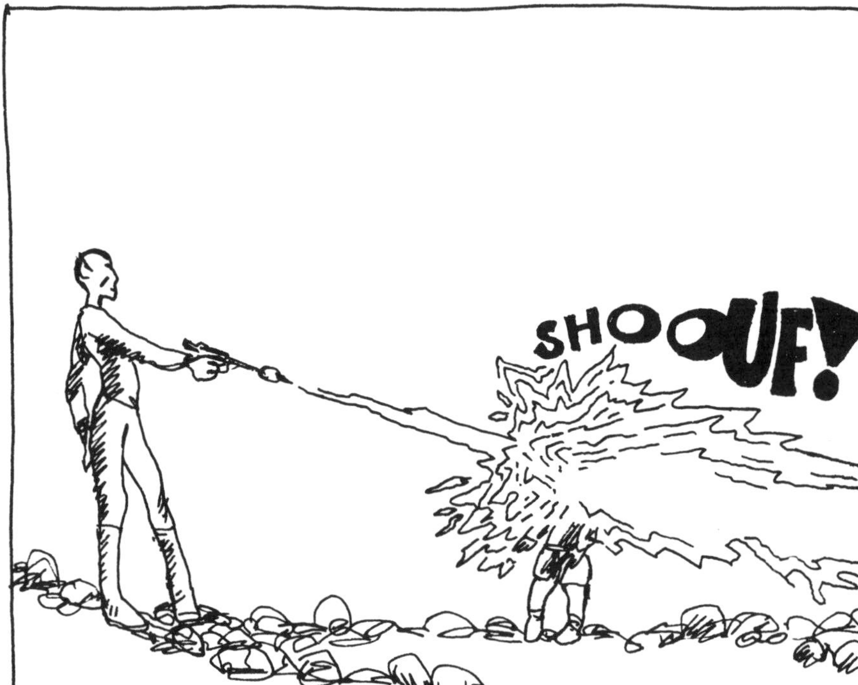
SHOOUF!

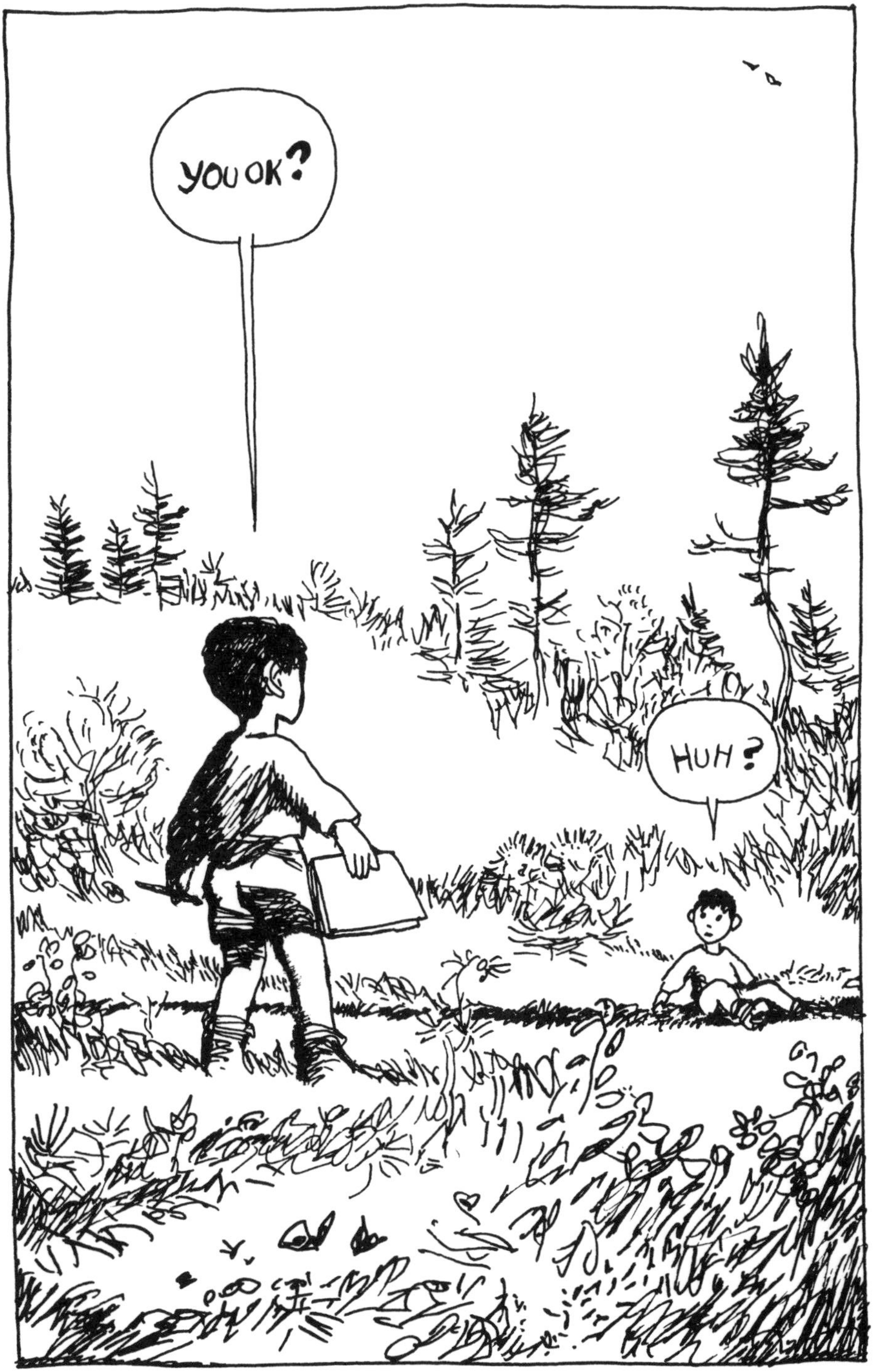
YOU OK?
HUH?

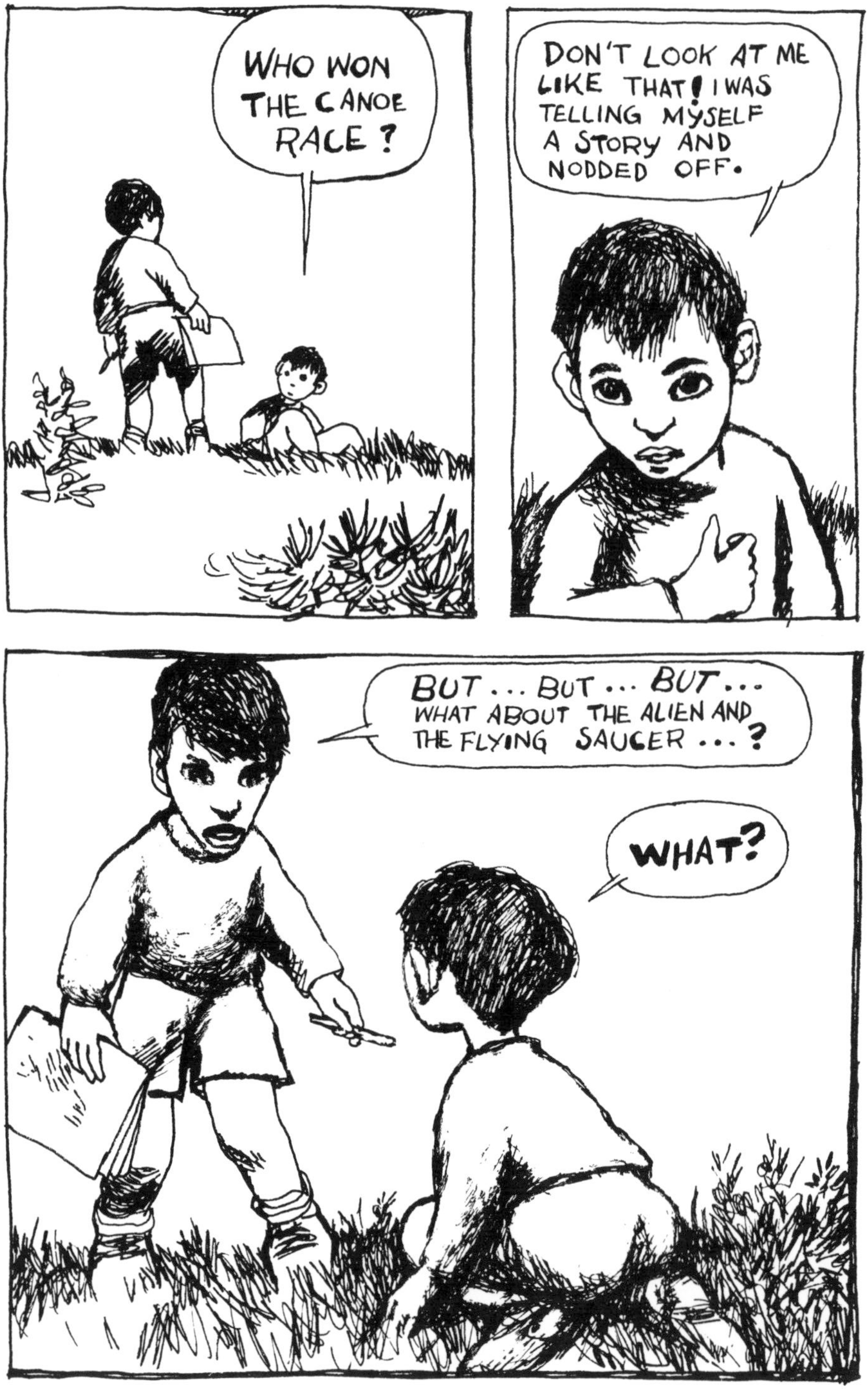
WHO WON THE CANOE RACE?
DON'T LOOK AT ME LIKE THAT! I WAS TELLING MYSELF A STORY AND NODDED OFF.
BUT ... BUT ... BUT ... WHAT ABOUT THE ALIEN AND THE FLYING SAUCER ...?
WHAT?

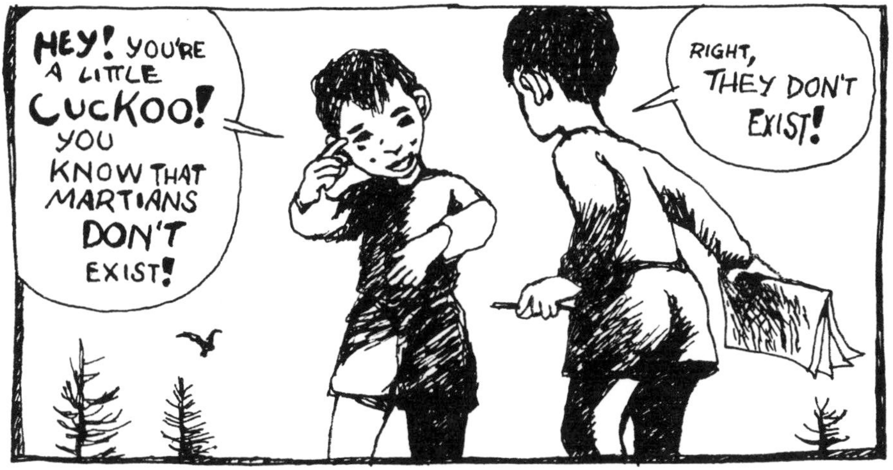
HEY! YOU'RE A LITTLE CUCKOO! YOU KNOW THAT MARTIANS DON'T EXIST!
RIGHT, THEY DON'T EXIST!

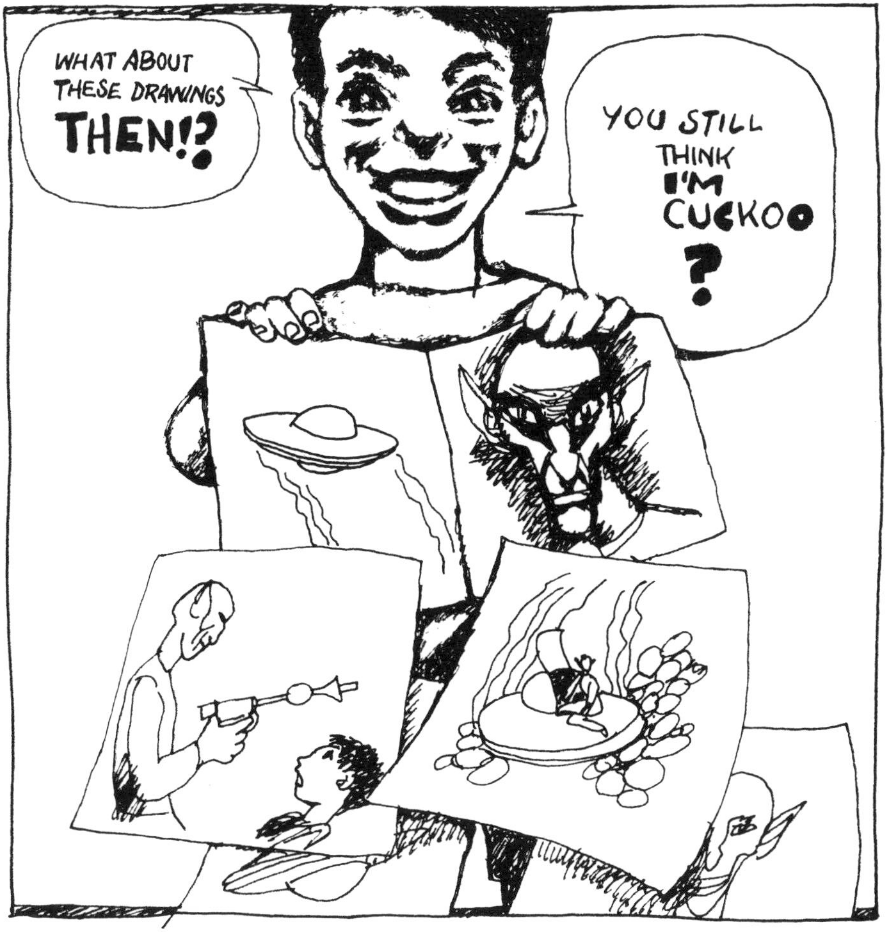
WHAT ABOUT THESE DRAWINGS THEN!?
YOU STILL THINK I'M CUCKOO ?

PIERO LIKED TO DRAW CARS.
I LIKED DRAWING HORSES BETTER.

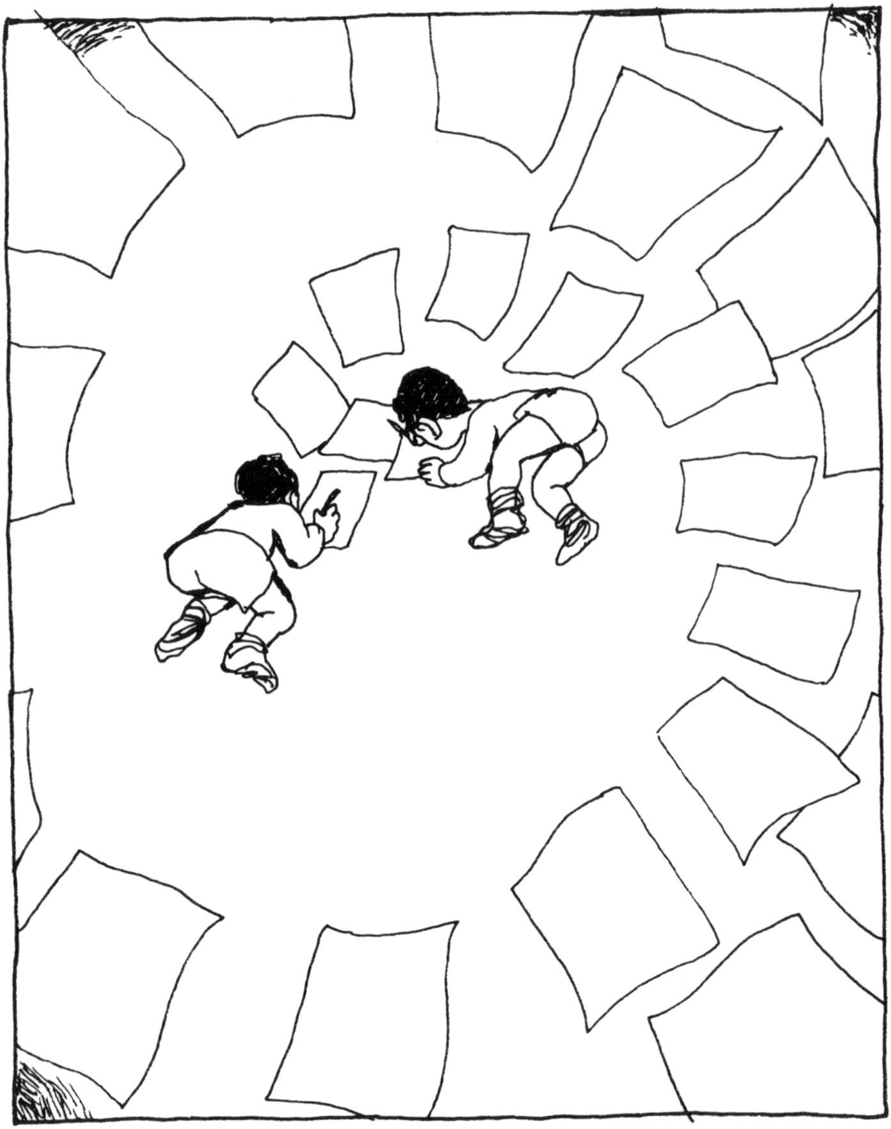

WHEN PIERO WAS FIVE I WAS SIX AND A HALF.
WE DIDN'T KNOW THAT TELEVISIONS HAD BEEN INVENTED OR THAT SOME PEOPLE ALREADY HAD THEM. WE HADN'T GONE TO PRESCHOOL.

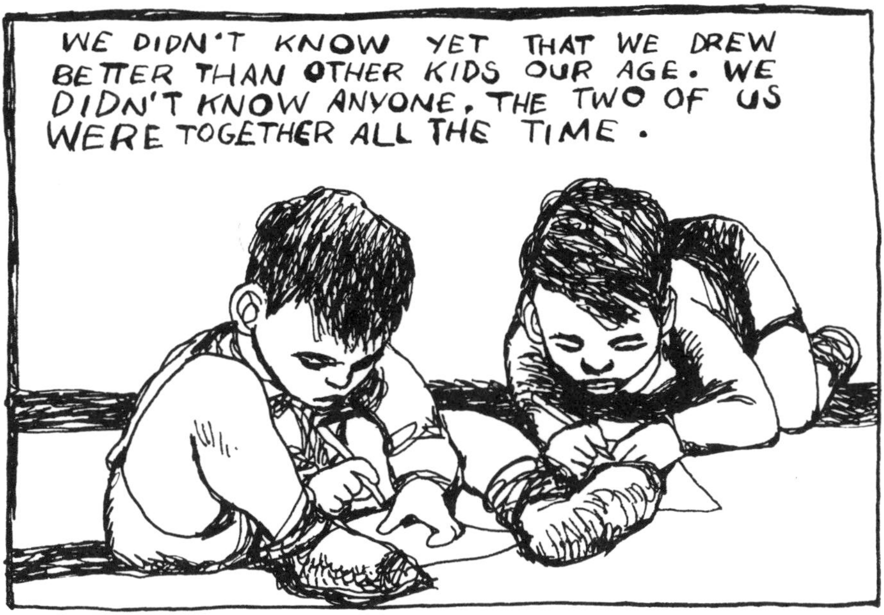
WE DIDN'T KNOW YET THAT WE DREW BETTER THAN OTHER KIDS OUR AGE. WE DIDN'T KNOW ANYONE, THE TWO OF US WERE TOGETHER ALL THE TIME.

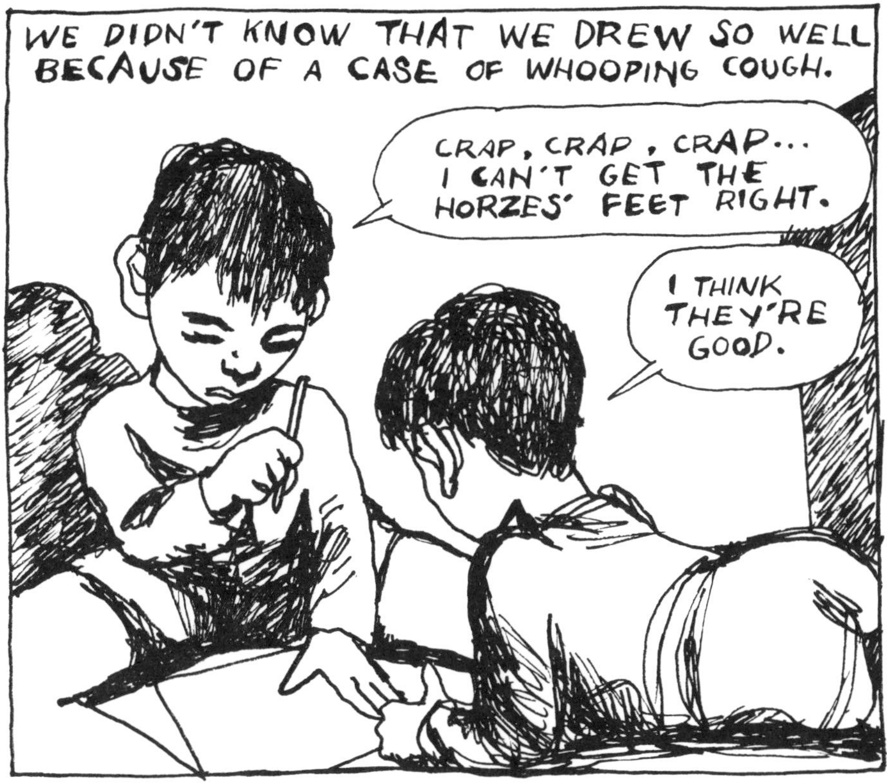
WE DIDN'T KNOW THAT WE DREW SO WELL BECAUSE OF A CASE OF WHOOPING COUGH.
CRAP, CRAP, CRAP... I CAN'T GET THE HORZES' FEET RIGHT.
I THINK THEY'RE GOOD.

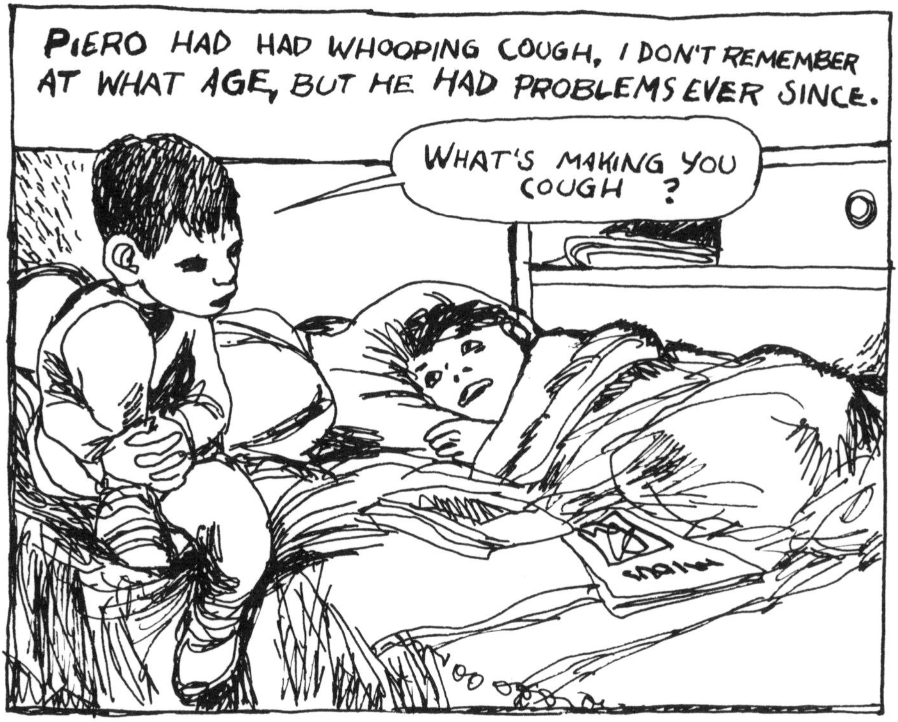
PIERO HAD HAD WHOOPING COUGH, I DON'T REMEMBER AT WHAT AGE, BUT HE HAD PROBLEMS EVER SINCE.
WHAT'S MAKING YOU COUGH ?

AND HE WAS SICK OFTEN.

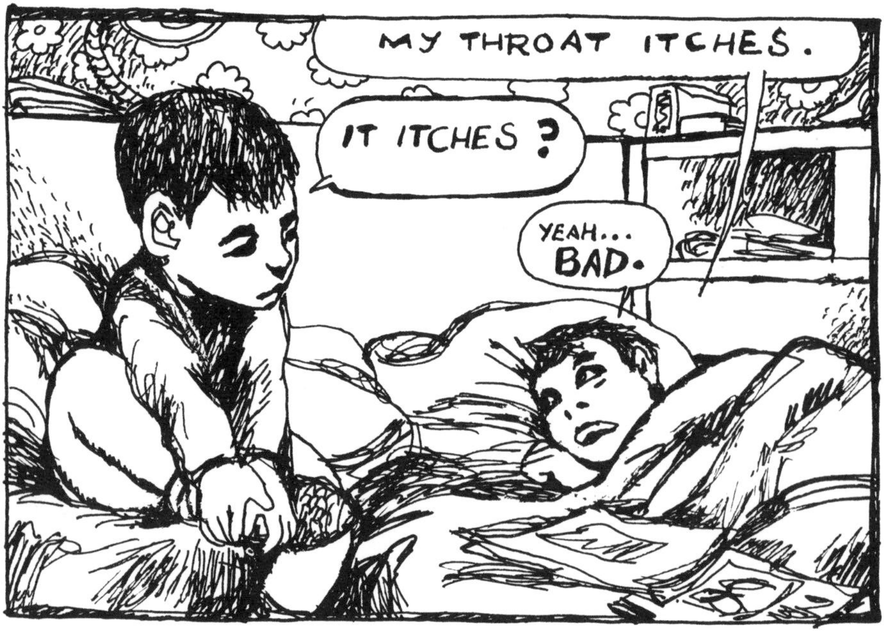
MY THROAT ITCHES.
IT ITCHES ?
YEAH... BAD.

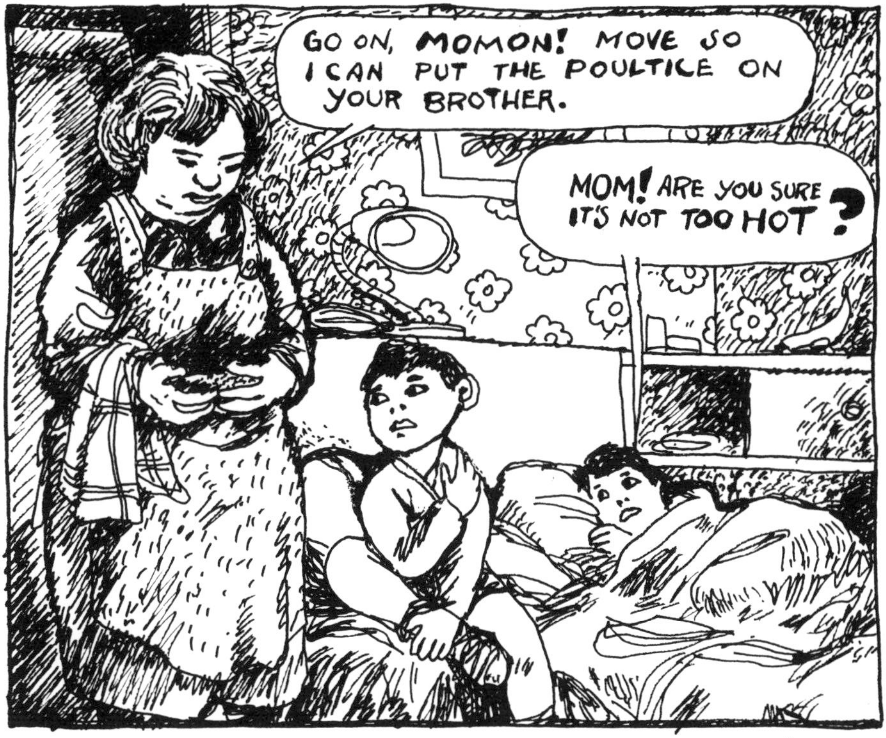
GO ON, MOMON! MOVE SO I CAN PUT THE POULTICE ON YOUR BROTHER.
MOM! ARE YOU SURE IT'S NOT TOO HOT?

THERE WERE MANY OF US LIVING IN A SMALL HOUSE.

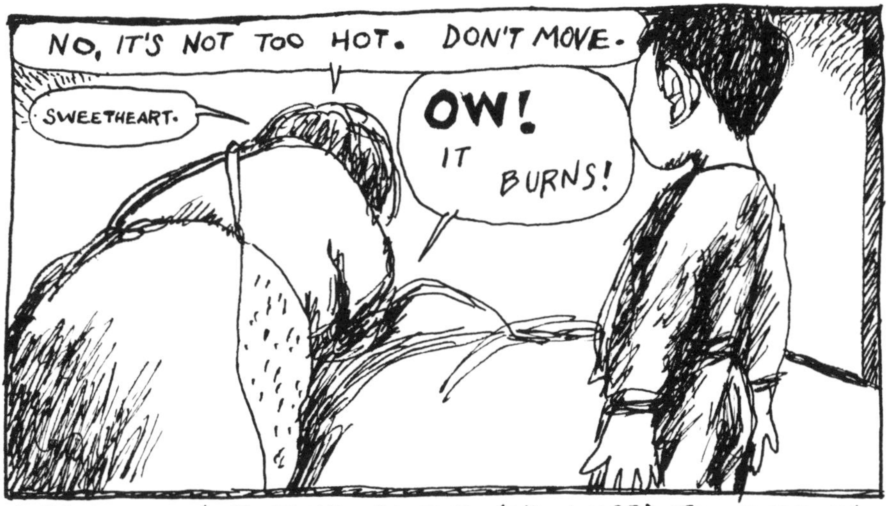
NO, IT'S NOT TOO HOT. DON'T MOVE.
SWEETHEART.
OW! IT BURNS!

WHICH MEANT THAT PIERO AND I USED TO SLEEP IN THE SAME BED.

THESE DAYS PEOPLE MIGHT SAY IT'S NOT A GOOD IDEA TO SLEEP WITH YOUR BROTHER.

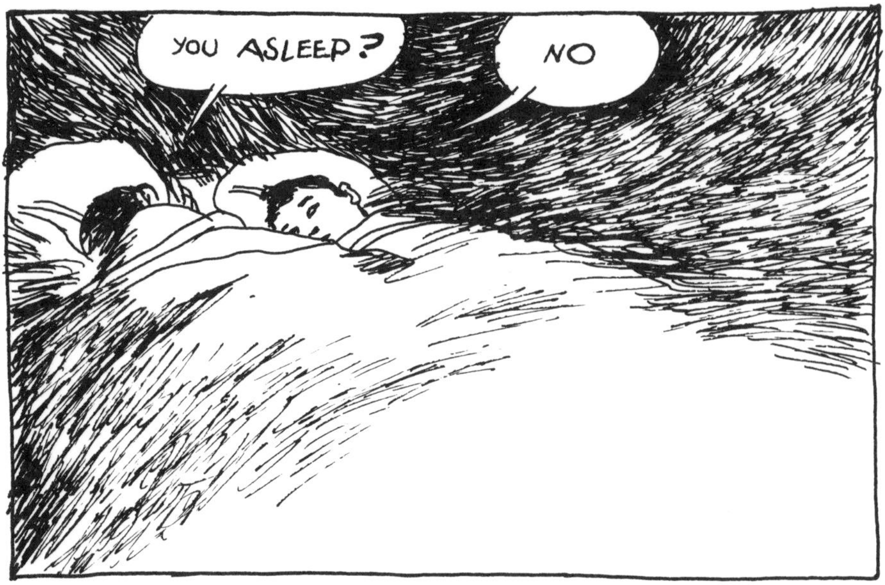

YOU ASLEEP?
NO

BUT TO US, IT WAS MARVELOUS.

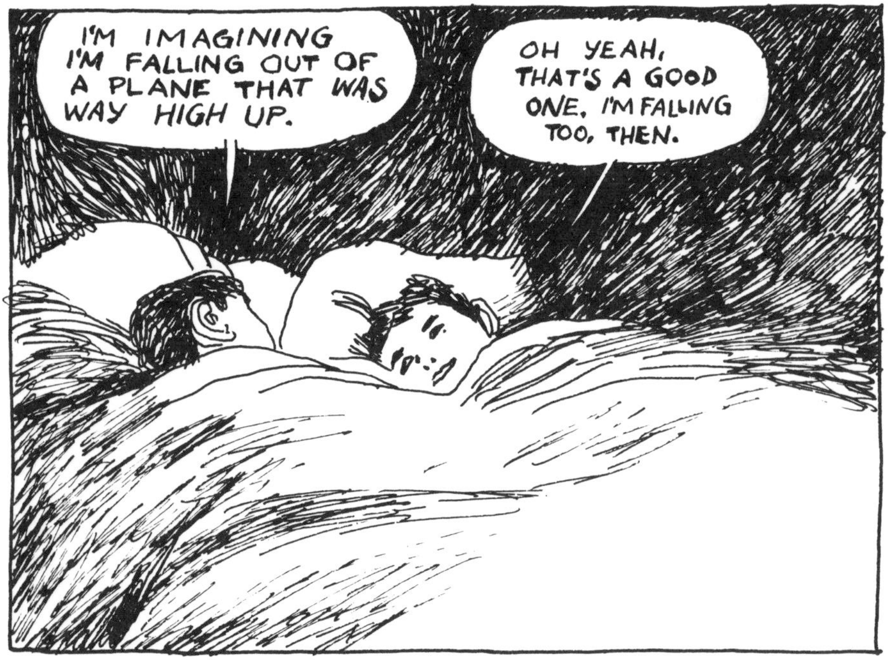

I'M IMAGINING I'M FALLING OUT OF A PLANE THAT WAS WAY HIGH UP.
OH YEAH, THAT'S A GOOD ONE. I'M FALLING TOO, THEN.

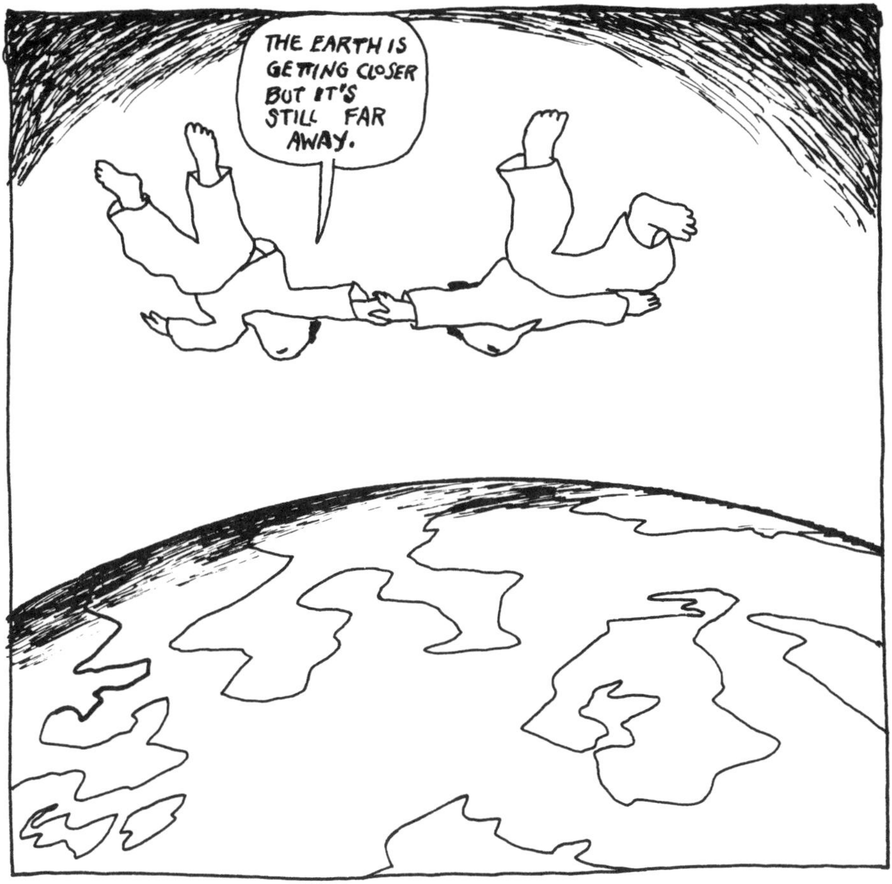
THE EARTH IS GETTING CLOSER BUT IT'S STILL FAR AWAY.

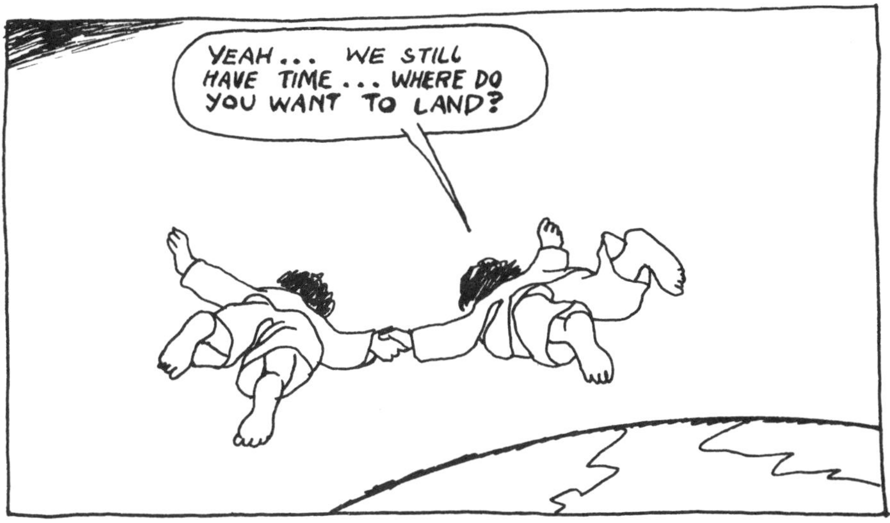
YEAH... WE STILL HAVE TIME... WHERE DO YOU WANT TO LAND?

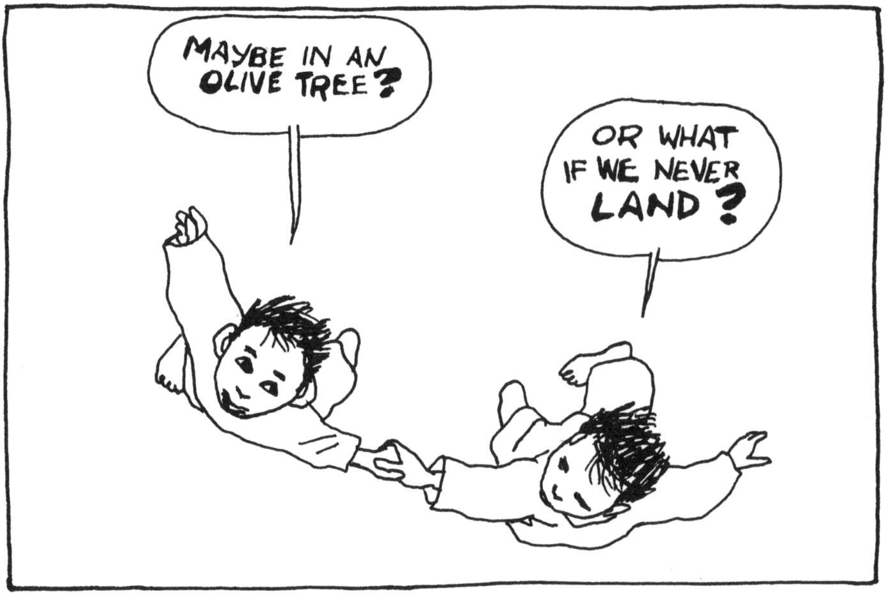
MAYBE IN AN OLIVE TREE?
OR WHAT IF WE NEVER LAND?

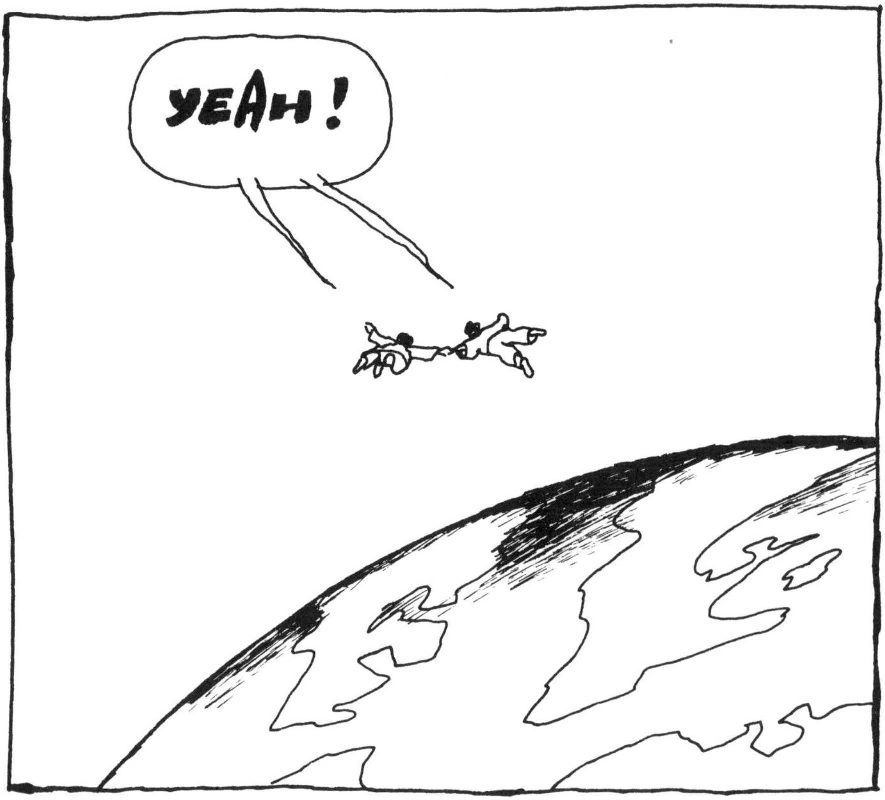
YEAH!

BECAUSE OF PIERO'S ILLNESS WE DIDN'T GO TO PRESCHOOL, BECAUSE OF HIS ILLNESS WE DIDN'T GO OUT TO PLAY BALL IN THE STREET WITH THE OTHER KIDS.

AND, BECAUSE IT WAS MORE PRACTICAL FOR OUR MOTHER, WE BOTH STARTED SCHOOL THE SAME YEAR.

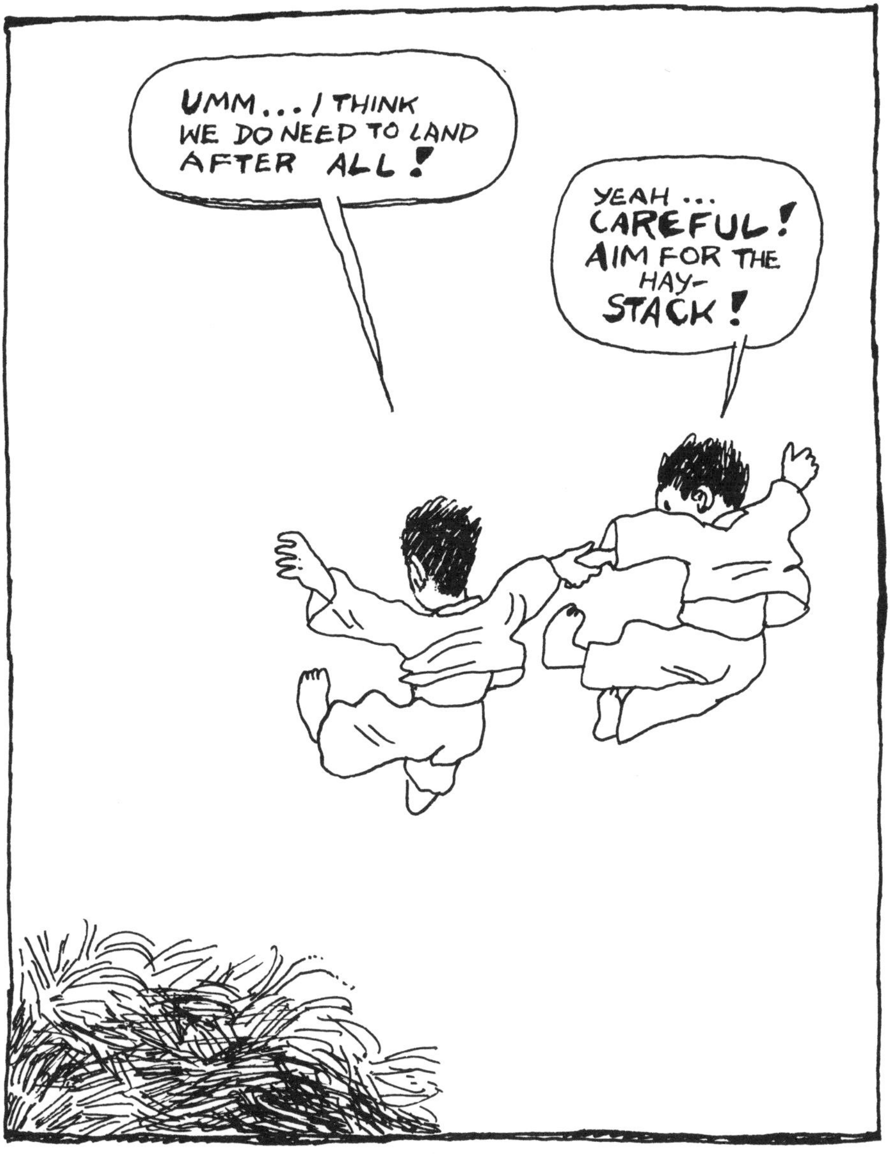
UMM.../ THINK WE DO NEED TO LAND AFTER ALL!
YEAH... CAREFUL! AIM FOR THE HAY-STACK!

BEFORE SCHOOL STARTED WE SPENT ANOTHER SUMMER IN VILLARS. THE DOCTOR RECOMMENDED IT BECAUSE OF ITS 1300-FOOT ALTITUDE.

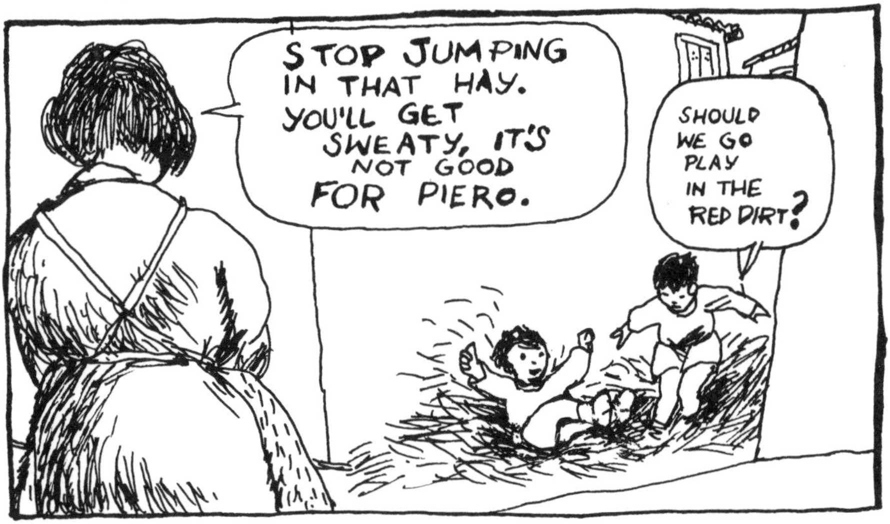
STOP JUMPING IN THAT HAY. YOU'LL GET SWEATY, IT'S NOT GOOD FOR PIERO.
SHOULD WE GO PLAY IN THE RED DIRT?

"RED DIRT" IS THE LOCAL CLAY THAT PEOPLE ONCE USED TO MAKE THE ROOF TILES IN OUR VILLAGE.

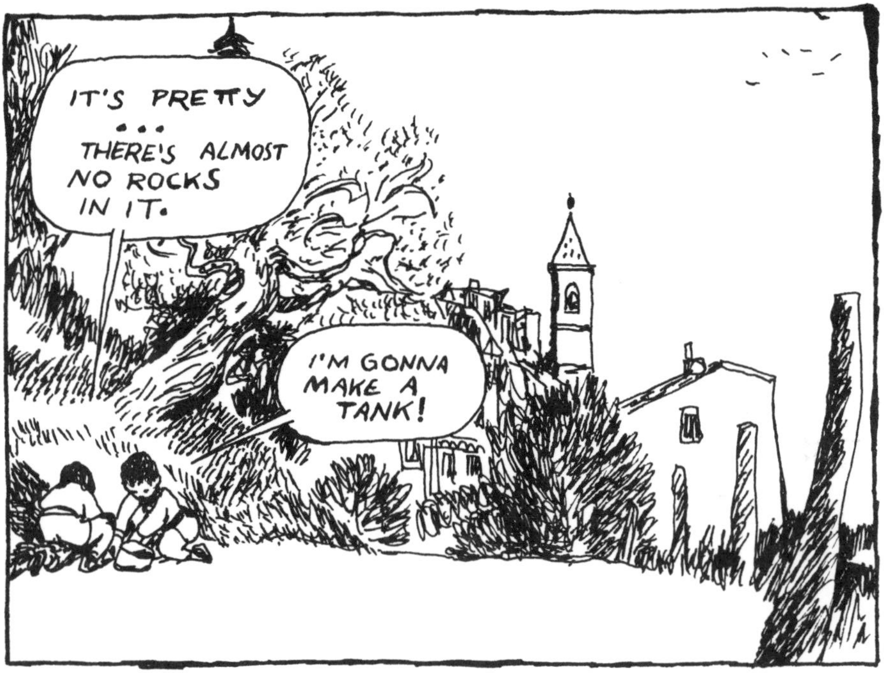
IT'S PRETTY ... THERE'S ALMOST NO ROCKS IN IT.
I'M GONNA MAKE A TANK!

WE WOULD USE THE RED DIRT TO MAKE TANKS, GUNS, COWS, SHEEP, AND LITTLE MEN.

PRETTY GOOD, RIGHT?

YEAH... THE COW NEEDS A TAIL.

THEN WE WOULD DESTROY THEM ...

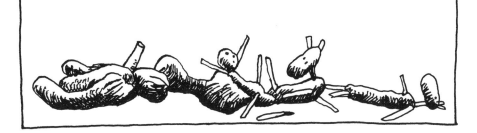

... INEVITABLY WE WOULD FINISH UP BY MAKING A SHEET, A BLANKET, TWO PILLOWS, A BOLSTER, A BED, AND TWO CHILDREN.

WE DIDN'T DESTROY THIS LAST CREATION. WE WOULD LEAVE IT BEHIND TO DRY UP IN SOME NOOK.

AND WE DREW EVERY DAY.

OUR FAVORITE GAME WAS TO TAKE A GIANT SHEET OF PAPER ...

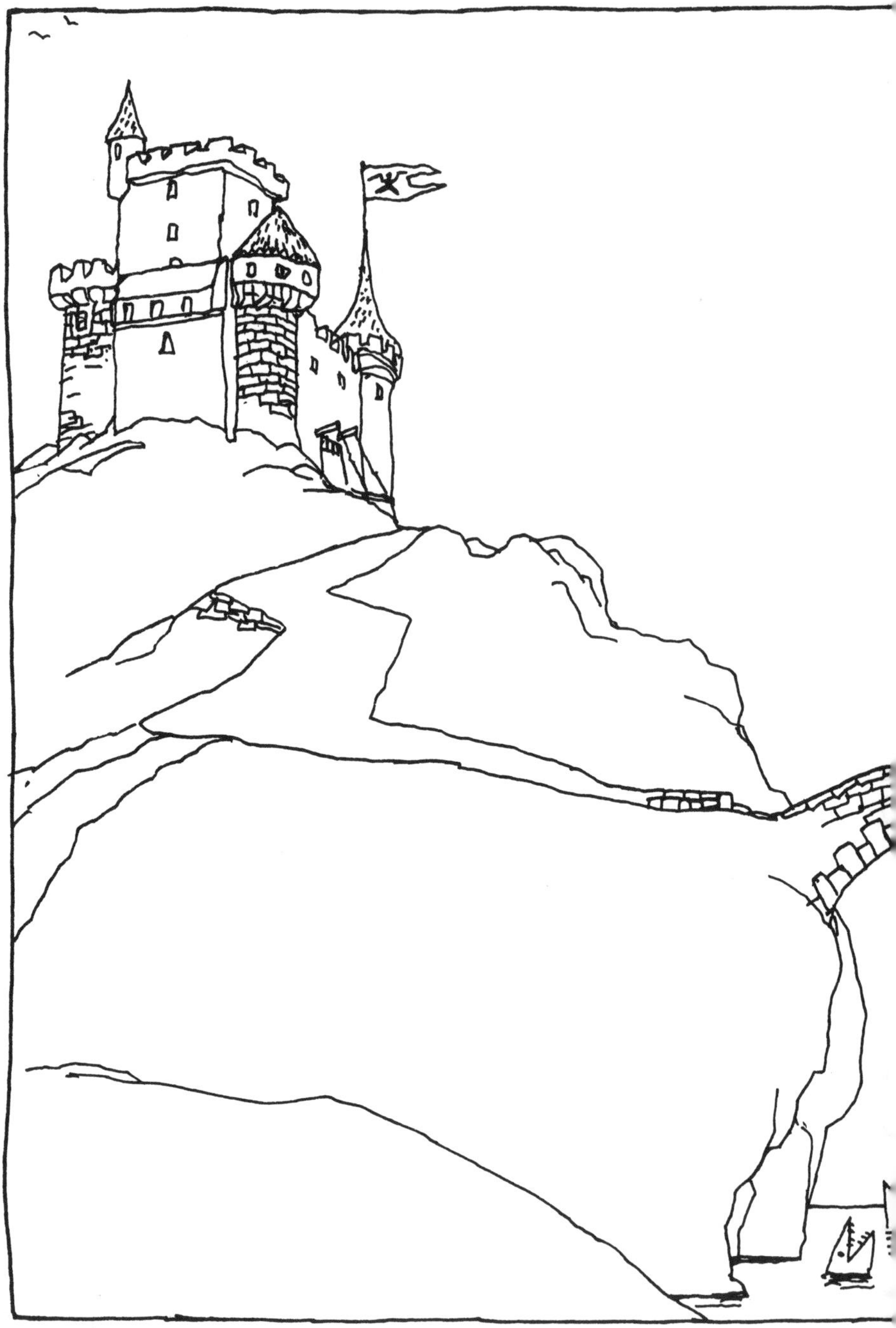

...ON EITHER SIDE OF THE PAPER WE WOULD EACH DRAW A CASTLE, WITH A FLAG.

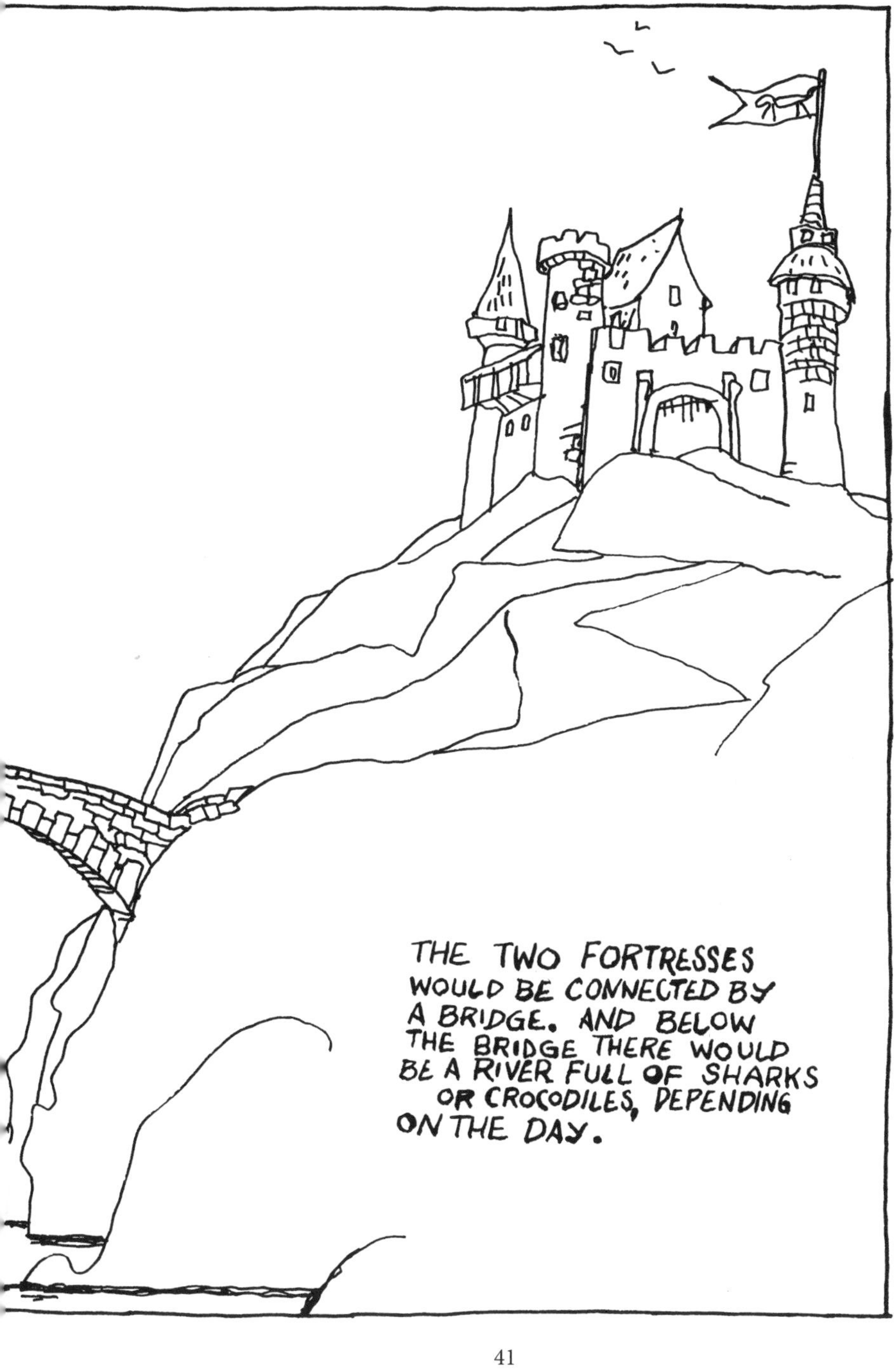
THE TWO FORTRESSES WOULD BE CONNECTED BY A BRIDGE. AND BELOW THE BRIDGE THERE WOULD BE A RIVER FULL OF SHARKS OR CROCODILES, DEPENDING ON THE DAY.

WHEN, AFTER STICKING OUT OUR TONGUES AND CHEWING OUR PENCILS, THE CASTLES WERE FINISHED...

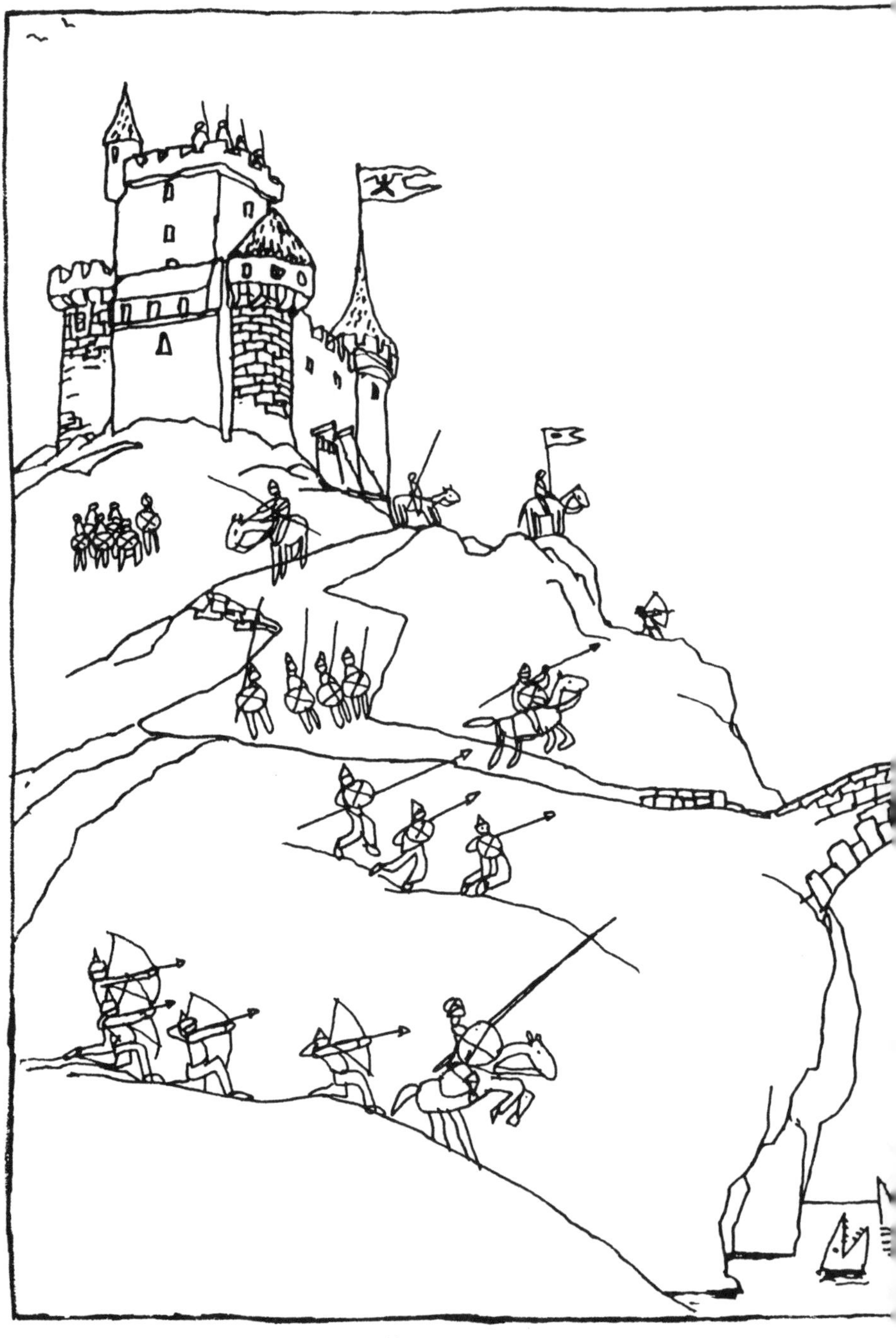

...THE BATTLE COULD BEGIN.

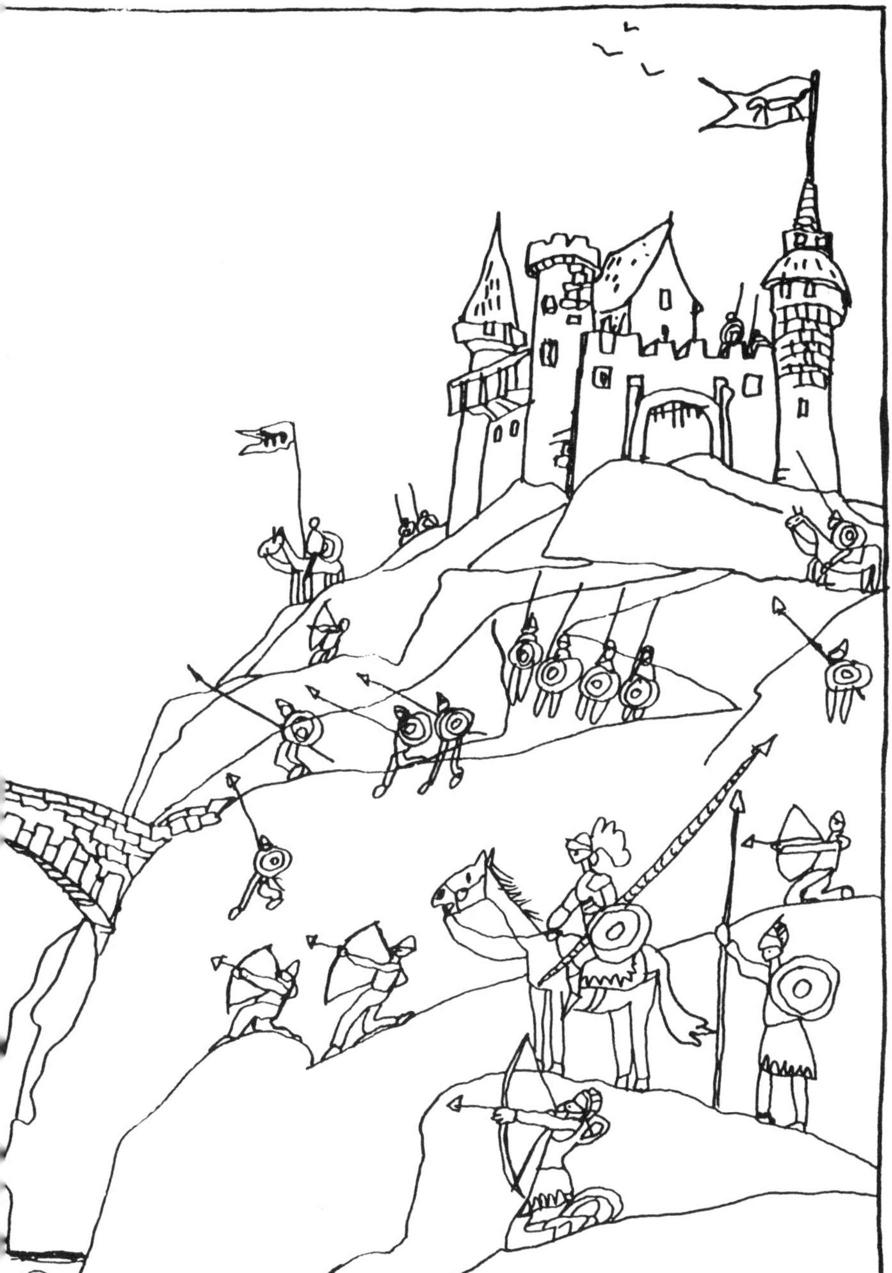

WE DIDN'T USE ERASERS, WE NEVER USED ERASERS VERY MUCH...

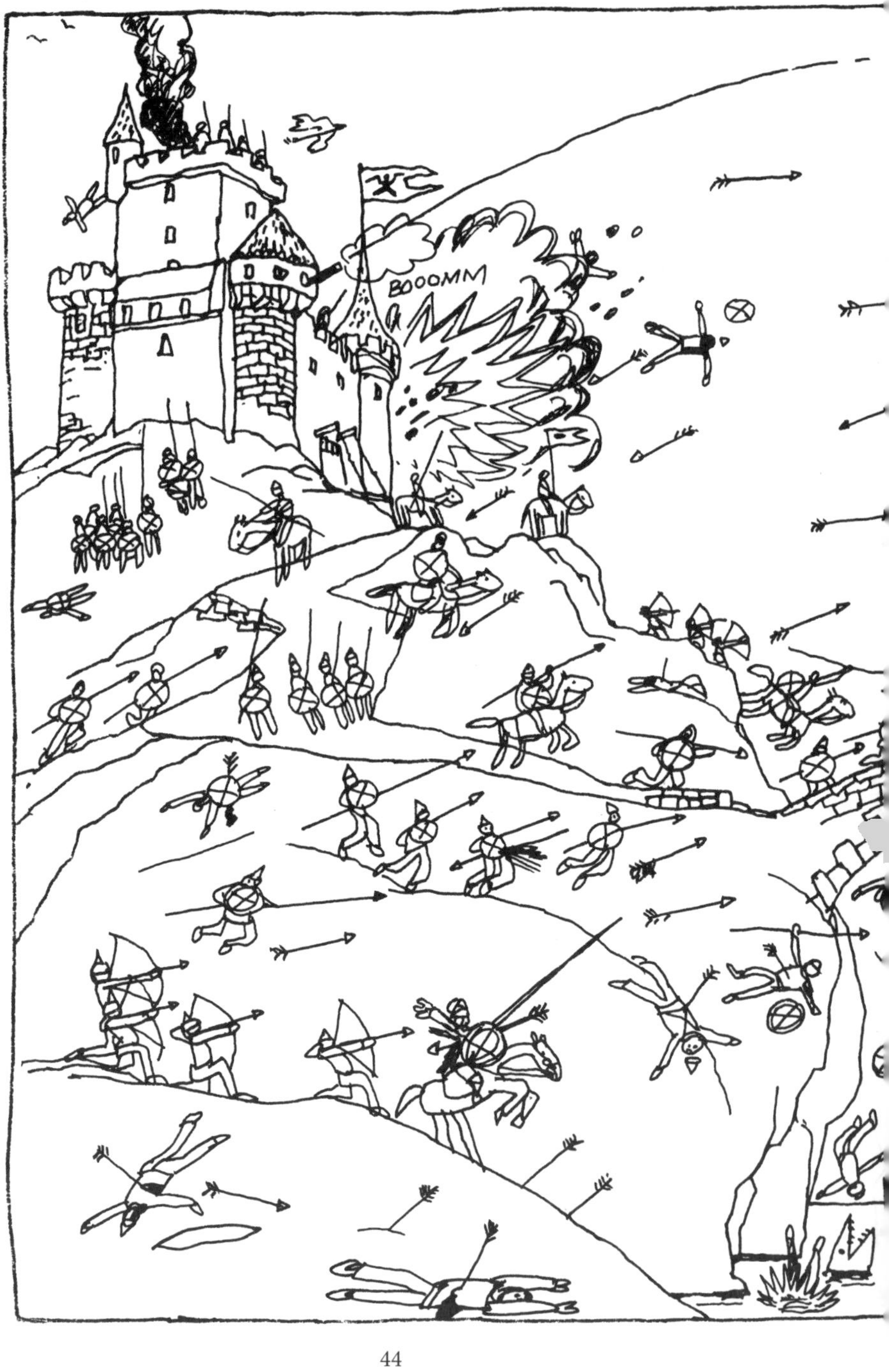
BOOOMM

... AND THE DEAD WERE PILED ON THE DEAD.

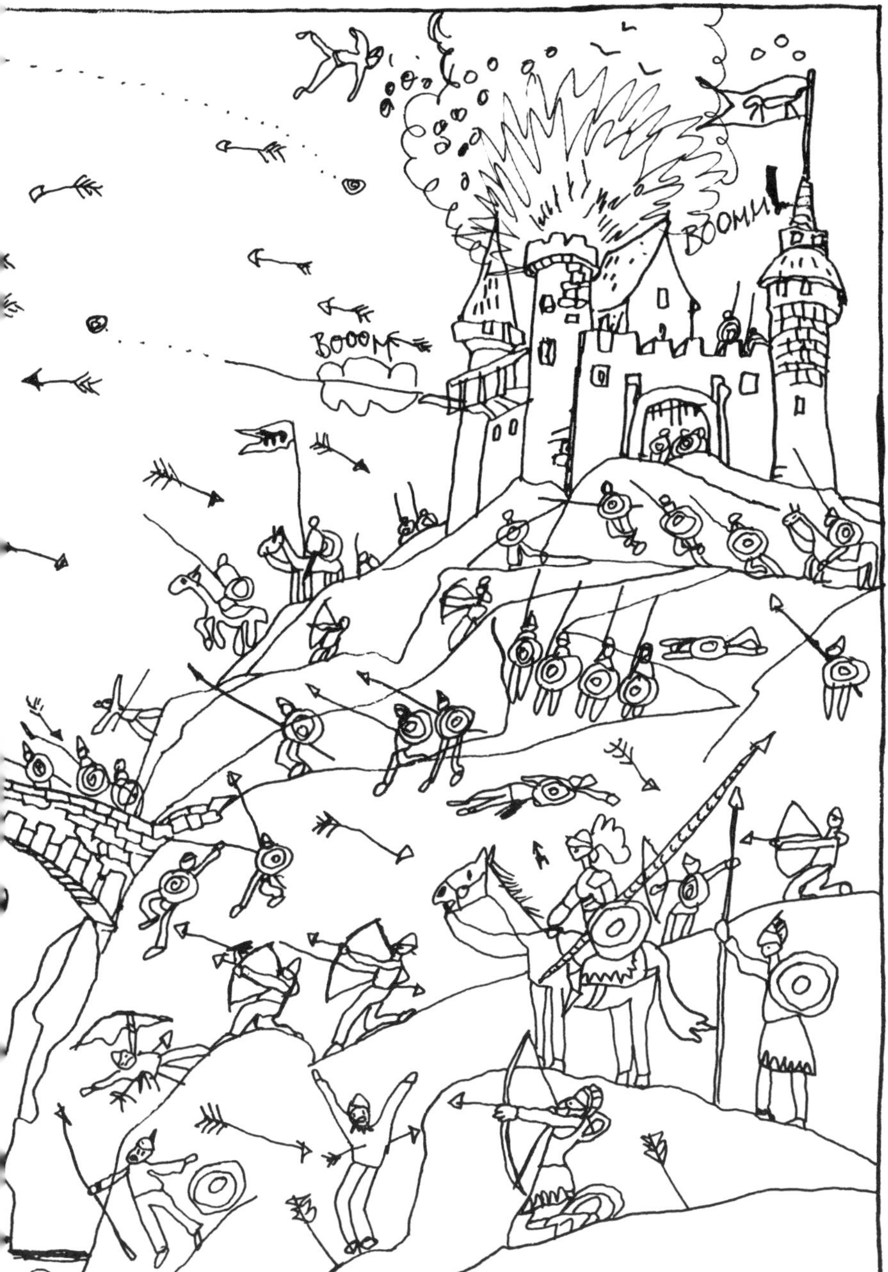
BOOMM!
BOOOM

BY THE END THERE WOULD BE NOTHING BUT SCRATCHES AND ILLEGIBLE MARKS...

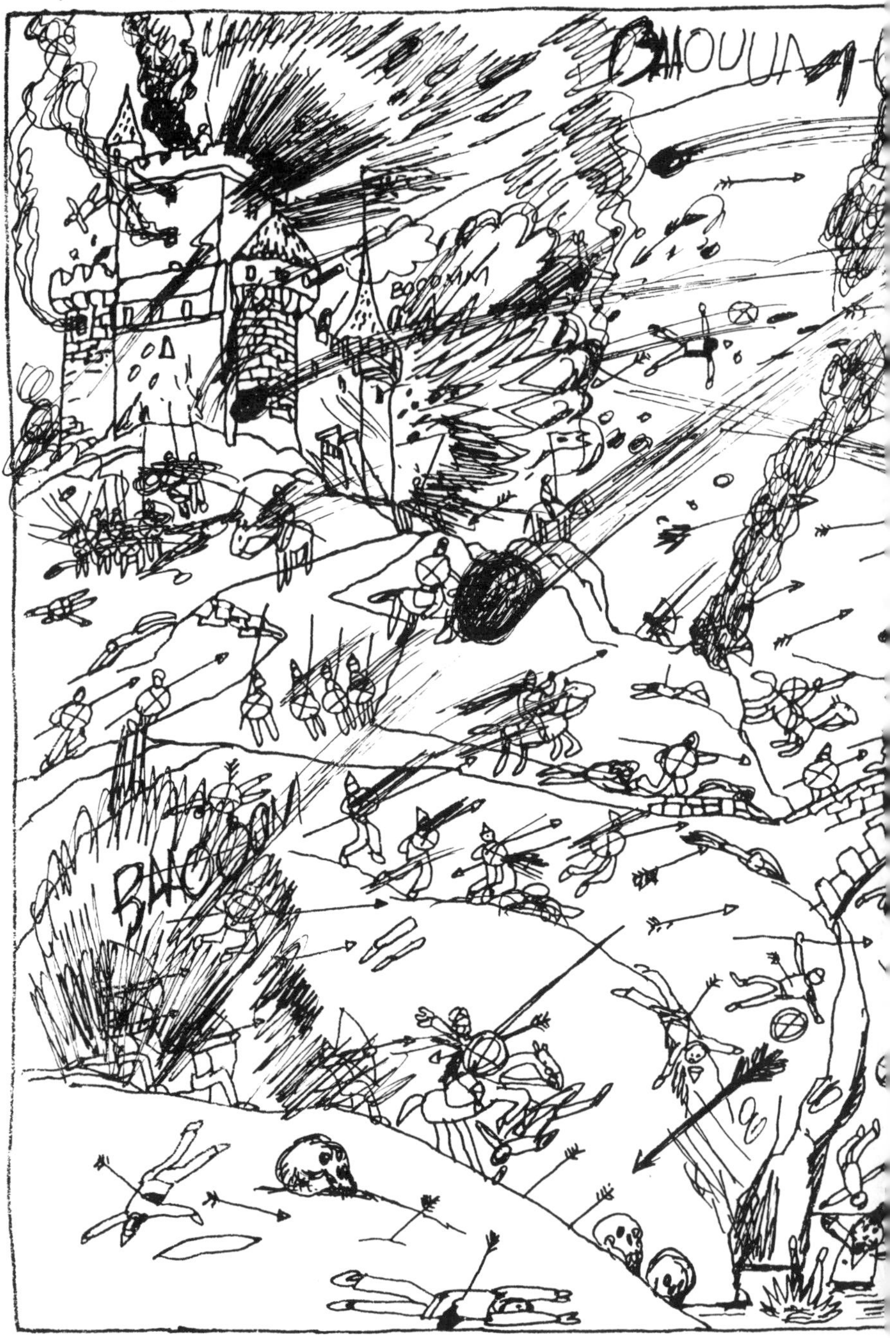
BAOUUM
BAOOOM

...WE WOULD HAVE TO STOP.

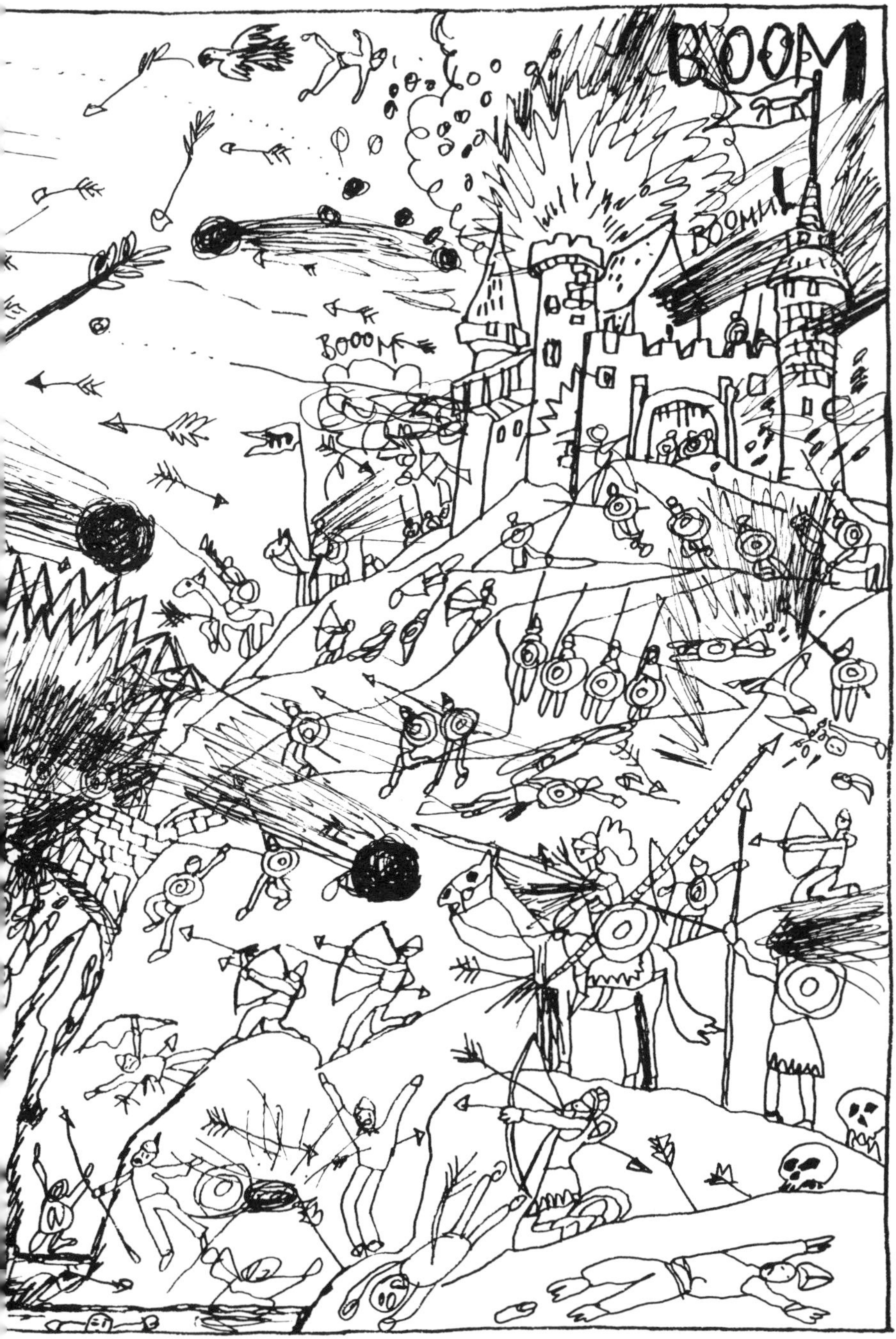
BOOM
BOOM!!
BOOOM

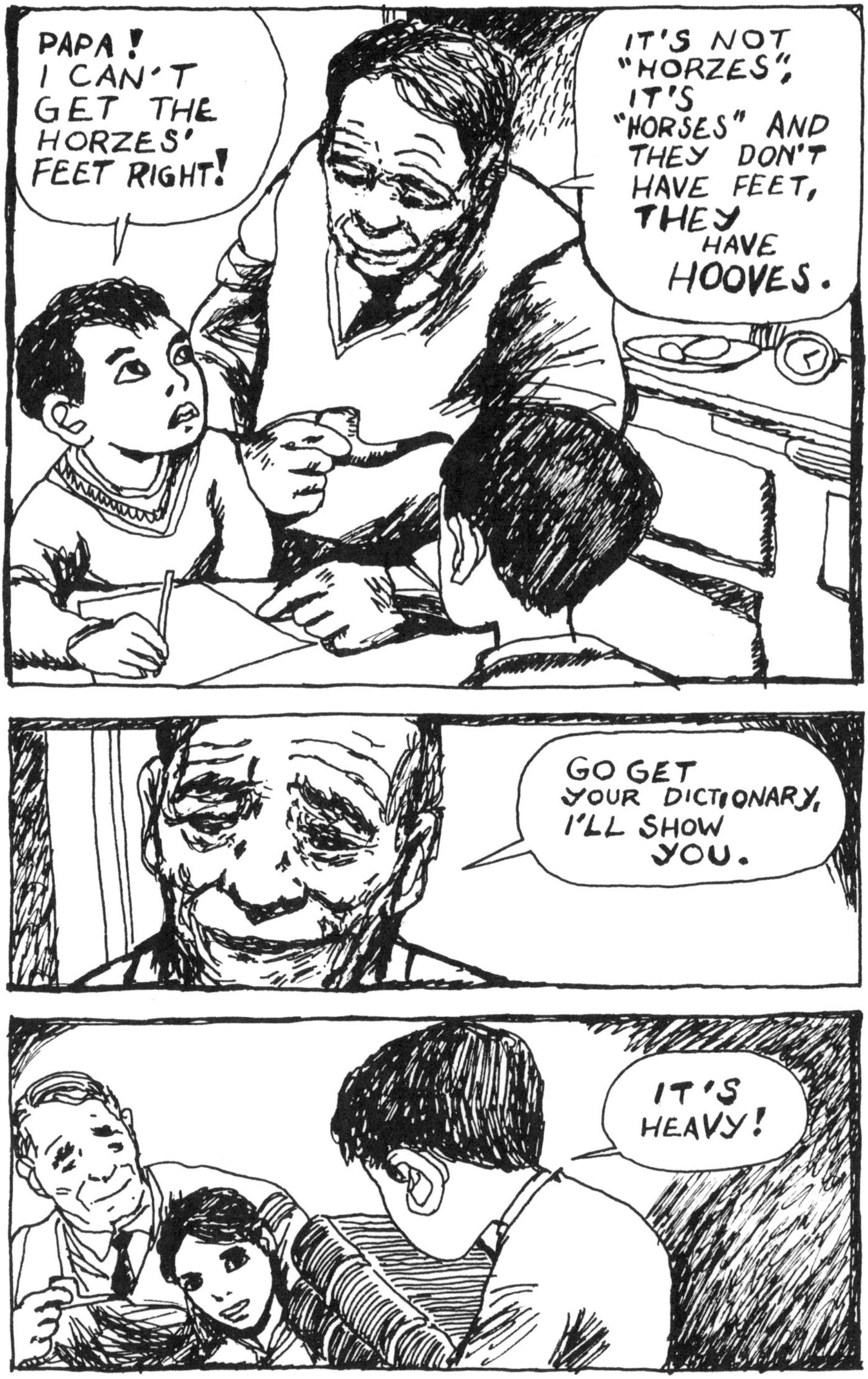
PAPA! I CAN'T GET THE HORZES' FEET RIGHT!
IT'S NOT "HORZES", IT'S "HORSES" AND THEY DON'T HAVE FEET, THEY HAVE HOOVES.
GO GET YOUR DICTIONARY, I'LL SHOW YOU.
IT'S HEAVY!

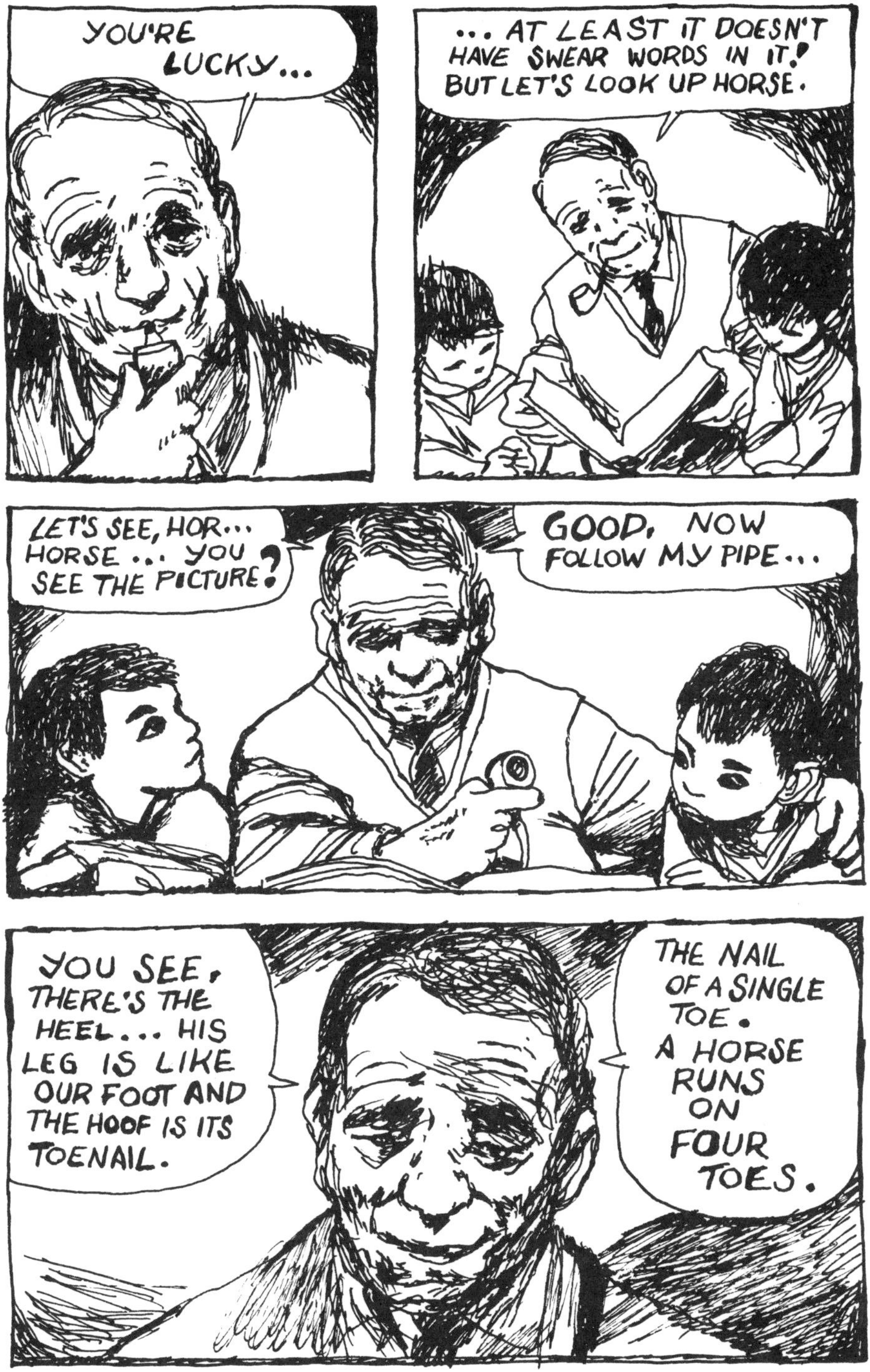
YOU'RE LUCKY...
... AT LEAST IT DOESN'T HAVE SWEAR WORDS IN IT! BUT LET'S LOOK UP HORSE.
LET'S SEE, HOR... HORSE ... YOU SEE THE PICTURE?
GOOD, NOW FOLLOW MY PIPE...
YOU SEE, THERE'S THE HEEL... HIS LEG IS LIKE OUR FOOT AND THE HOOF IS ITS TOENAIL.
THE NAIL OF A SINGLE TOE. A HORSE RUNS ON FOUR TOES.

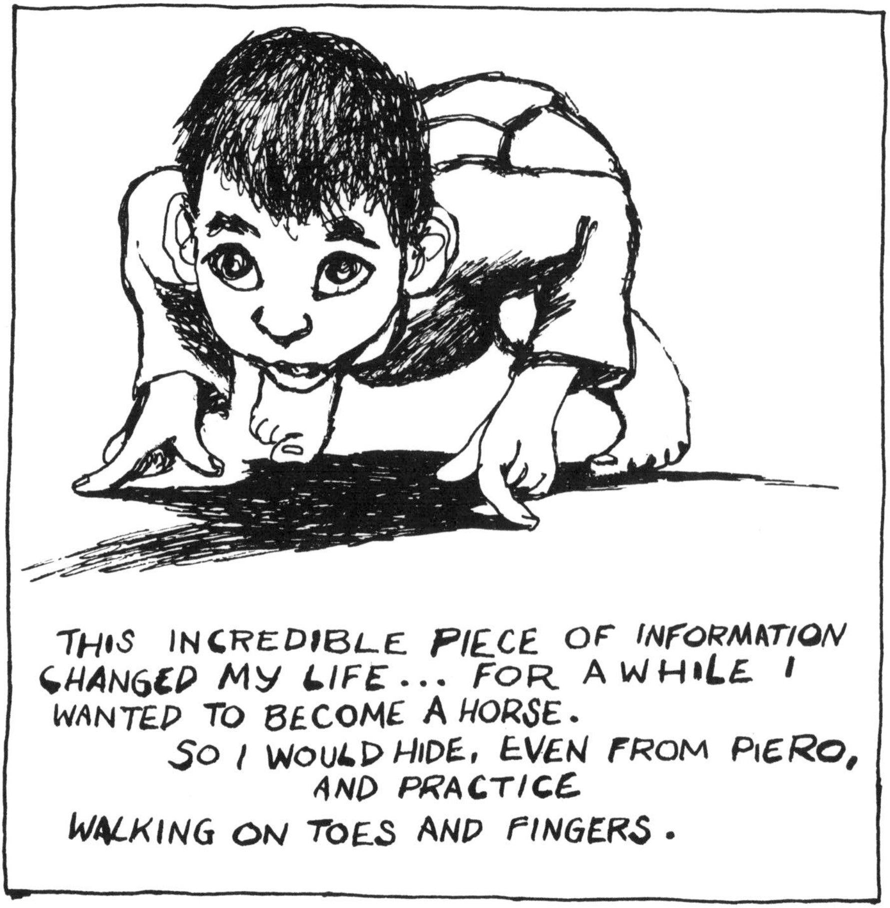
THIS INCREDIBLE PIECE OF INFORMATION CHANGED MY LIFE... FOR A WHILE I WANTED TO BECOME A HORSE.
SO I WOULD HIDE, EVEN FROM PIERO, AND PRACTICE
WALKING ON TOES AND FINGERS.

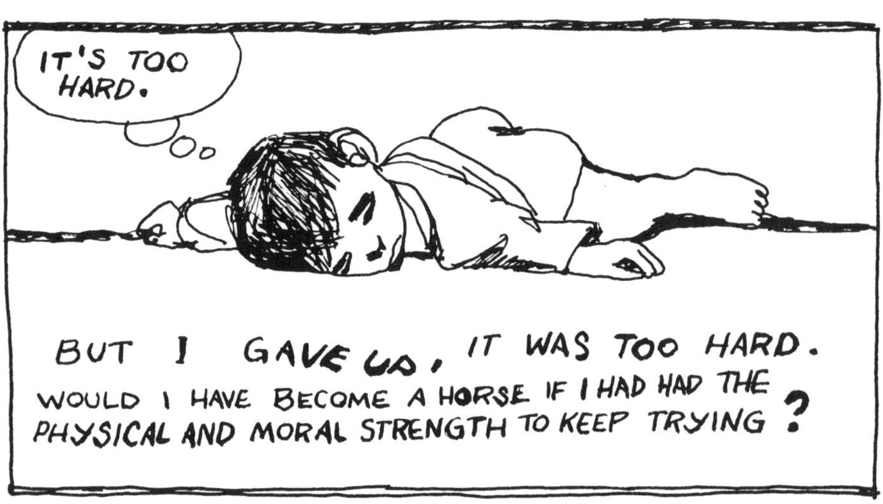
IT'S TOO HARD.
BUT I GAVE UP, IT WAS TOO HARD.
WOULD I HAVE BECOME A HORSE IF I HAD HAD THE PHYSICAL AND MORAL STRENGTH TO KEEP TRYING?

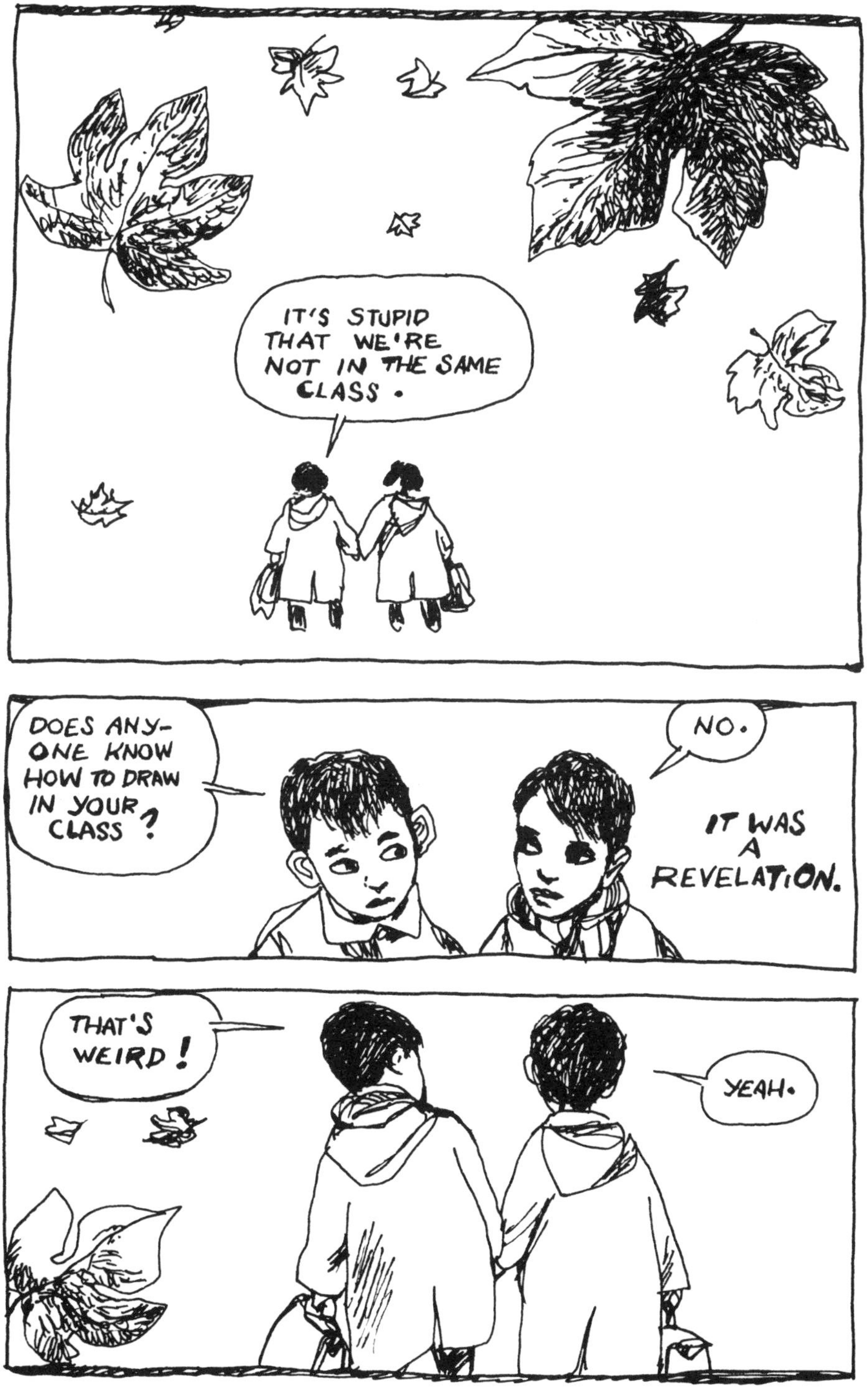
IT'S STUPID THAT WE'RE NOT IN THE SAME CLASS.
DOES ANYONE KNOW HOW TO DRAW IN YOUR CLASS?
NO.
IT WAS A REVELATION.
THAT'S WEIRD!
YEAH.

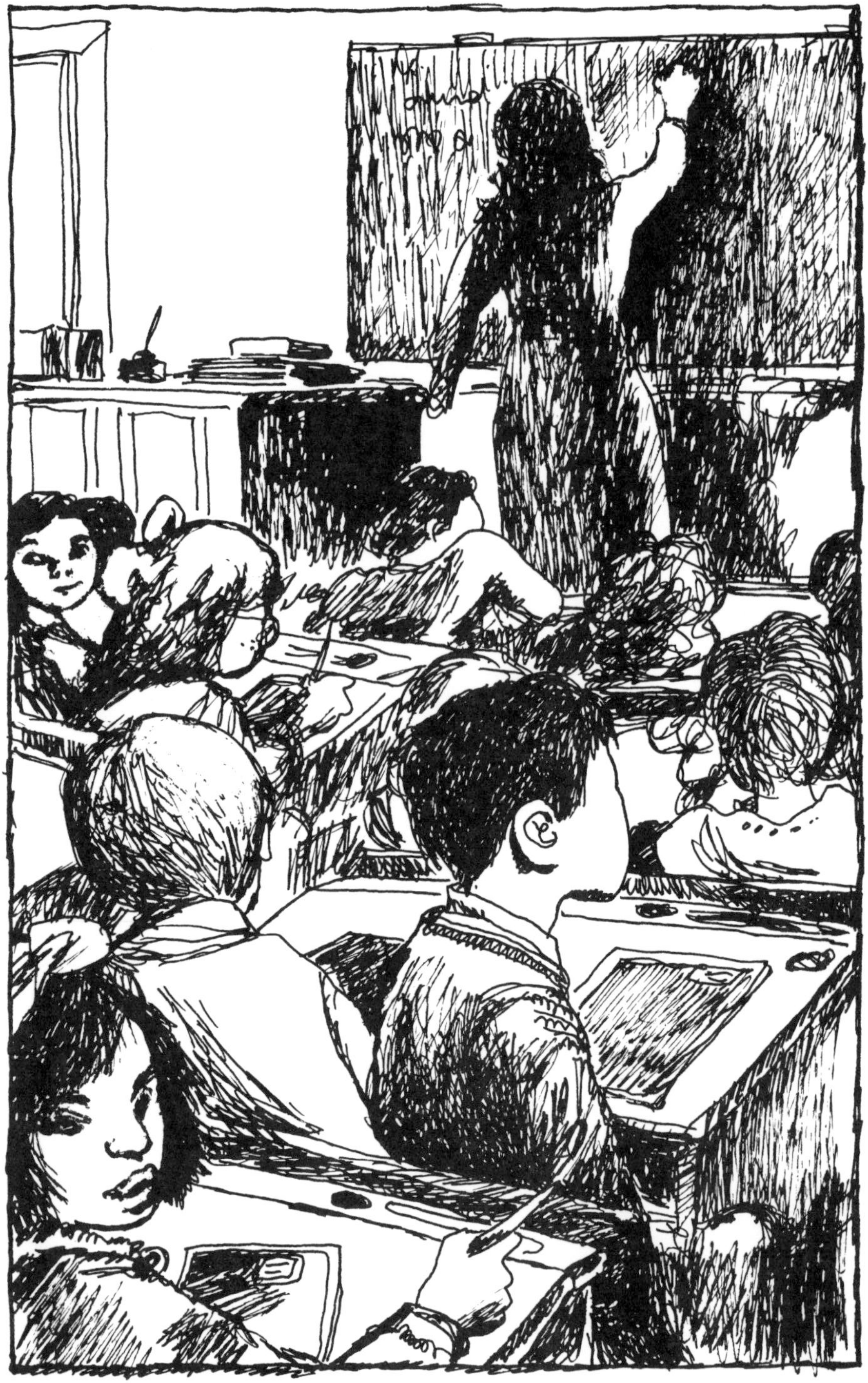

SCHOOL, OTHER PEOPLE. FIGURING OUT THAT WE HAD SOMETHING OTHER KIDS DIDN'T HAVE.

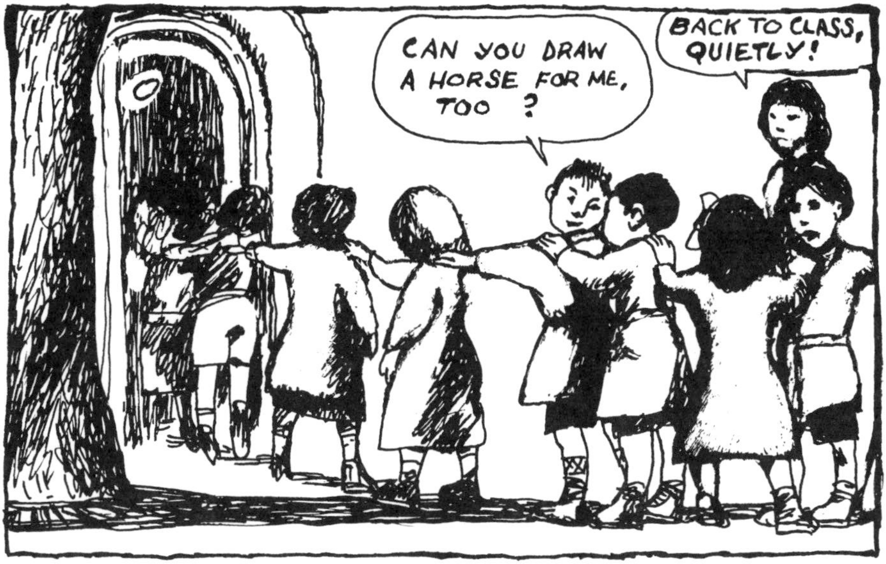
CAN YOU DRAW A HORSE FOR ME, TOO ?
BACK TO CLASS, QUIETLY!

EXISTING.
THE KID WHO REALIZES WITHIN THE FIRST HOUR OF GYM CLASS THAT HE RUNS FASTER THAN THE OTHERS WILL KEEP RUNNING... HE'LL BE "THE KID WHO RUNS FAST."

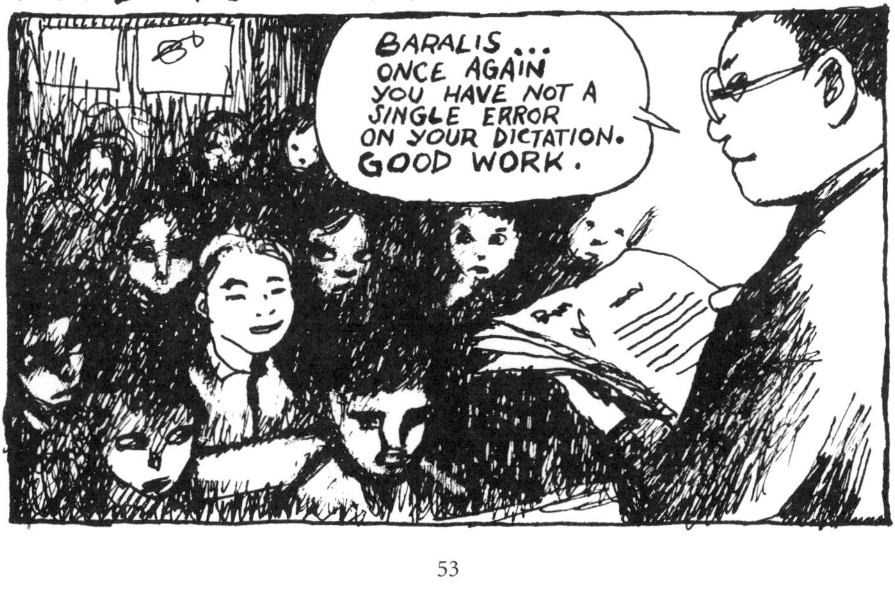
BARALIS... ONCE AGAIN YOU HAVE NOT A SINGLE ERROR ON YOUR DICTATION. GOOD WORK.

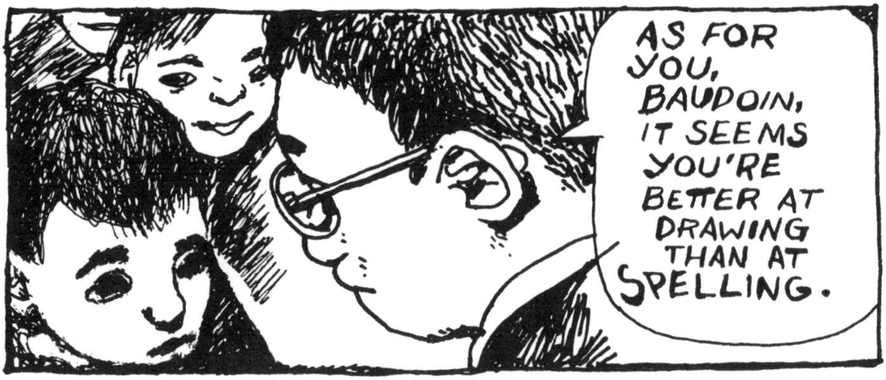
AS FOR YOU, BAUDOIN, IT SEEMS YOU'RE BETTER AT DRAWING THAN AT SPELLING.

I COULDN'T RUN FAST.

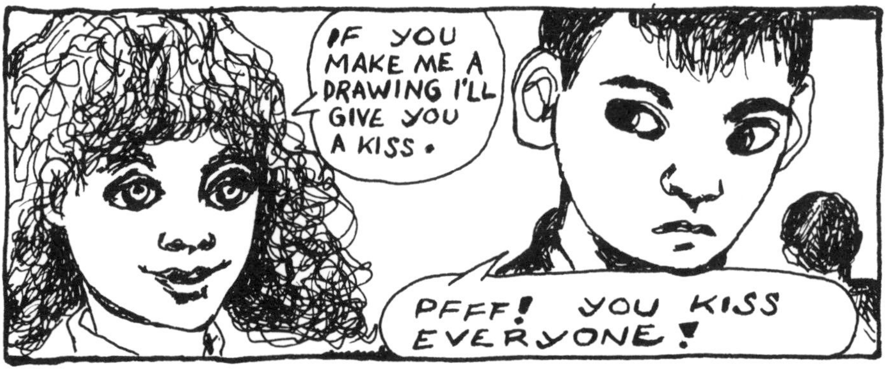
IF YOU MAKE ME A DRAWING I'LL GIVE YOU A KISS.
PFFF! YOU KISS EVERYONE!

I WAS TERRIBLE AT EVERYTHING, EXCEPT MAYBE GEOGRAPHY.

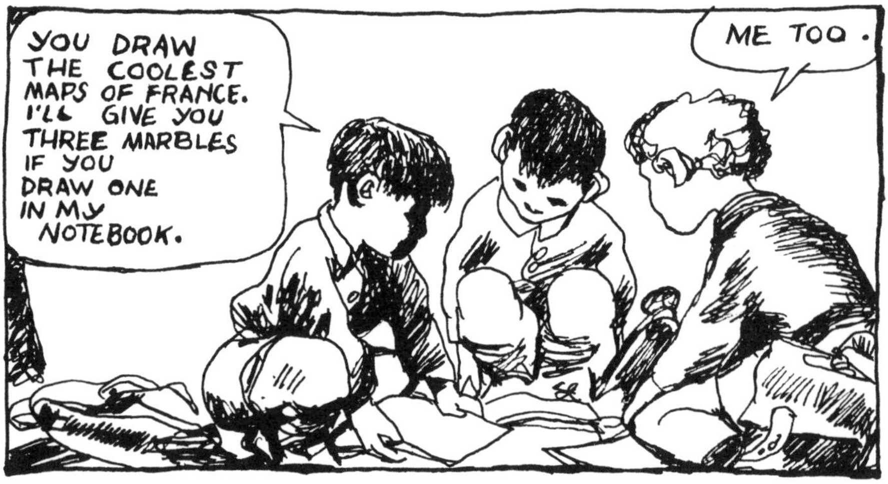
YOU DRAW THE COOLEST MAPS OF FRANCE. I'LL GIVE YOU THREE MARBLES IF YOU DRAW ONE IN MY NOTEBOOK.
ME TOO.

WITH PIERO IT WAS THE SAME... EXCEPT HE MANAGED TO SCORE ½ POINT MORE THAN ME PRETTY MUCH ACROSS THE BOARD.

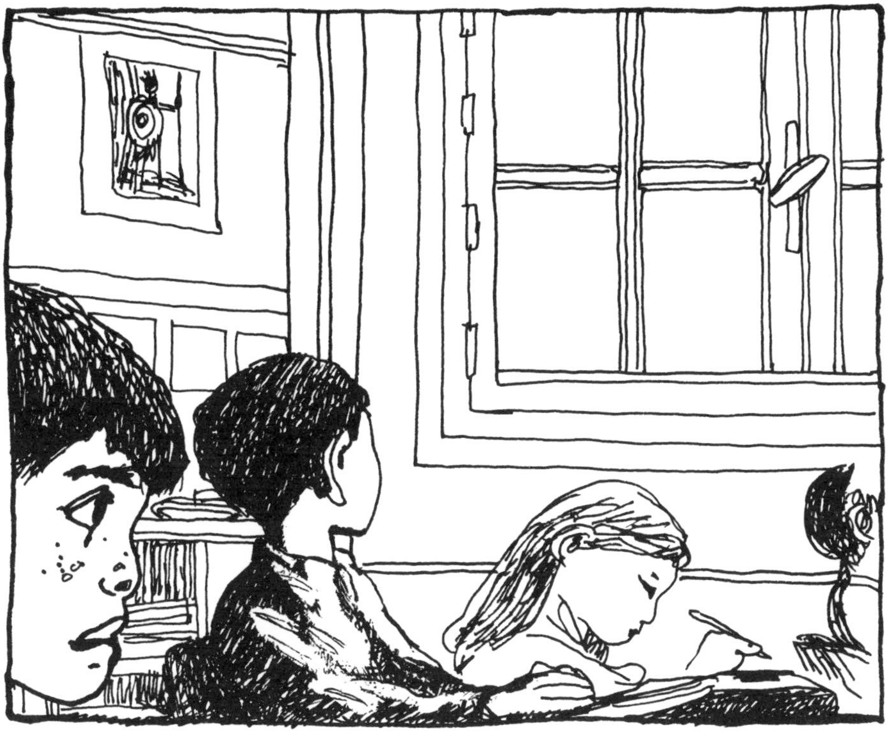

WHAT INTERESTED ME MOST IN THE CLASSROOM WAS THE WINDOW ...

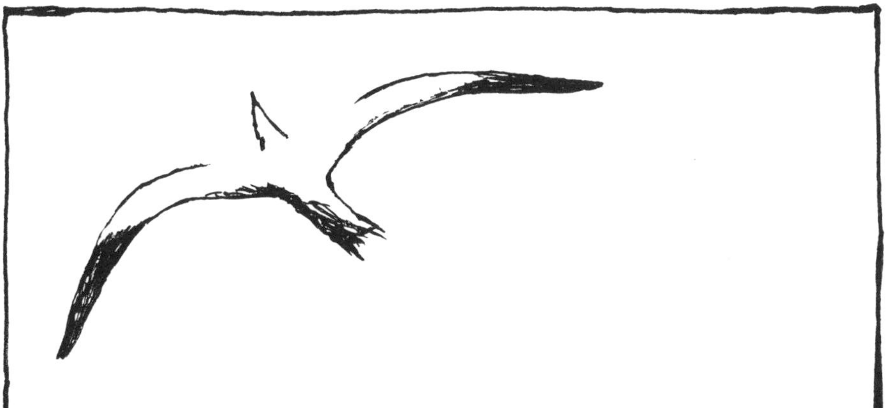

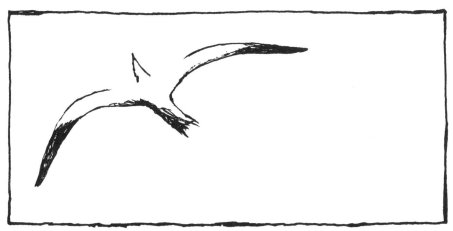

... AND MOST OF ALL WHAT WAS HAPPENING ON THE OTHER SIDE.

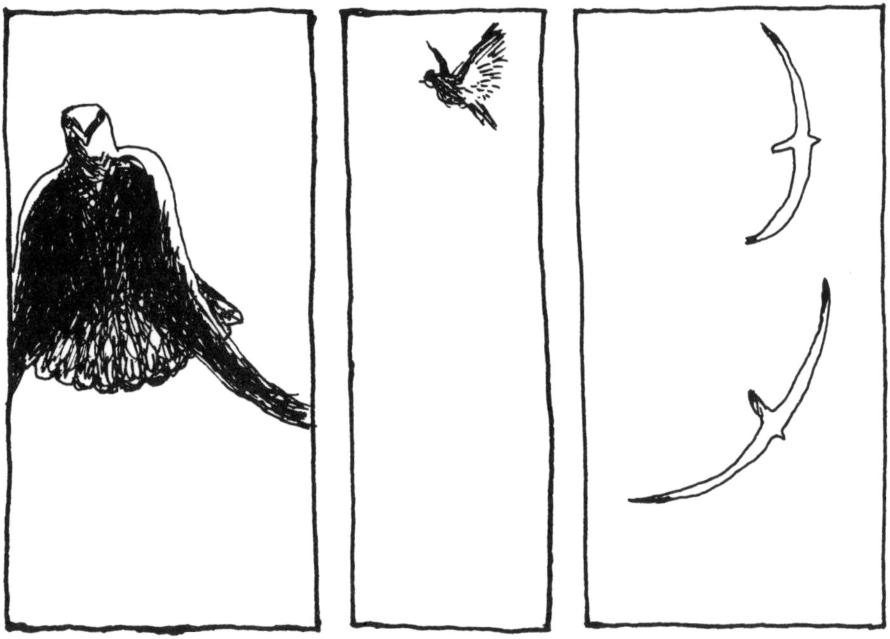

THANKS TO SCHOOL I BECAME A GREAT EXPERT IN THE COMPARATIVE STUDY OF THE FLIGHT OF PIGEONS, SPARROWS, AND SEAGULLS.

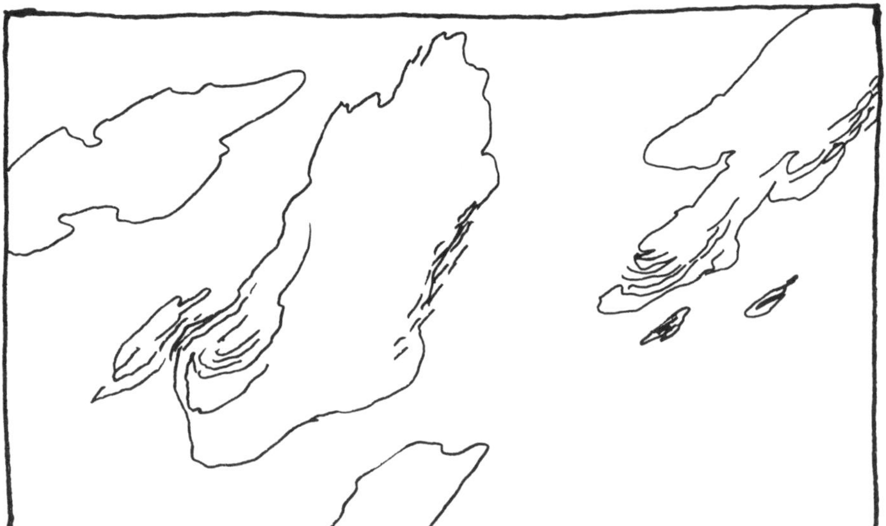

... AS WELL AS IN THE MYSTERIES OF THE FORMATION AND DISSOLUTION OF CLOUDS.

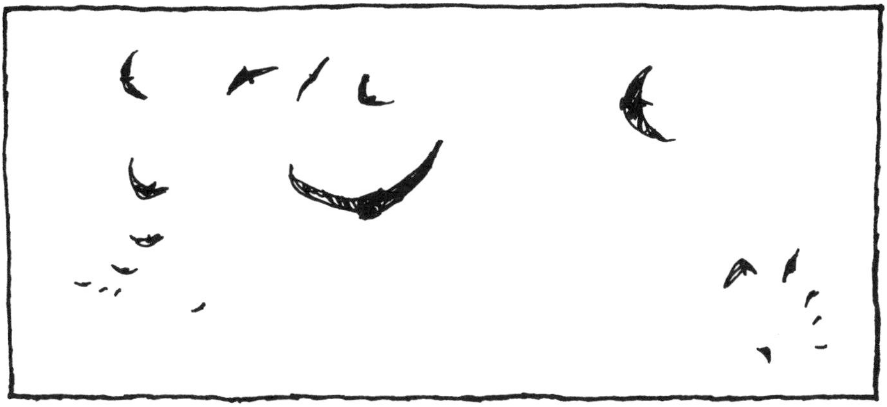

AND, WHEN SPRING RETURNED, ALL MY ATTENTION BECAME FOCUSED ON THE SWALLOWS AND THE SWIFTS, THOSE CALLIGRAPHERS IN THE SKY.

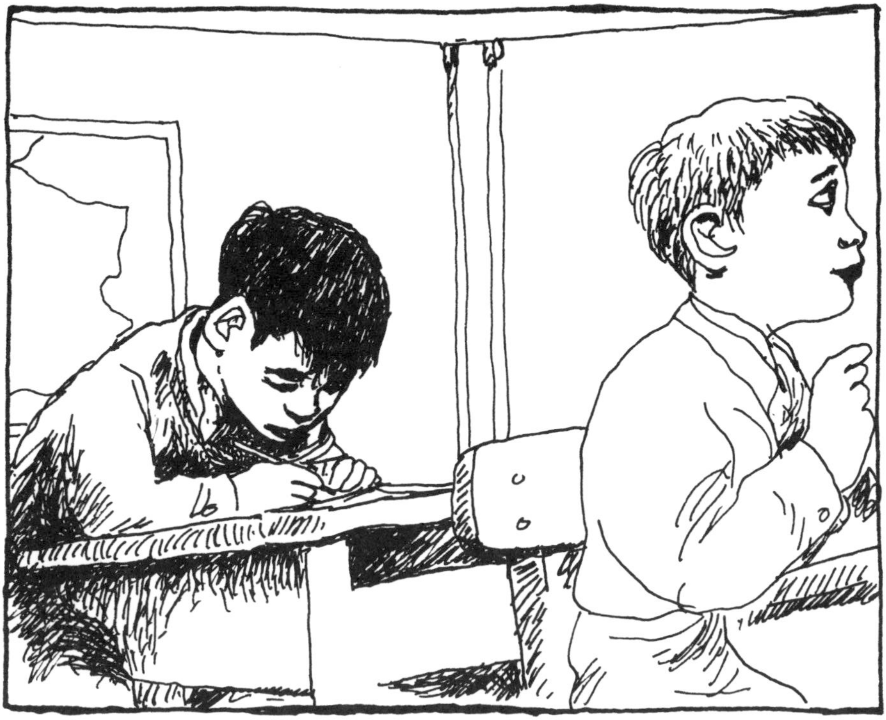

THERE WERE OTHER SCHOLARS OF NOTHING AT SCHOOL. BUT I WAS THE ONLY ONE WHO INSCRIBED THE FRUITS OF MY RESEARCH ON THE WOODEN DESKTOPS.

TEACHERS ARE INTELLIGENT PEOPLE. THEY QUICKLY REALIZED THAT I WAS NOT TO BE DISTURBED.

BUT SINCE THEY WERE RESPONSIBLE FOR THE SCHOOL'S FURNISHINGS...

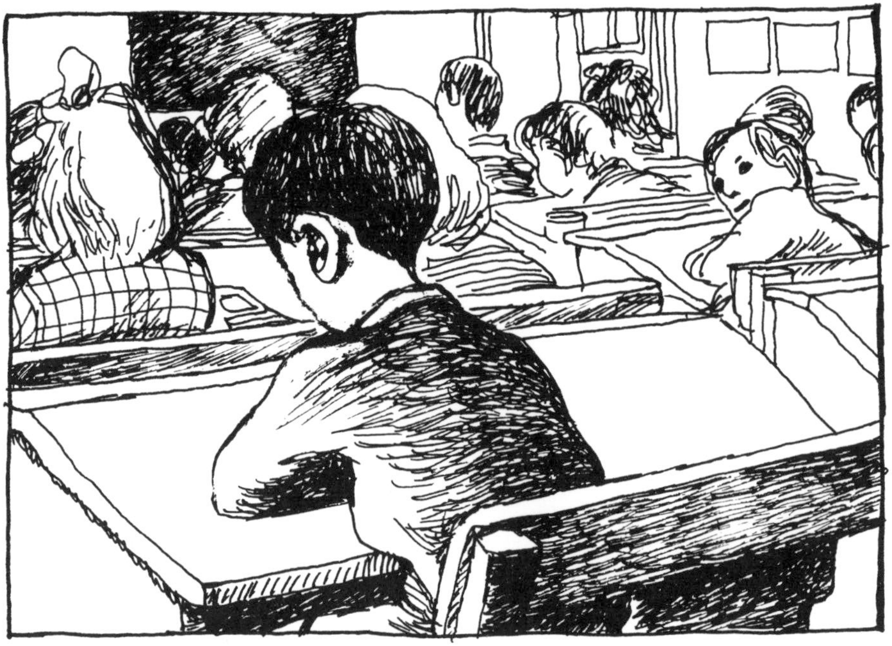

...THEY WERE QUICK TO FIGURE OUT THAT THEY NEEDED TO LEAVE ME AT ONE DESK AND NOT MOVE ME FOR THE REST OF THE SCHOOL YEAR.

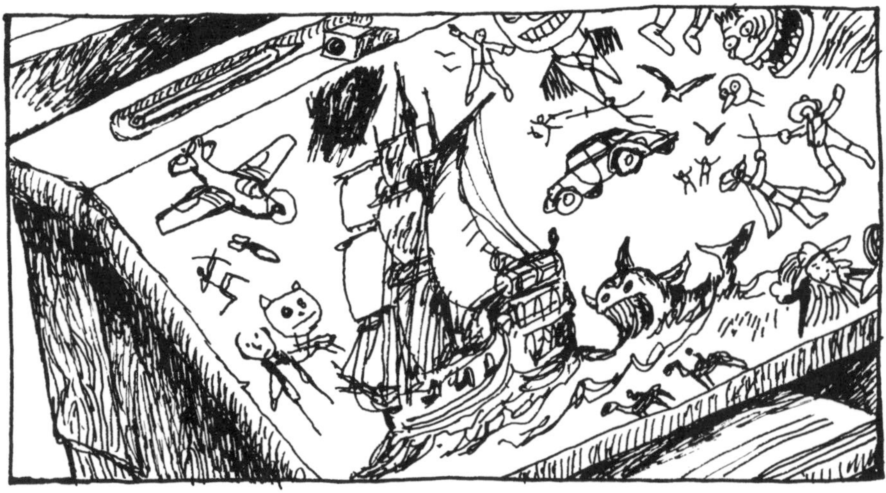

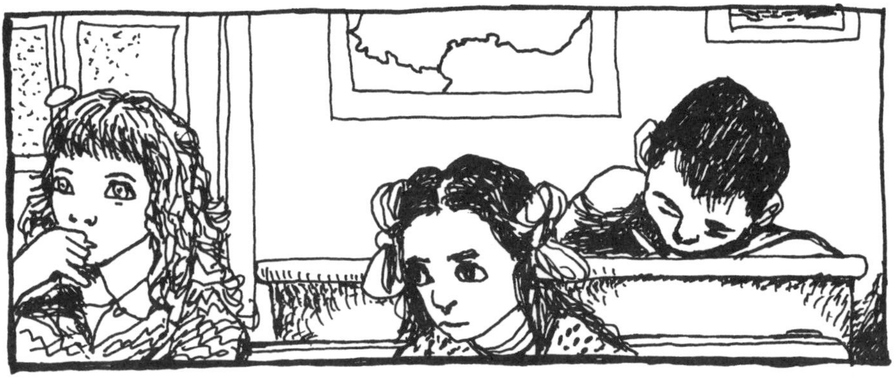

I WAS A QUIET, WELL-BEHAVED STUDENT, SO QUIET THAT ONE YEAR THEY FORGOT ABOUT ME AND I HAD TO REPEAT A YEAR. I SPENT TWO YEARS IN THE SAME SEAT, AT THE SAME DESK.

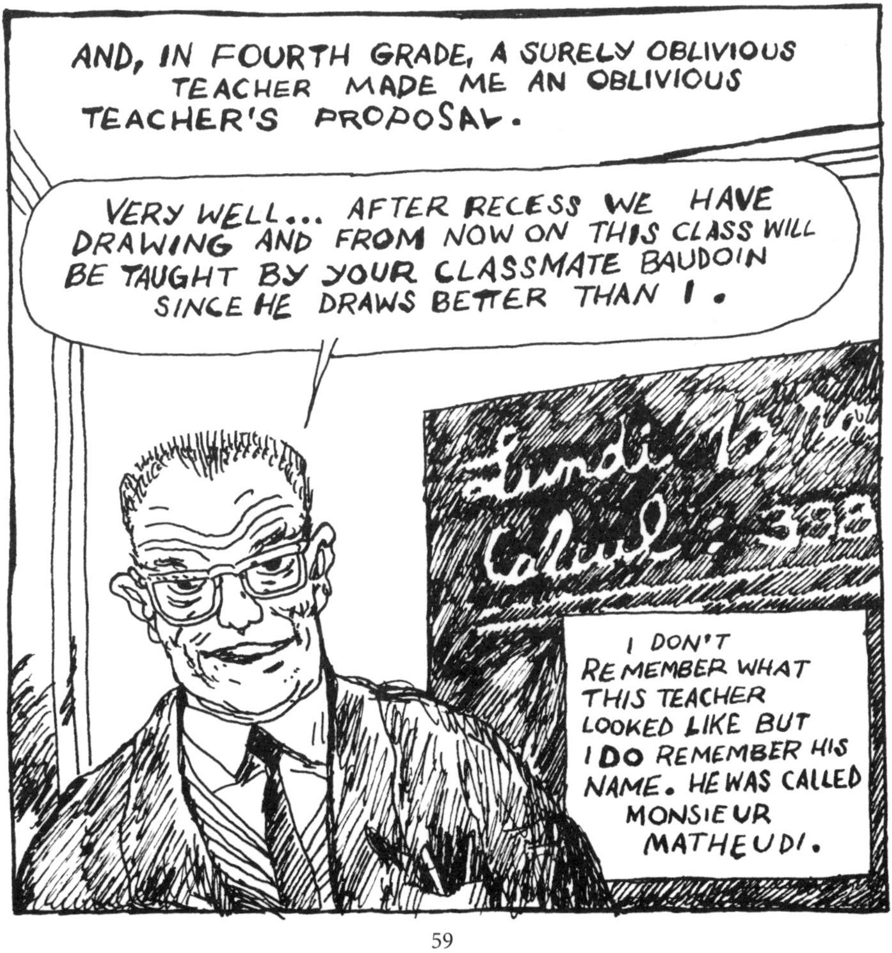
AND, IN FOURTH GRADE, A SURELY OBLIVIOUS TEACHER MADE ME AN OBLIVIOUS TEACHER'S PROPOSAL.
VERY WELL... AFTER RECESS WE HAVE DRAWING AND FROM NOW ON THIS CLASS WILL BE TAUGHT BY YOUR CLASSMATE BAUDOIN SINCE HE DRAWS BETTER THAN I.
I DON'T REMEMBER WHAT THIS TEACHER LOOKED LIKE BUT I DO REMEMBER HIS NAME. HE WAS CALLED MONSIEUR MATHEUDI.

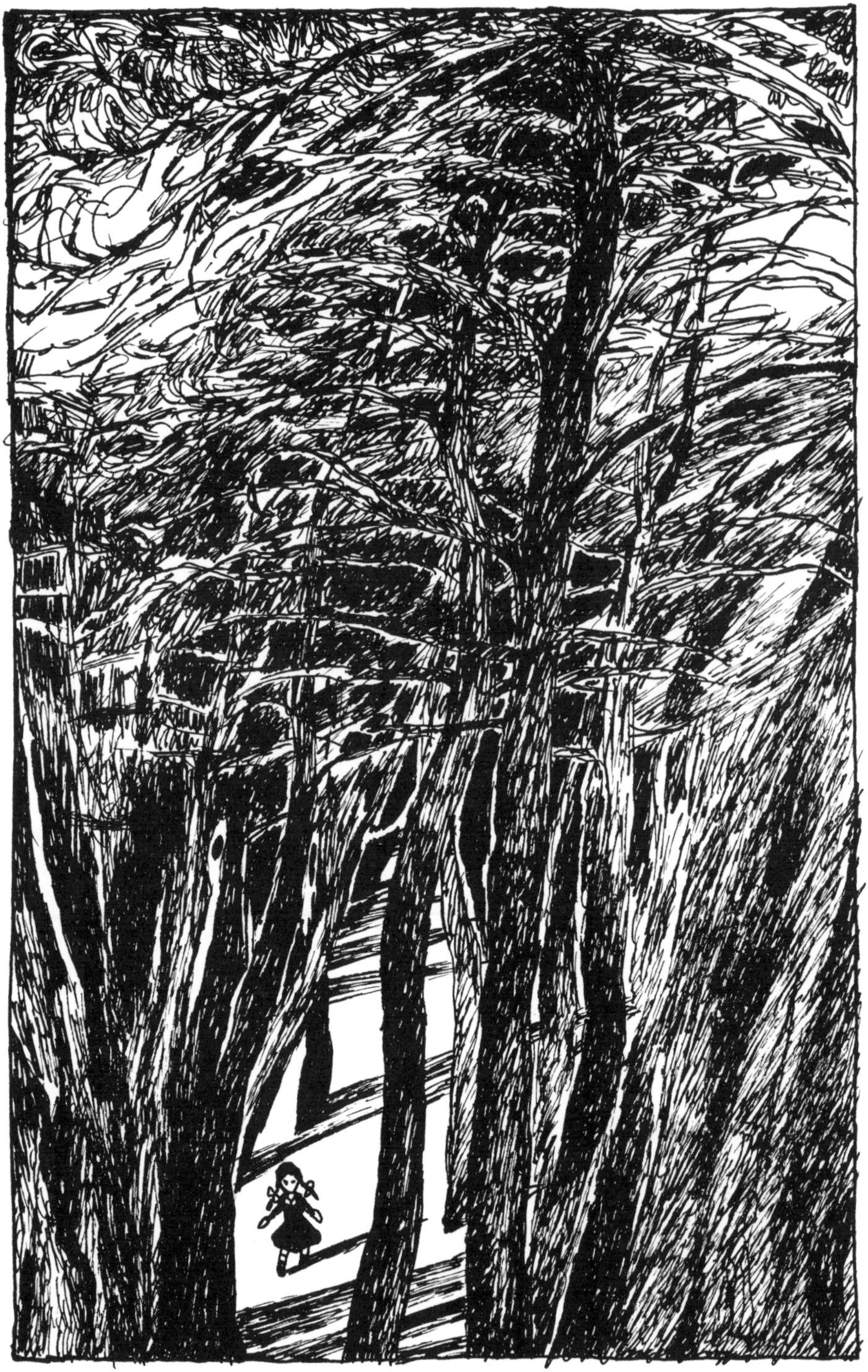

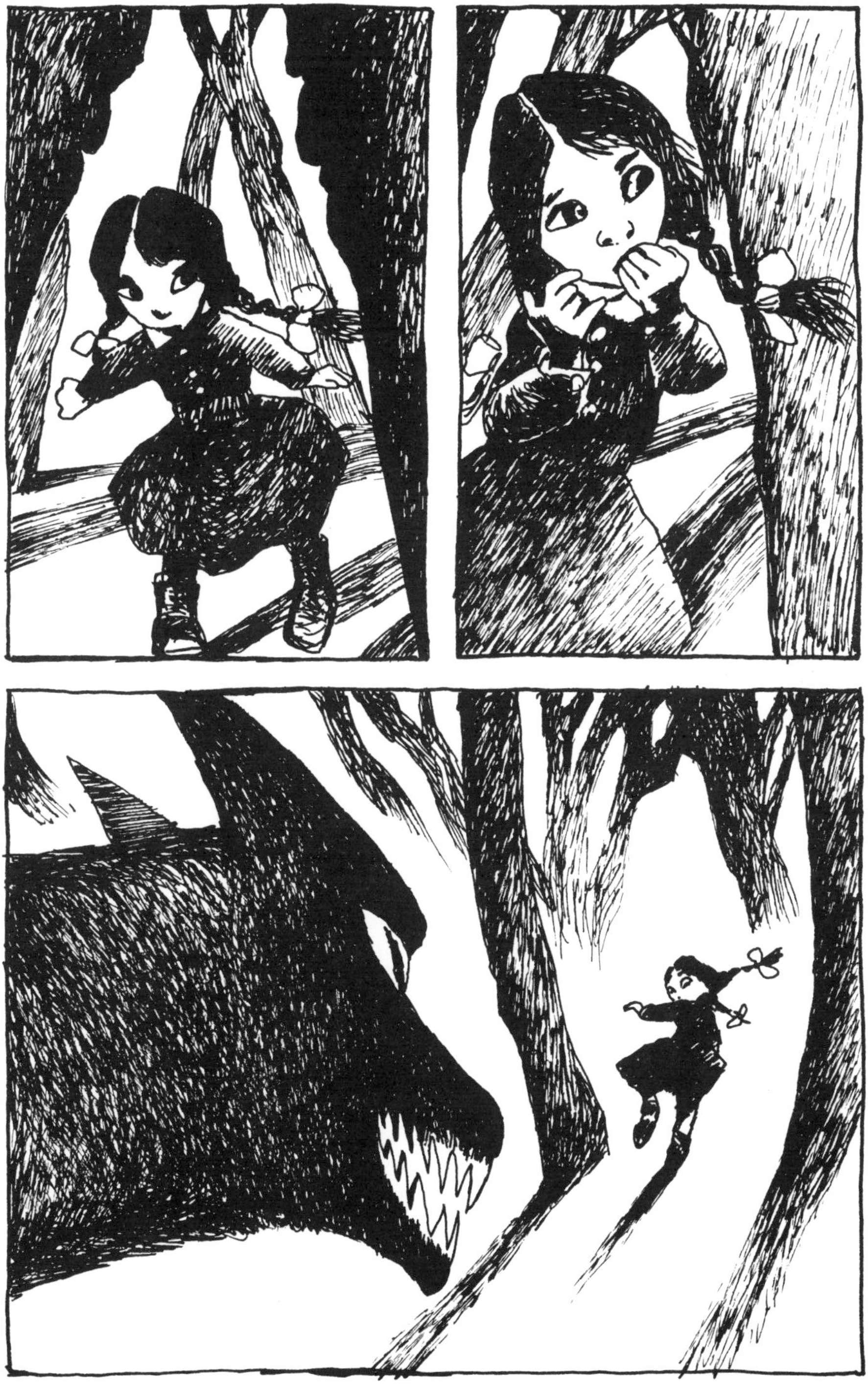

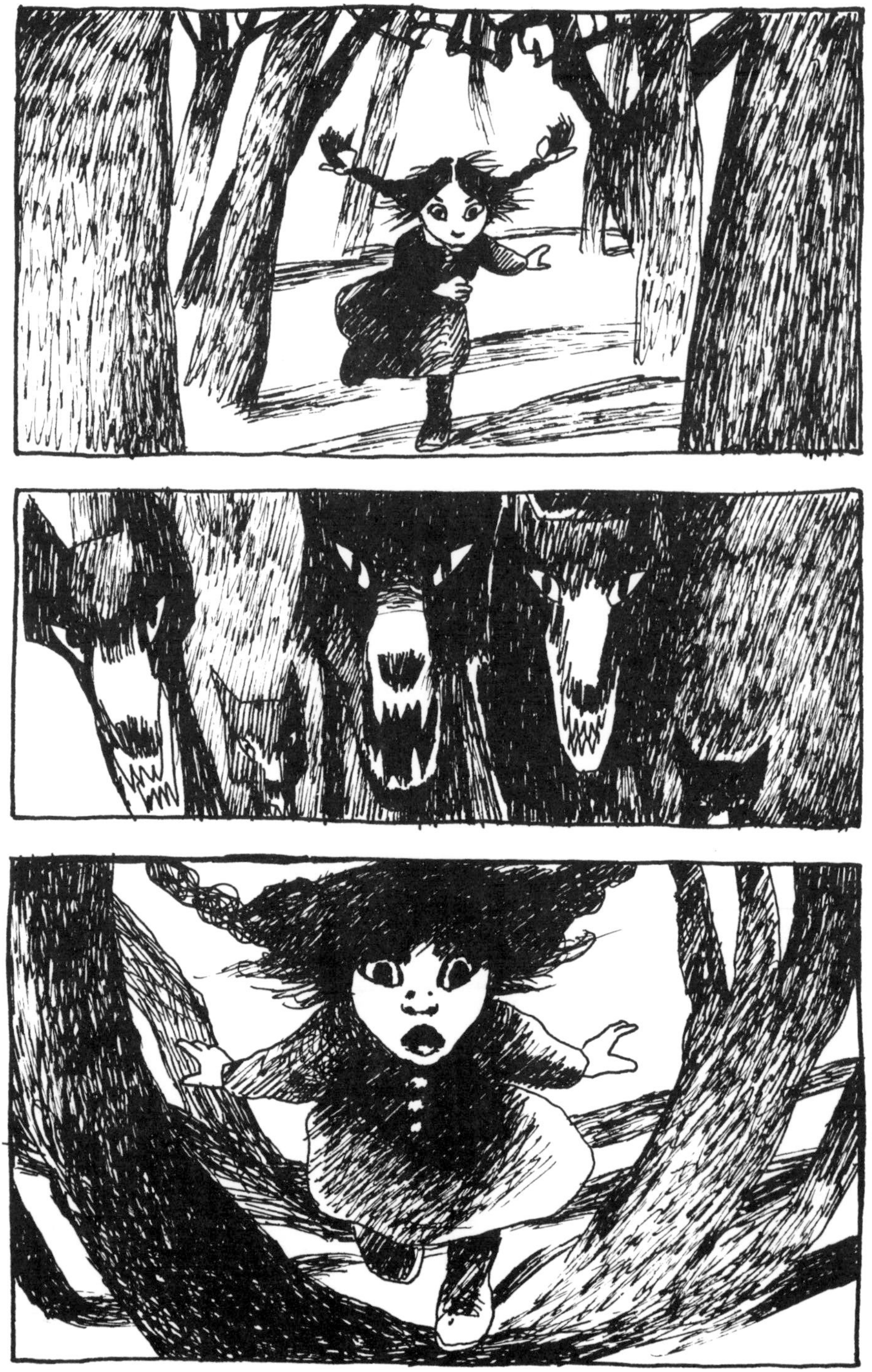

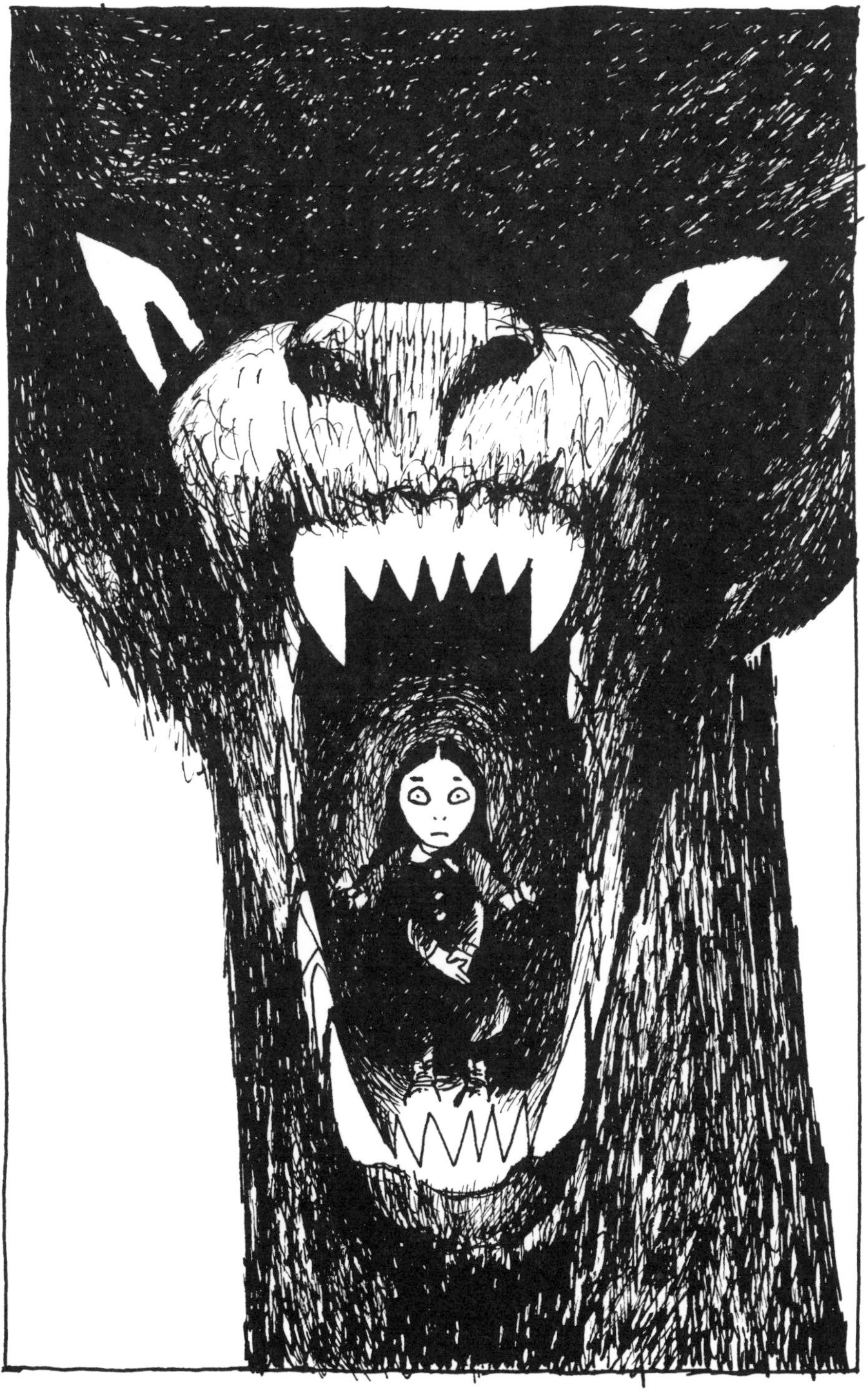

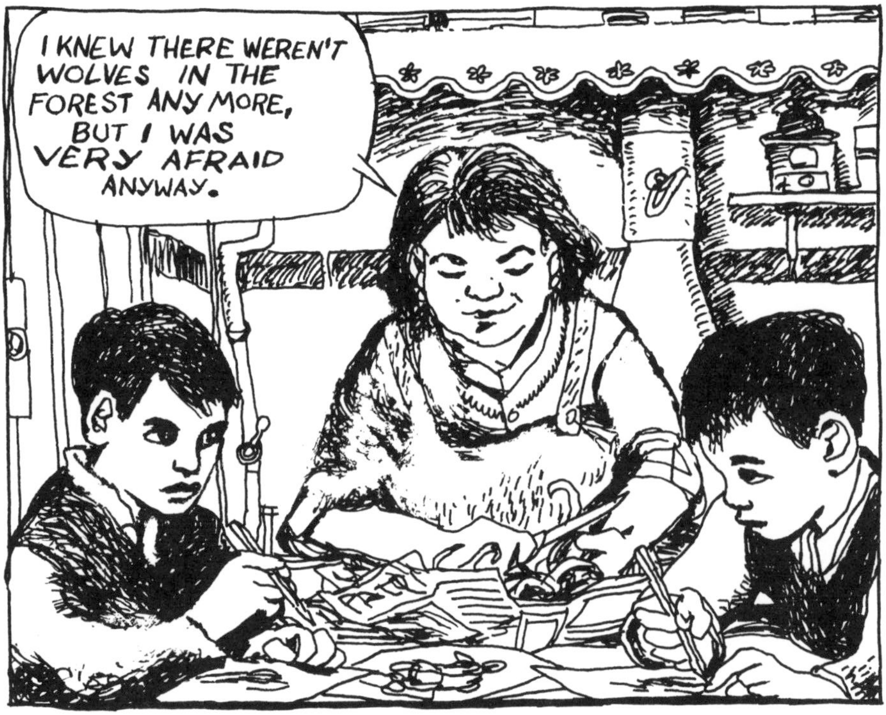
I KNEW THERE WEREN'T WOLVES IN THE FOREST ANY MORE, BUT I WAS VERY AFRAID ANYWAY.

WE WERE AFRAID OF THE WOLF IN THE FOREST, TOO. BUT YOU NEED A BIG FOREST AND AROUND NICE ALL WE HAD WERE DIFFERENT SORTS OF GARDENS SO WE HAD TO COME UP WITH OTHER FEARS.

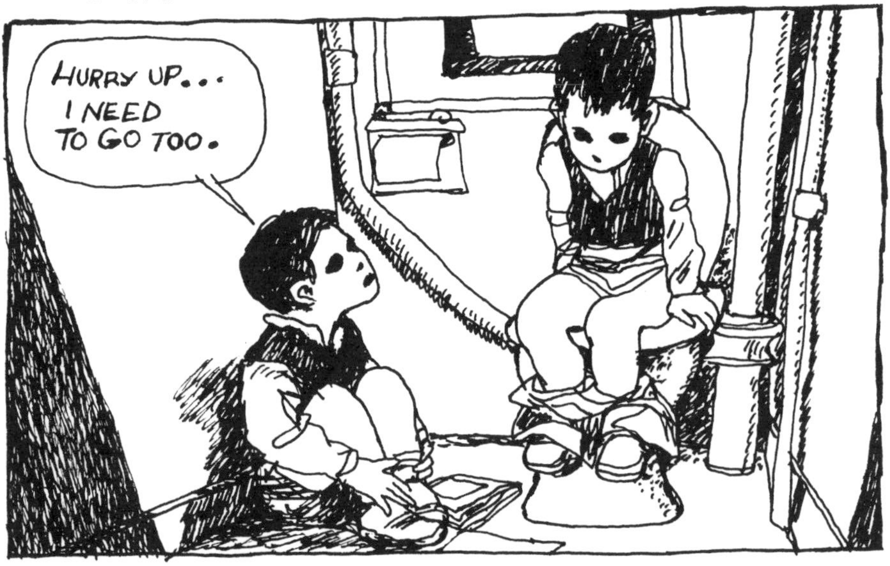
HURRY UP... I NEED TO GO TOO.

CAREFUL!
GO AHEAD!

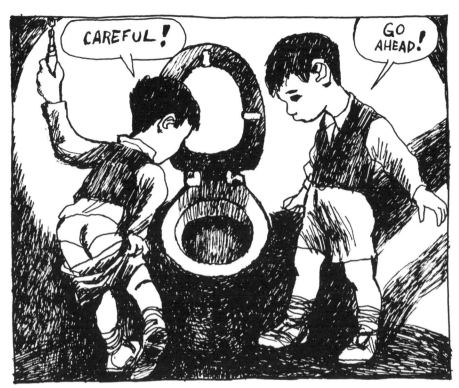

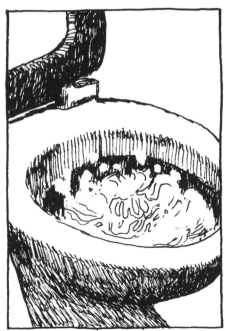

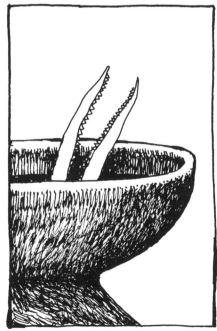

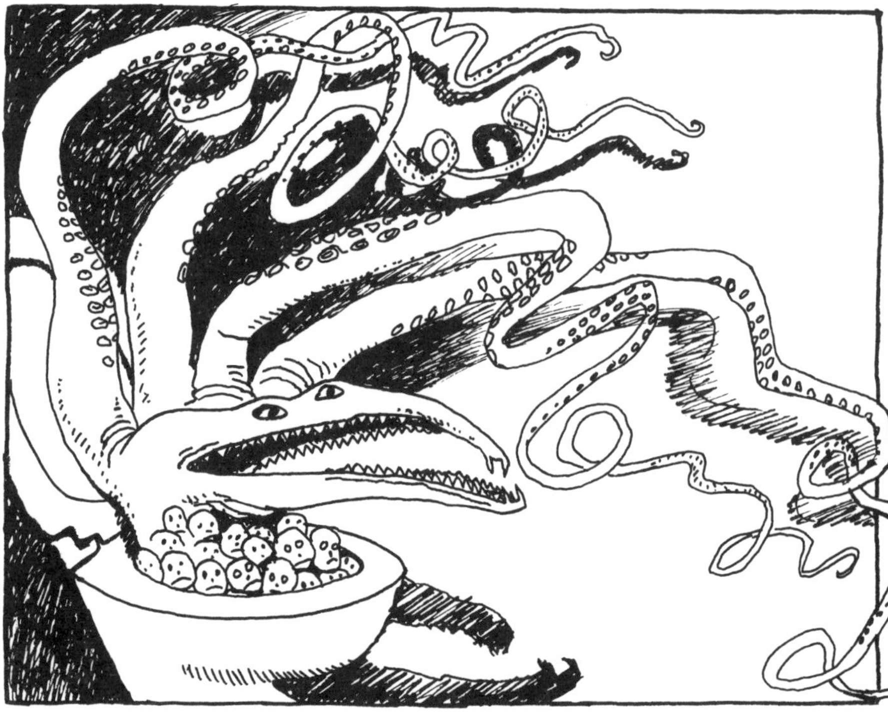

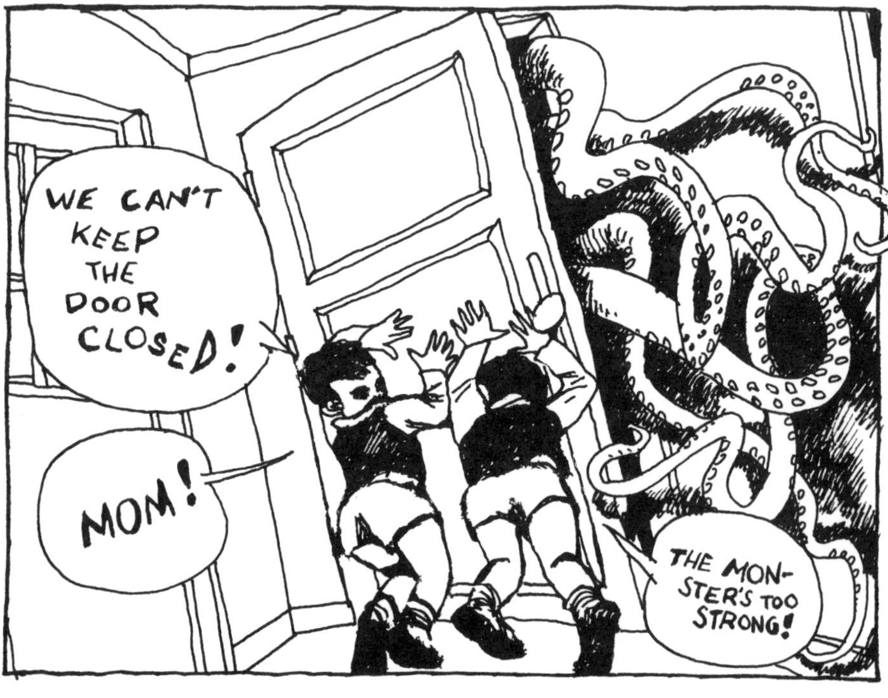
WE CAN'T KEEP THE DOOR CLOSED!
MOM!
THE MONSTER'S TOO STRONG!

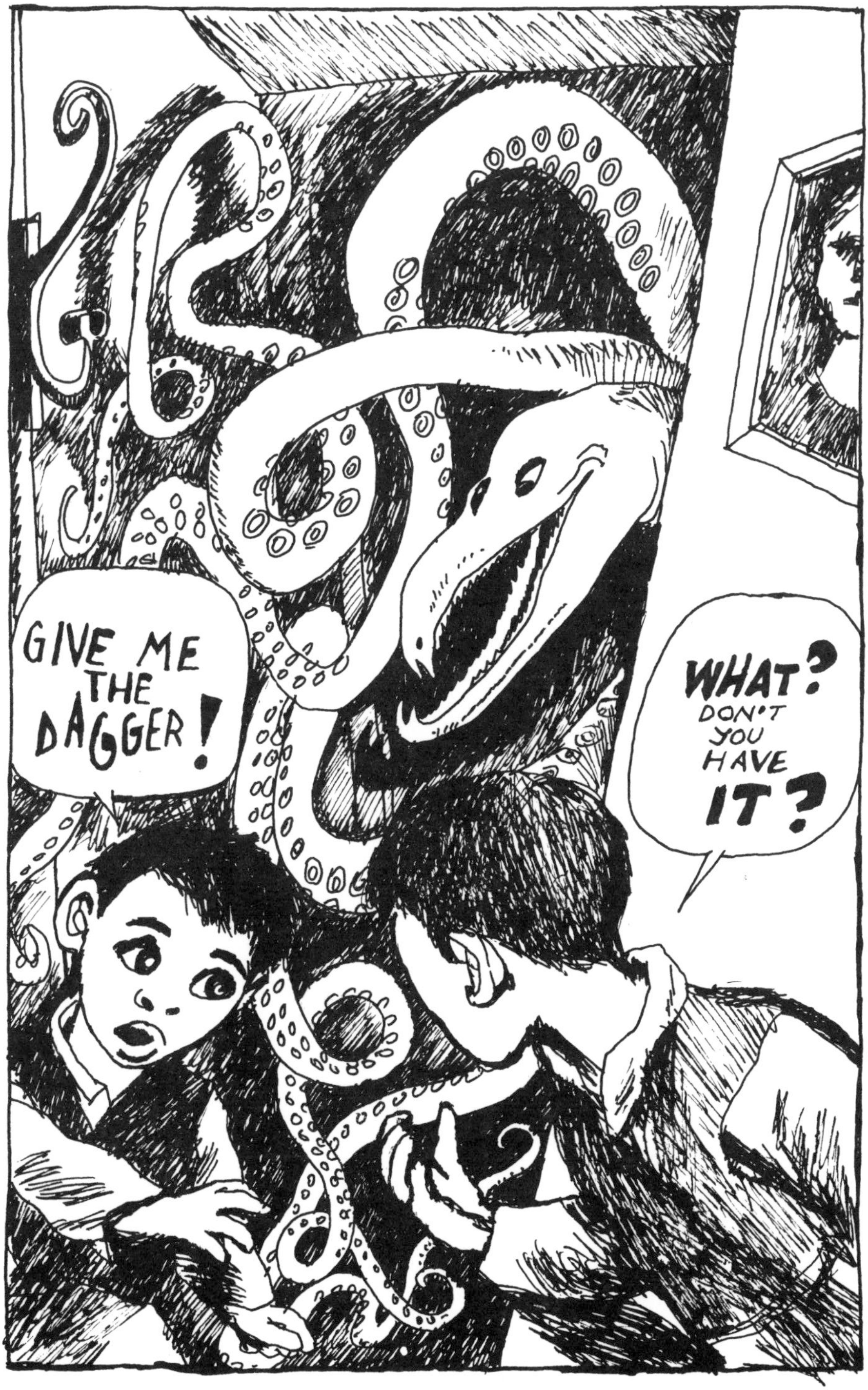
GIVE ME THE DAGGER!
WHAT? DON'T YOU HAVE IT?

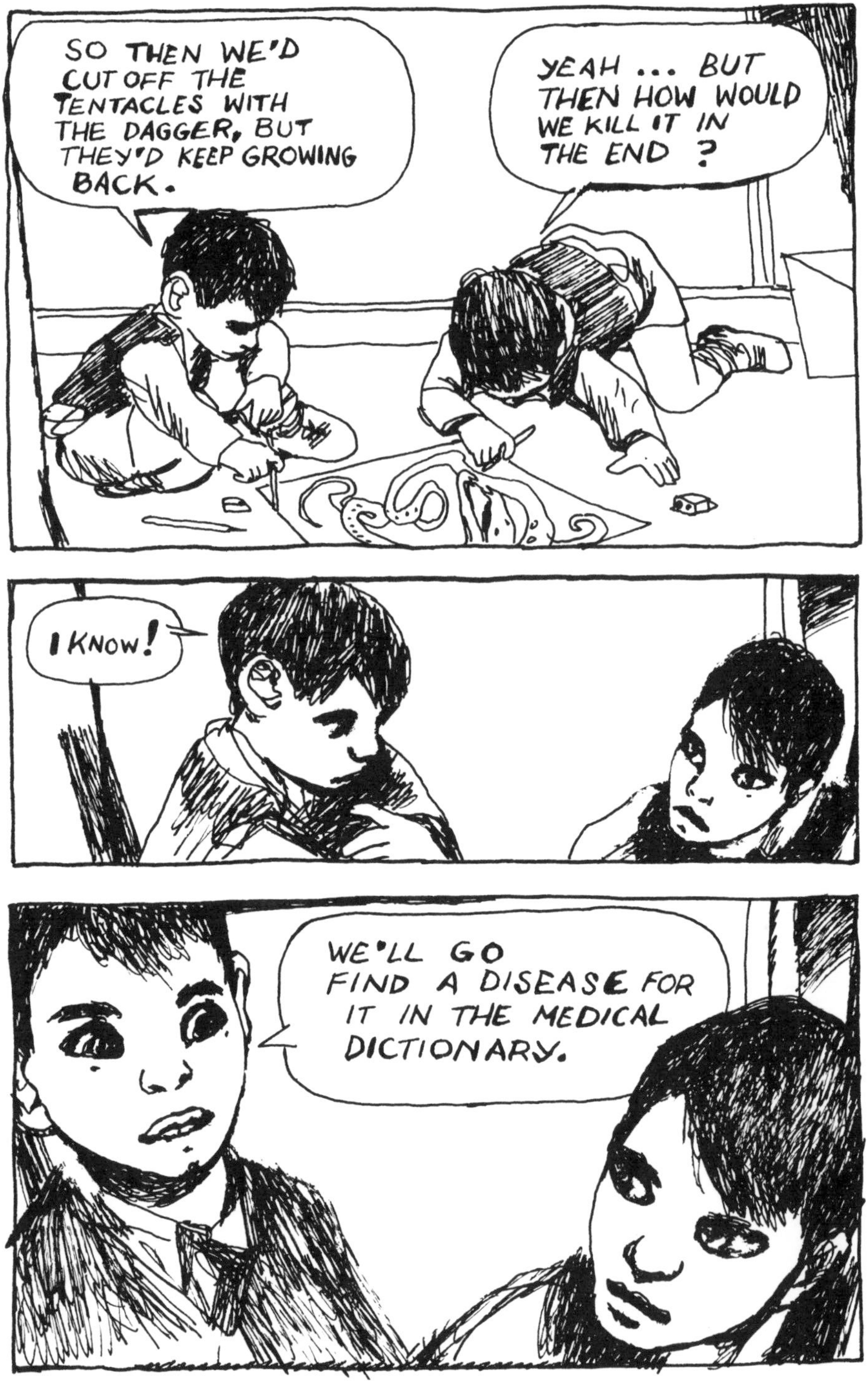
SO THEN WE'D CUT OFF THE TENTACLES WITH THE DAGGER, BUT THEY'D KEEP GROWING BACK.
YEAH ... BUT THEN HOW WOULD WE KILL IT IN THE END ?
I KNOW!
WE'LL GO FIND A DISEASE FOR IT IN THE MEDICAL DICTIONARY.

THE MEDICAL DICTIONARY: IT WAS OUR GREATEST FEAR.

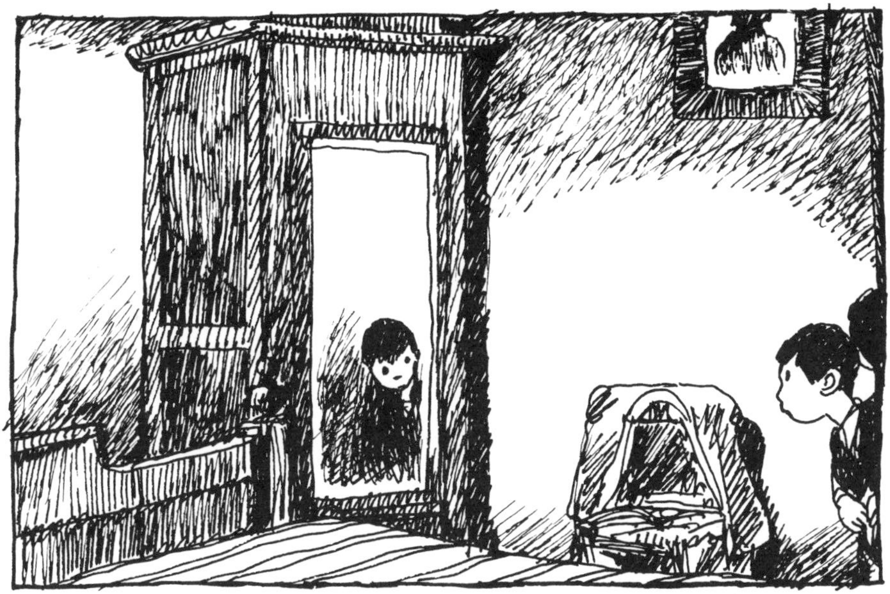

IT WAS KEPT IN THE MIRRORED ARMOIRE IN OUR PARENTS' ROOM.

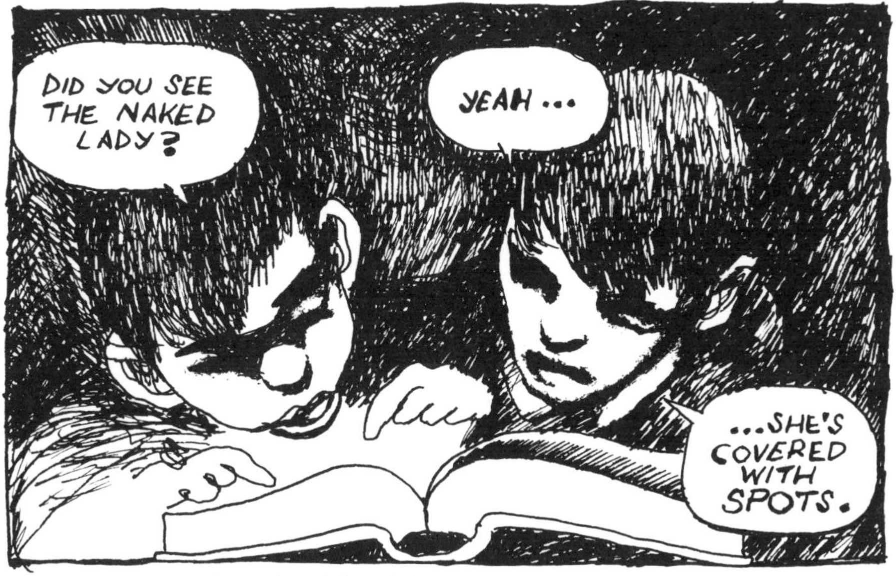
DID YOU SEE THE NAKED LADY?
YEAH...
...SHE'S COVERED WITH SPOTS.

WE WERE SURE WE WOULD CATCH THE DISEASES IF WE ACCIDENTALLY TOUCHED THE ILLUSTRATIONS.

AND WHEN NIGHT FELL, THE MEMORIES OF THOSE HORRORS REMAINED IMPRINTED ON OUR CLOSED EYELIDS.

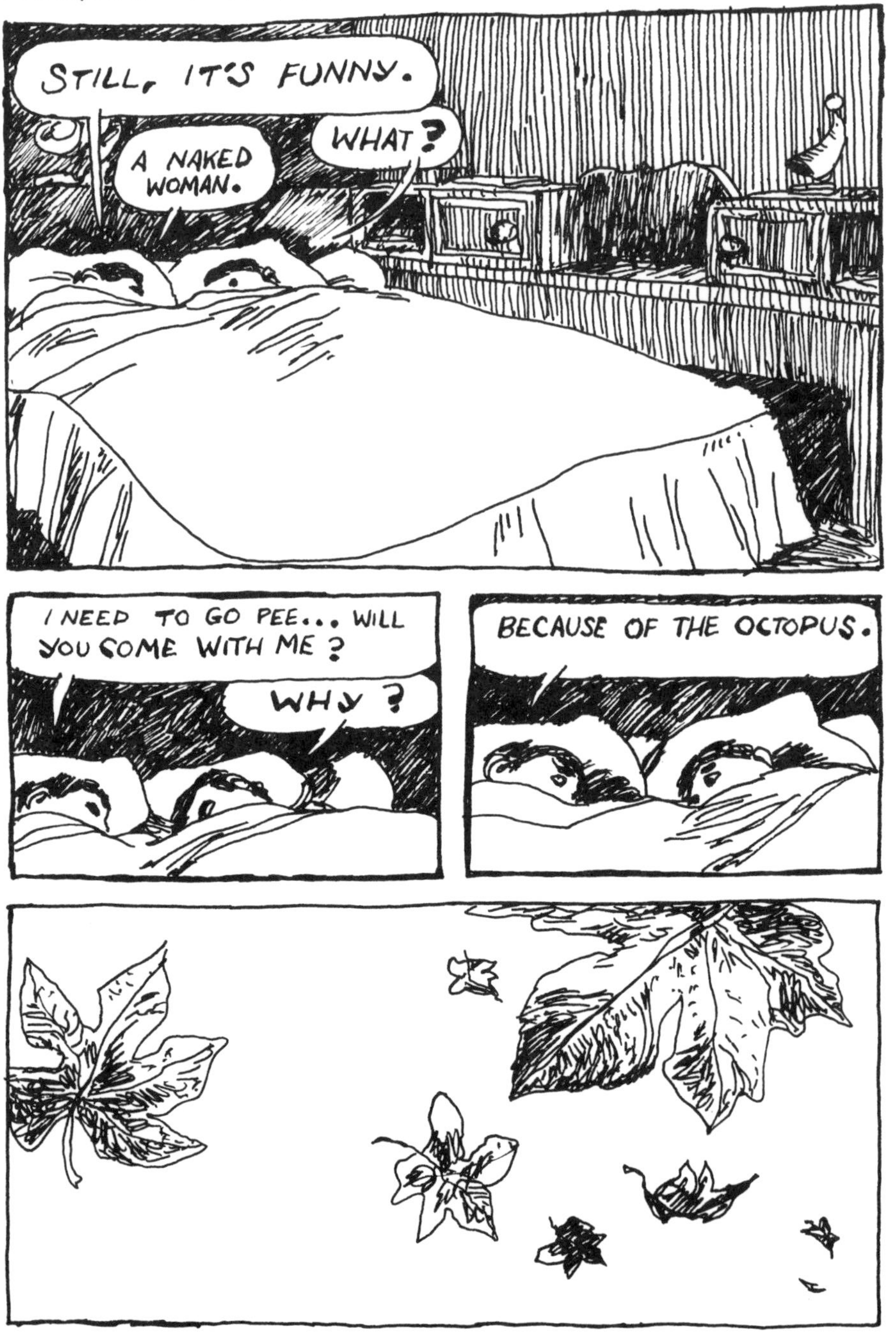
STILL, IT'S FUNNY.
A NAKED WOMAN.
WHAT?
I NEED TO GO PEE... WILL YOU COME WITH ME?
WHY?
BECAUSE OF THE OCTOPUS.

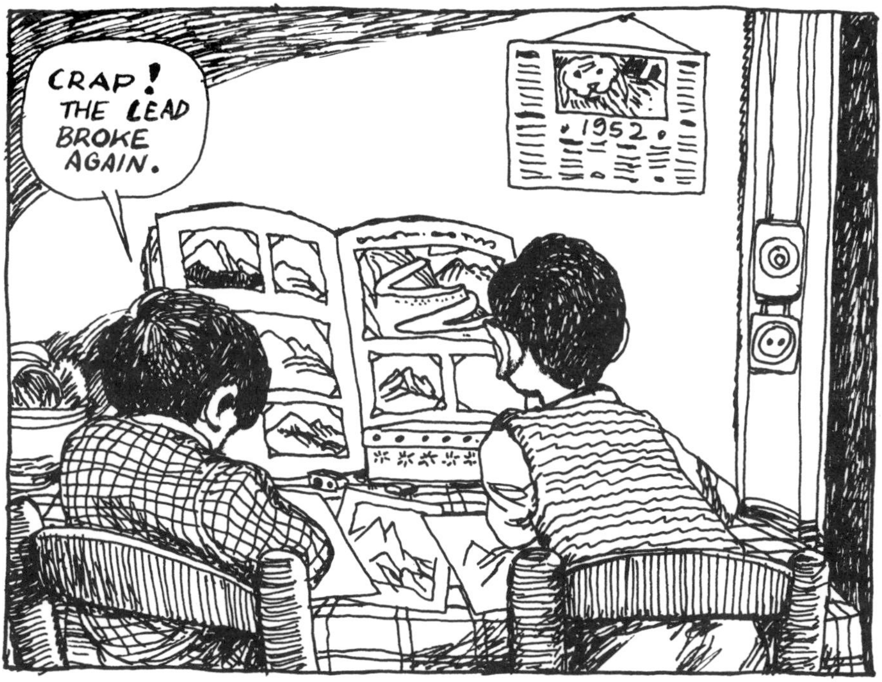
CRAP! THE LEAD BROKE AGAIN.
1952

THERE WEREN'T A LOT OF PICTURES IN OUR HOUSE. FOR A LONG TIME, THE ONLY BOOK WE HAD WITH PICTURES IN IT WAS AN ALBUM OF PHOTOS OF SWITZERLAND. THAT'S HOW PIERO AND I LEARNED HOW TO DRAW THE GOTTHARD PASS AND ITS WINDING ROADS.

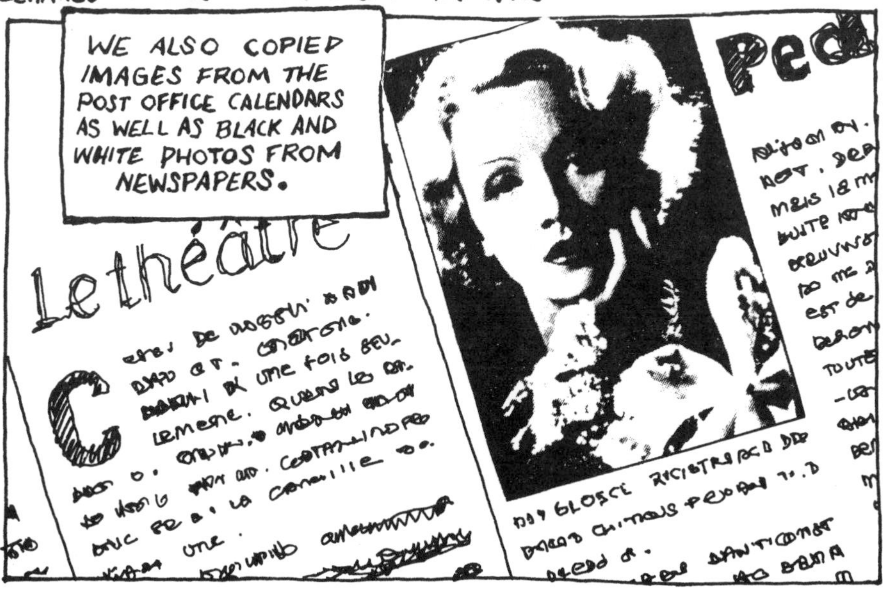
WE ALSO COPIED IMAGES FROM THE POST OFFICE CALENDARS AS WELL AS BLACK AND WHITE PHOTOS FROM NEWSPAPERS.
Le théâtre

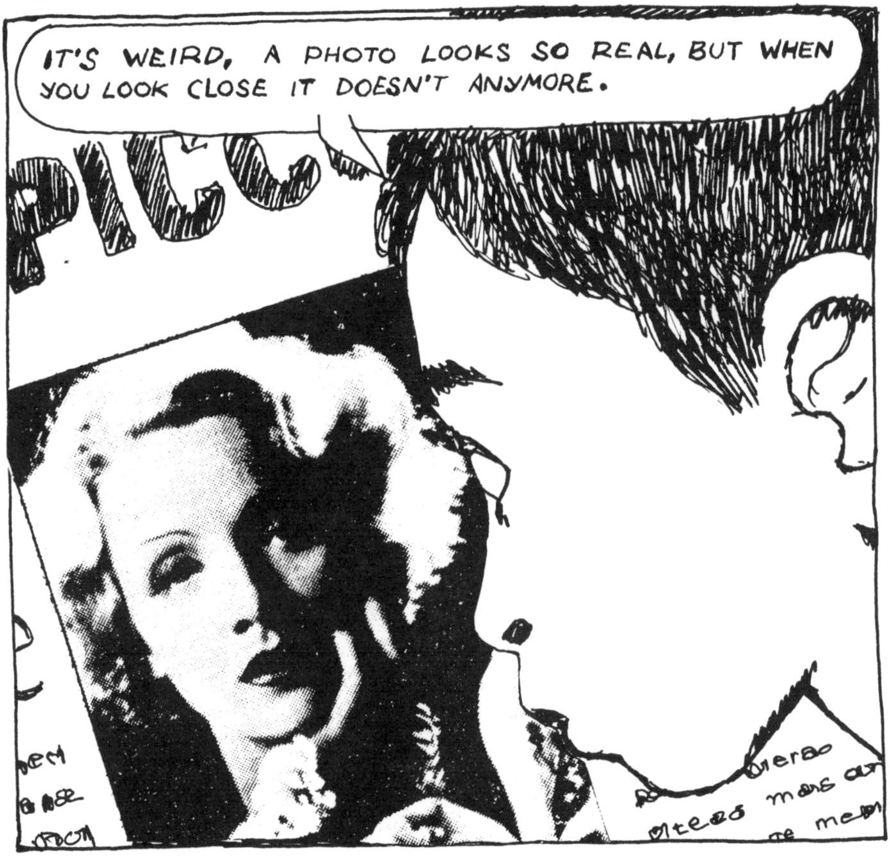
IT'S WEIRD, A PHOTO LOOKS SO REAL, BUT WHEN YOU LOOK CLOSE IT DOESN'T ANYMORE.

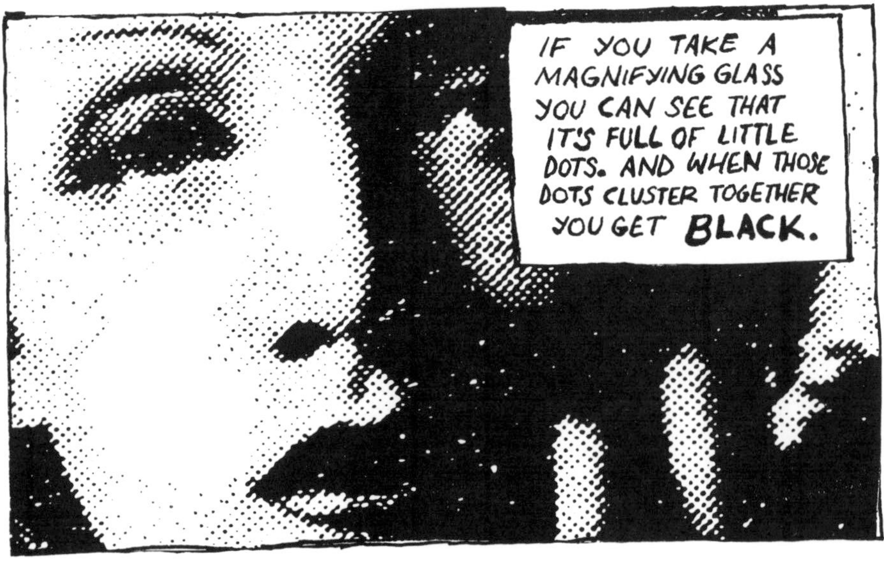
IF YOU TAKE A MAGNIFYING GLASS YOU CAN SEE THAT IT'S FULL OF LITTLE DOTS. AND WHEN THOSE DOTS CLUSTER TOGETHER YOU GET BLACK.

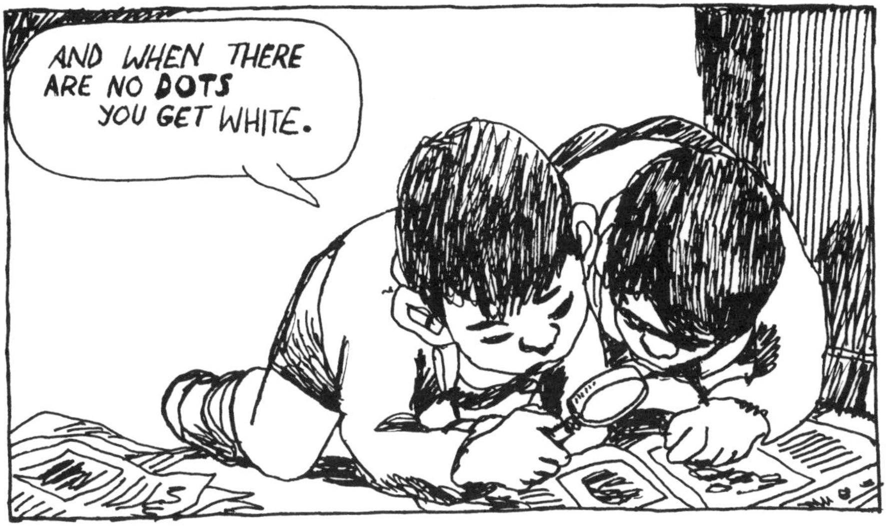
AND WHEN THERE ARE NO DOTS YOU GET WHITE.

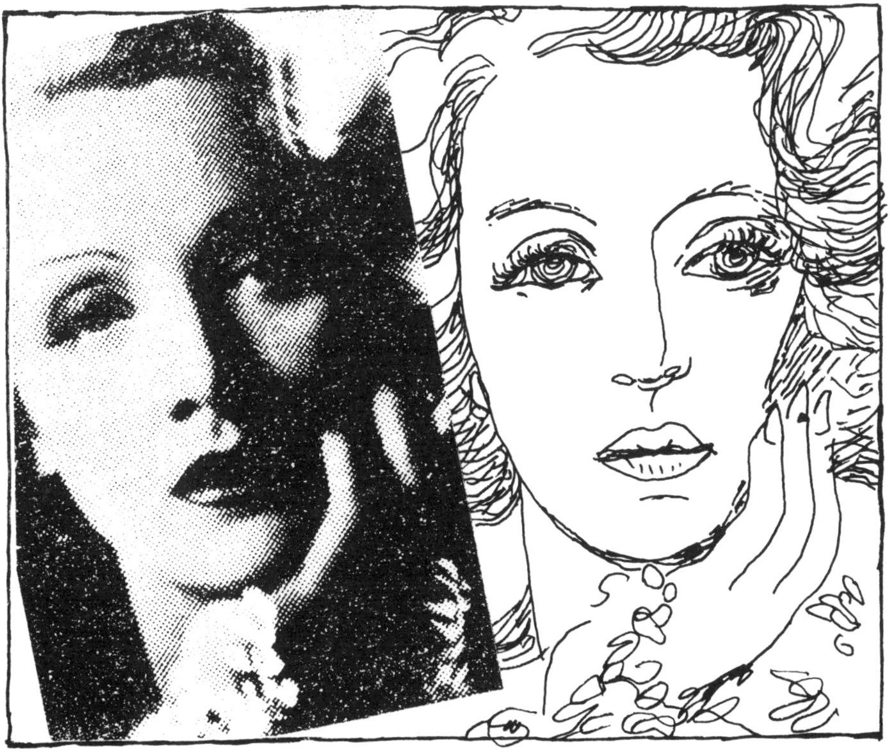

MOST OF ALL, IT'S NOT LIKE THE DRAWINGS IN ILLUSTRATED BOOKS.
THERE ARE NO CONTOURS, NO DESCRIPTIVE LINES.
THERE ARE ONLY SPLOTCHES, ONLY MARKS.

WHEN I
DISCOVERED THIS
NEW GAME,
I SPENT A LOT
OF TIME
ON IT.

I COPIED PHOTOS,
SIMPLIFYING
THE MARKS
MORE AND
MORE TO SEE
AT WHAT
POINT MY
BLACK SCRIBBLES
BECAME
NOTHING
BUT SCRIBBLES.

LOOKING OUT OUR WINDOW, PIERO STILL SAW OUTLINES OF CARS, WHILE I SAW ONLY MARKS AND HIGHLIGHTS.

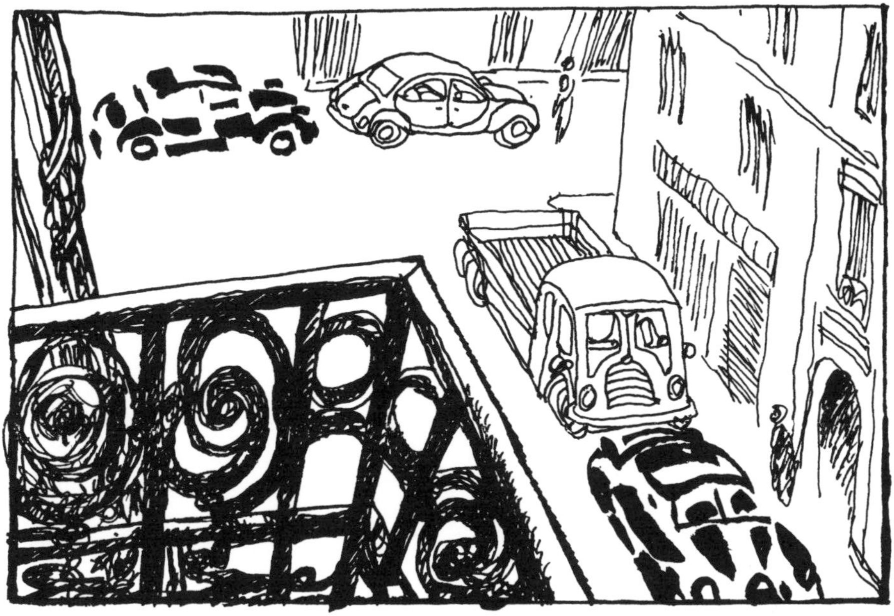

AT THAT POINT WE WERE BETWEEN ELEVEN AND THIRTEEN YEARS OLD AND I HAD A VAGUE INTUITION THAT I WAS GOING TO DEVOTE MUCH OF MY TIME TO THE STUDY OF MARKS AND **LINES**... WITHOUT **EVER MANAGING** TO **UNDERSTAND** THEM...

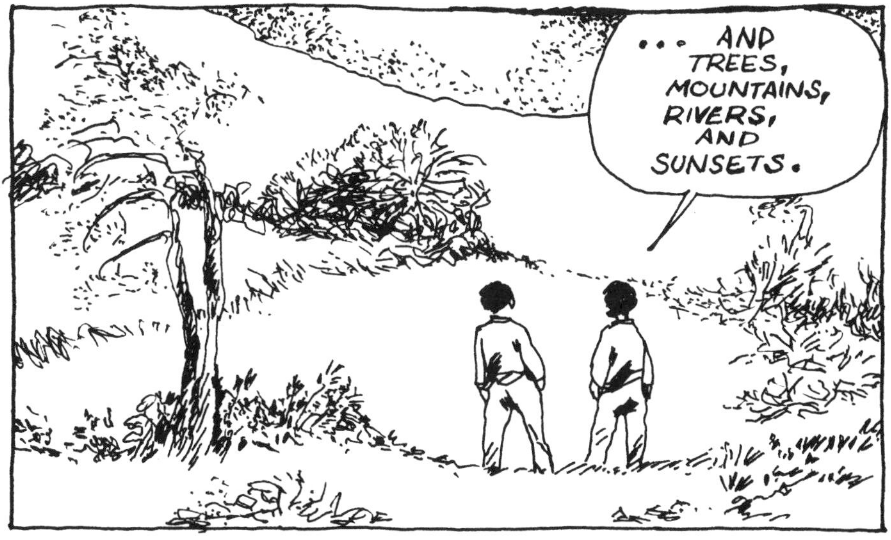
... AND TREES, MOUNTAINS, RIVERS, AND SUNSETS.

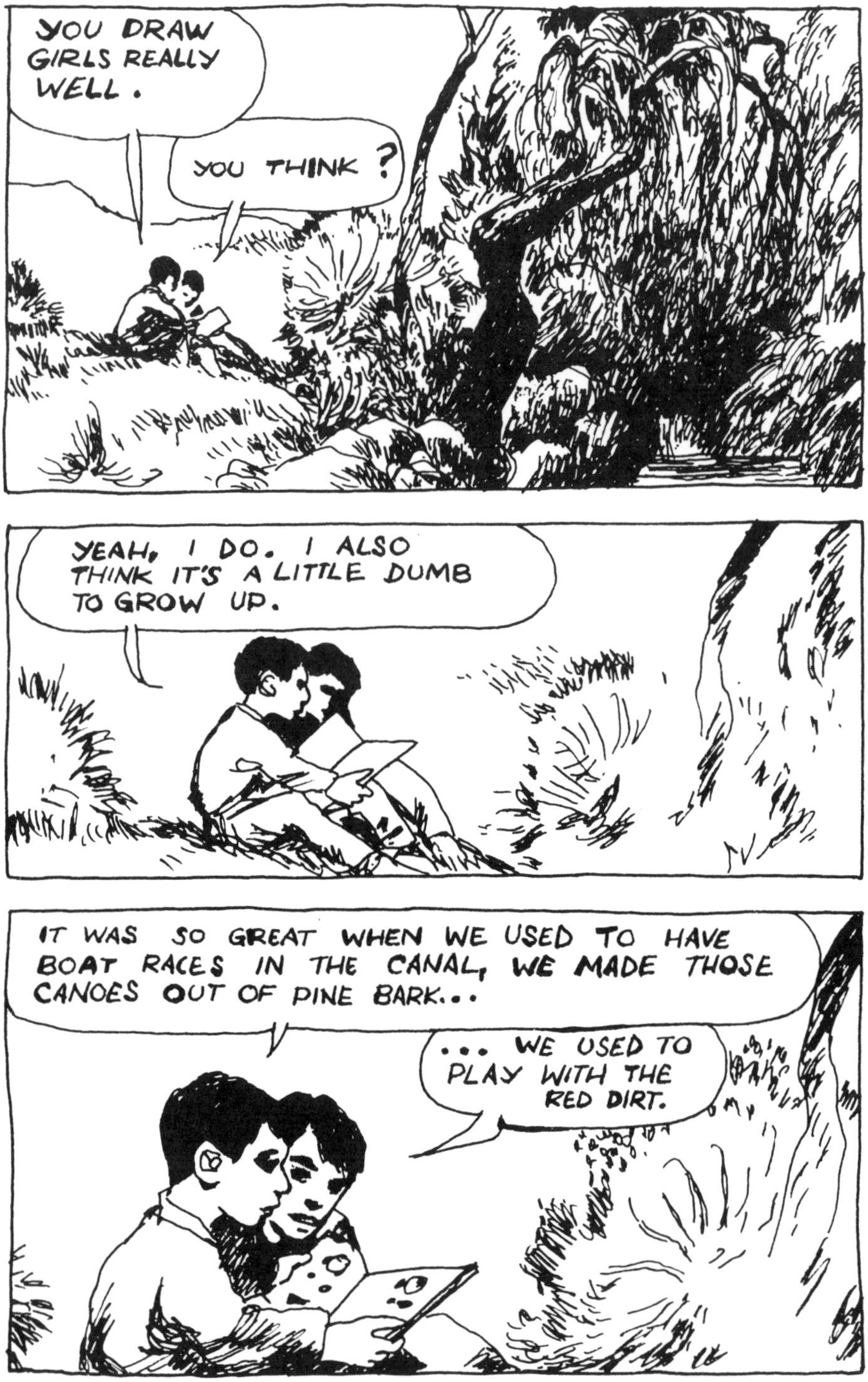
YOU DRAW GIRLS REALLY WELL.
YOU THINK?
YEAH, I DO. I ALSO THINK IT'S A LITTLE DUMB TO GROW UP.
IT WAS SO GREAT WHEN WE USED TO HAVE BOAT RACES IN THE CANAL, WE MADE THOSE CANOES OUT OF PINE BARK...
... WE USED TO PLAY WITH THE RED DIRT.

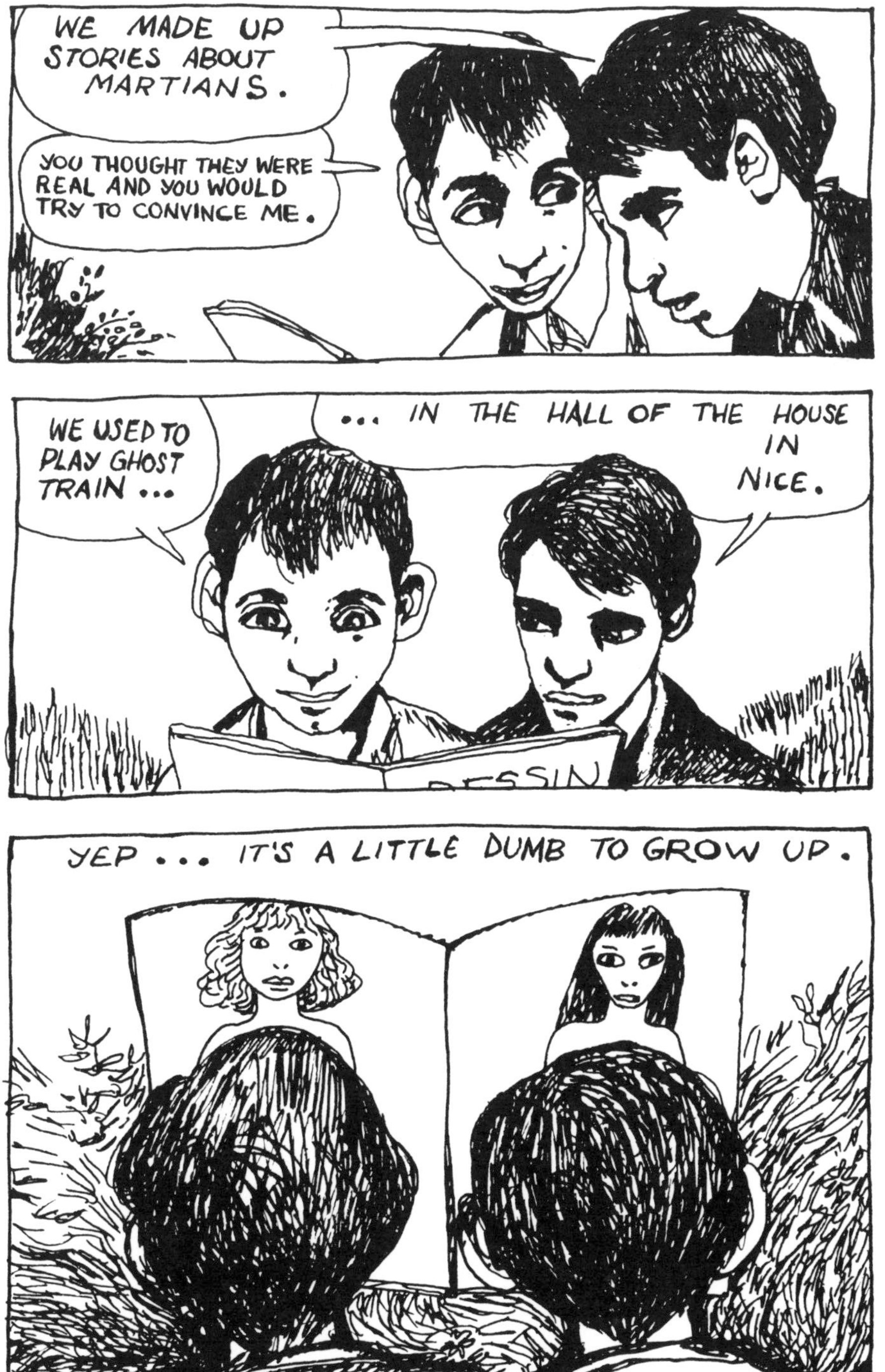
WE MADE UP STORIES ABOUT MARTIANS.
YOU THOUGHT THEY WERE REAL AND YOU WOULD TRY TO CONVINCE ME.
WE USED TO PLAY GHOST TRAIN ...
... IN THE HALL OF THE HOUSE IN NICE.
YEP ... IT'S A LITTLE DUMB TO GROW UP.

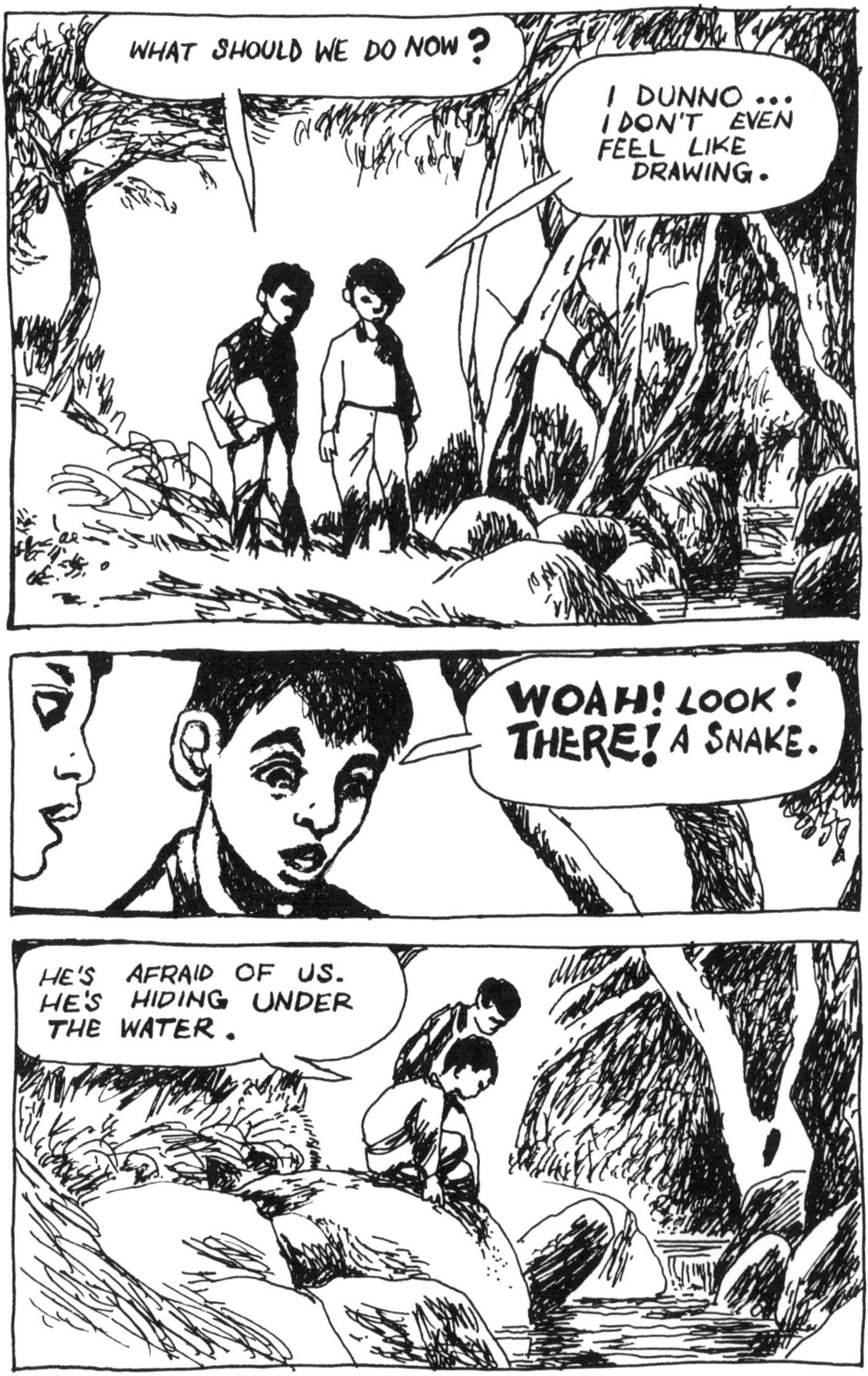
WHAT SHOULD WE DO NOW?
I DUNNO ... I DON'T EVEN FEEL LIKE DRAWING.
WOAH! LOOK! THERE! A SNAKE.
HE'S AFRAID OF US. HE'S HIDING UNDER THE WATER.

HE HAS NOWHERE TO HIDE UNDER THE WATER ... HOW LONG DO YOU THINK HE CAN GO WITHOUT BREATHING?

SHOULD WE COUNT?

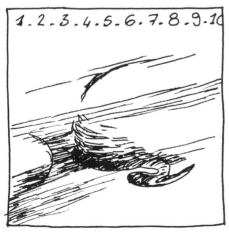

1 . 2 . 3 . 4 . 5 . 6 . 7 . 8 . 9 . 1

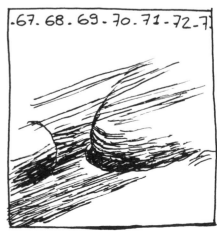

. 67 . 68 . 69 . 70 . 71 . 72 . 7

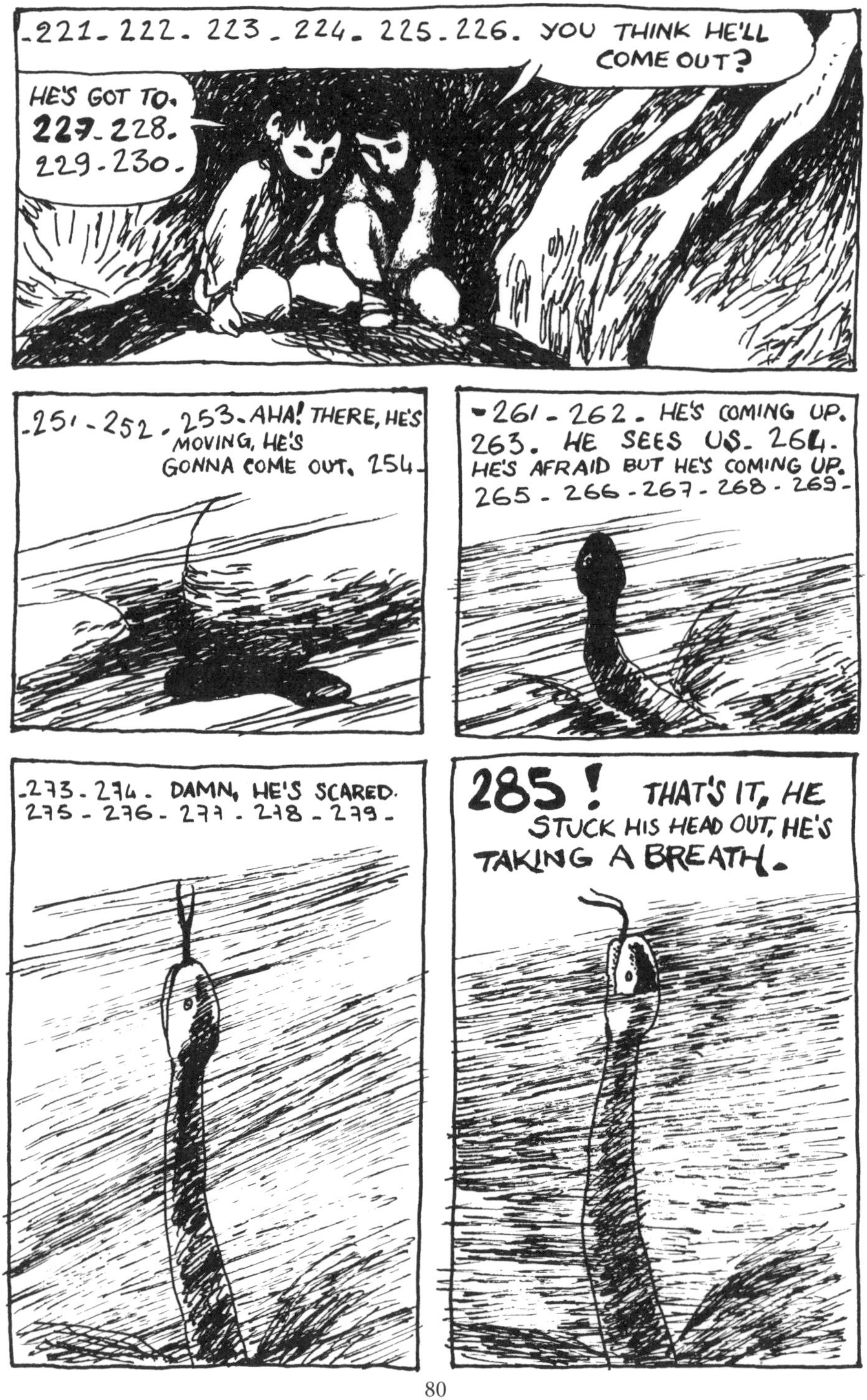
-221-222-223-224-225-226- YOU THINK HE'LL COME OUT?
HE'S GOT TO. 227-228. 229-230-
-251-252-253-AHA! THERE, HE'S MOVING, HE'S GONNA COME OUT. 254-
-261-262. HE'S COMING UP. 263. HE SEES US. 264. HE'S AFRAID BUT HE'S COMING UP. 265-266-267-268-269-
-273-274- DAMN, HE'S SCARED. 275-276-277-278-279-
285! THAT'S IT, HE STUCK HIS HEAD OUT, HE'S TAKING A BREATH.

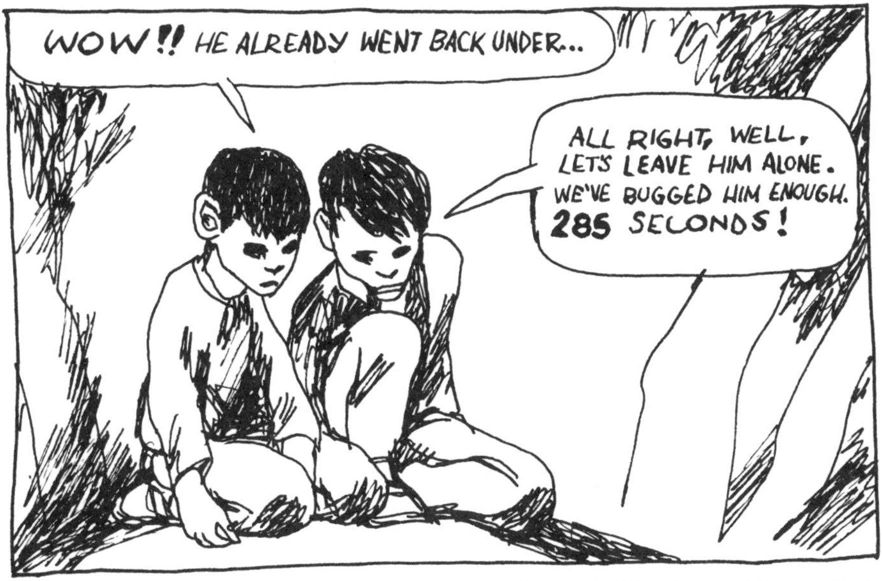
WOW!! HE ALREADY WENT BACK UNDER...
ALL RIGHT, WELL, LET'S LEAVE HIM ALONE. WE'VE BUGGED HIM ENOUGH. 285 SECONDS!

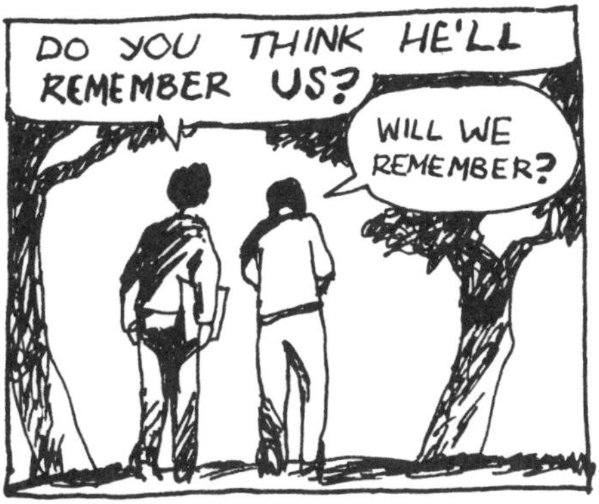
DO YOU THINK HE'LL REMEMBER US?
WILL WE REMEMBER?

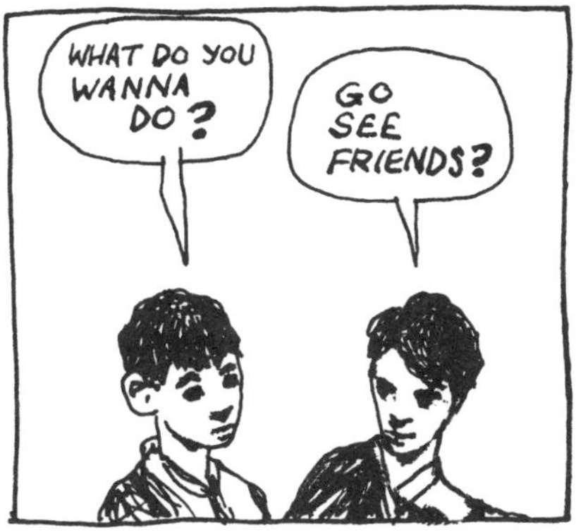
WHAT DO YOU WANNA DO?
GO SEE FRIENDS?

FRIENDS AND CLASSMATES AND... THE SNAKE HAD GONE 285 SECONDS WITHOUT BREATHING. HOW LONG COULD WE GO WITHOUT THE OXYGEN OF FRIENDSHIP?

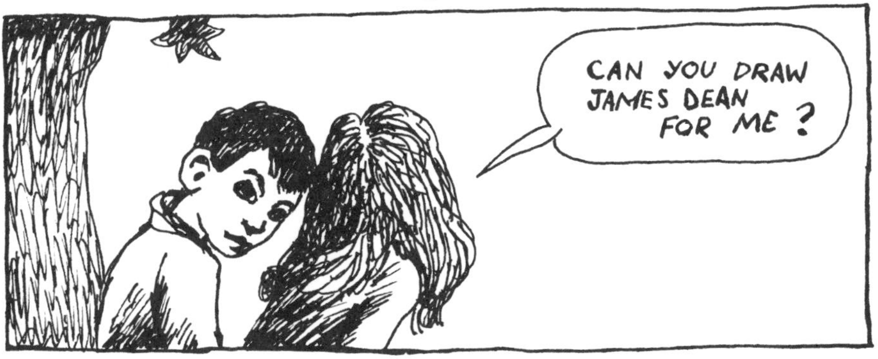
CAN YOU DRAW JAMES DEAN FOR ME?

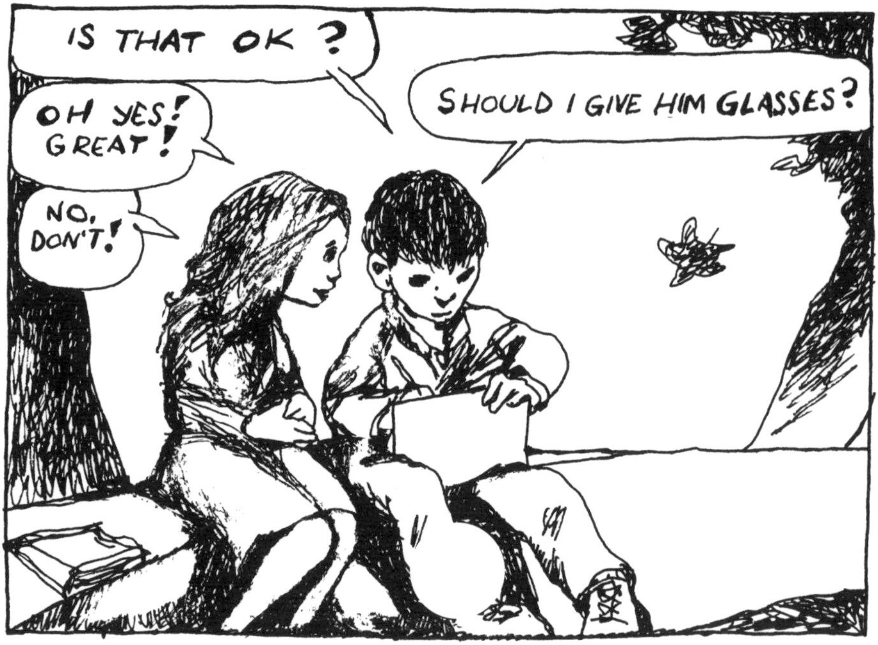
IS THAT OK ?
OH YES! GREAT!
NO, DON'T!
SHOULD I GIVE HIM GLASSES?

I WASN'T CRAZY ABOUT JAMES DEAN. MAINLY BECAUSE HE WAS HANDSOME. HE WAS BLOND, HE HAD BLUE EYES. I'M A BRUNETTE WITH HAZEL EYES. AT LEAST HE WORE GLASSES.

STILL, I OWED A LOT TO AMERICAN MOVIES. THAT'S HOW I EARNED MY FIRST INCOME.

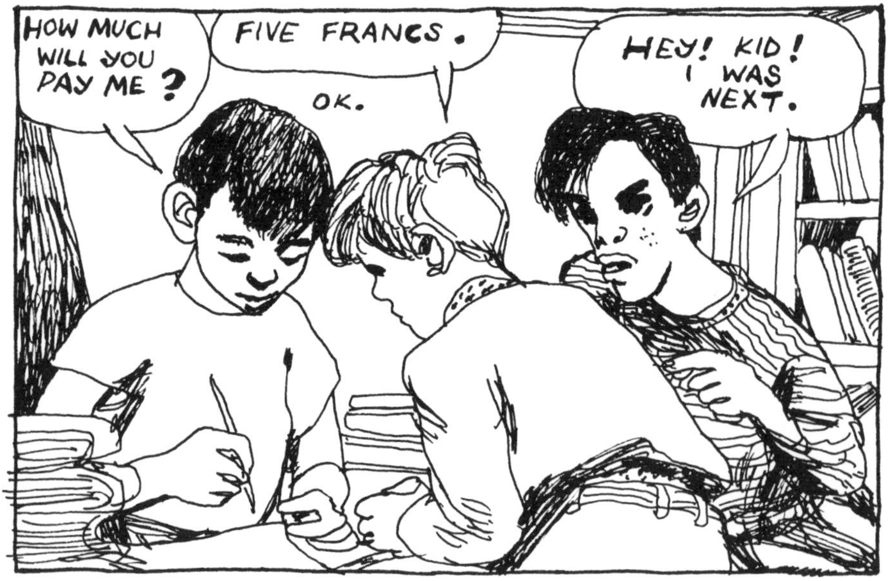
HOW MUCH WILL YOU PAY ME?
FIVE FRANCS.
OK.
HEY! KID! I WAS NEXT.

I HADN'T EVEN SEEN THE MOVIE. IT WAS CALLED "BLACKBOARD JUNGLE."

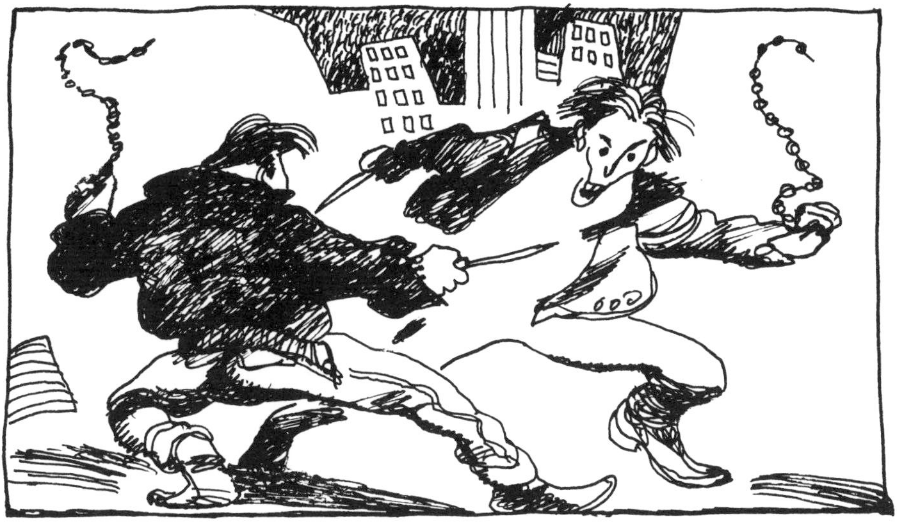

600

THERE WAS A FIGHT SCENE BETWEEN GANG MEMBERS WITH KNIVES, MAYBE THE FIRST ONE EVER FILMED. I IMAGINED WHAT IT MIGHT LOOK LIKE, DREW IT, AND SOLD SEVERAL DOZEN COPIES.

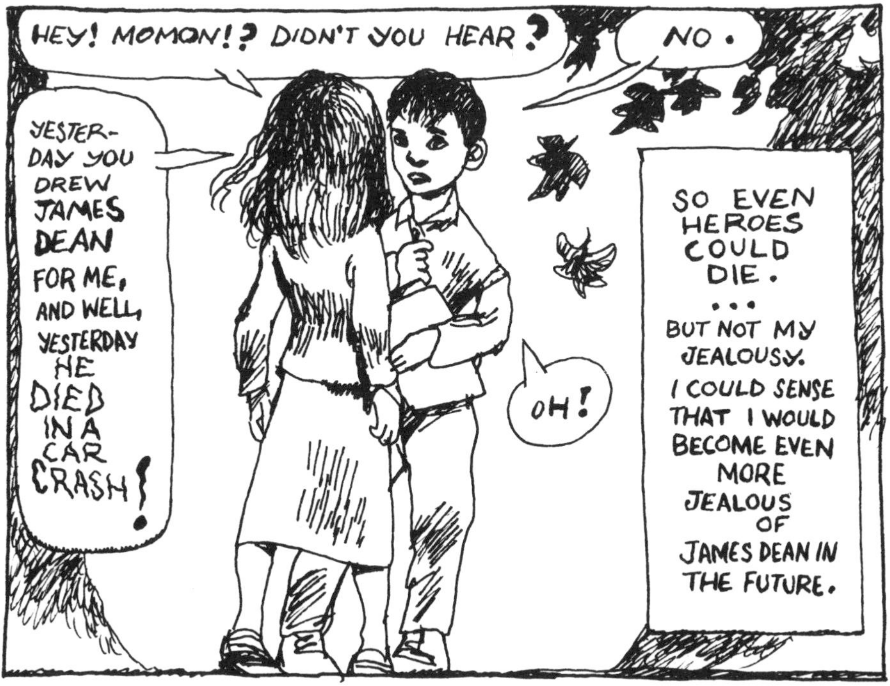

HEY! MOMON!? DIDN'T YOU HEAR?
NO.
YESTERDAY YOU DREW JAMES DEAN FOR ME, AND WELL, YESTERDAY HE DIED IN A CAR CRASH!
OH!
SO EVEN HEROES COULD DIE. ... BUT NOT MY JEALOUSY. I COULD SENSE THAT I WOULD BECOME EVEN MORE JEALOUS OF JAMES DEAN IN THE FUTURE.

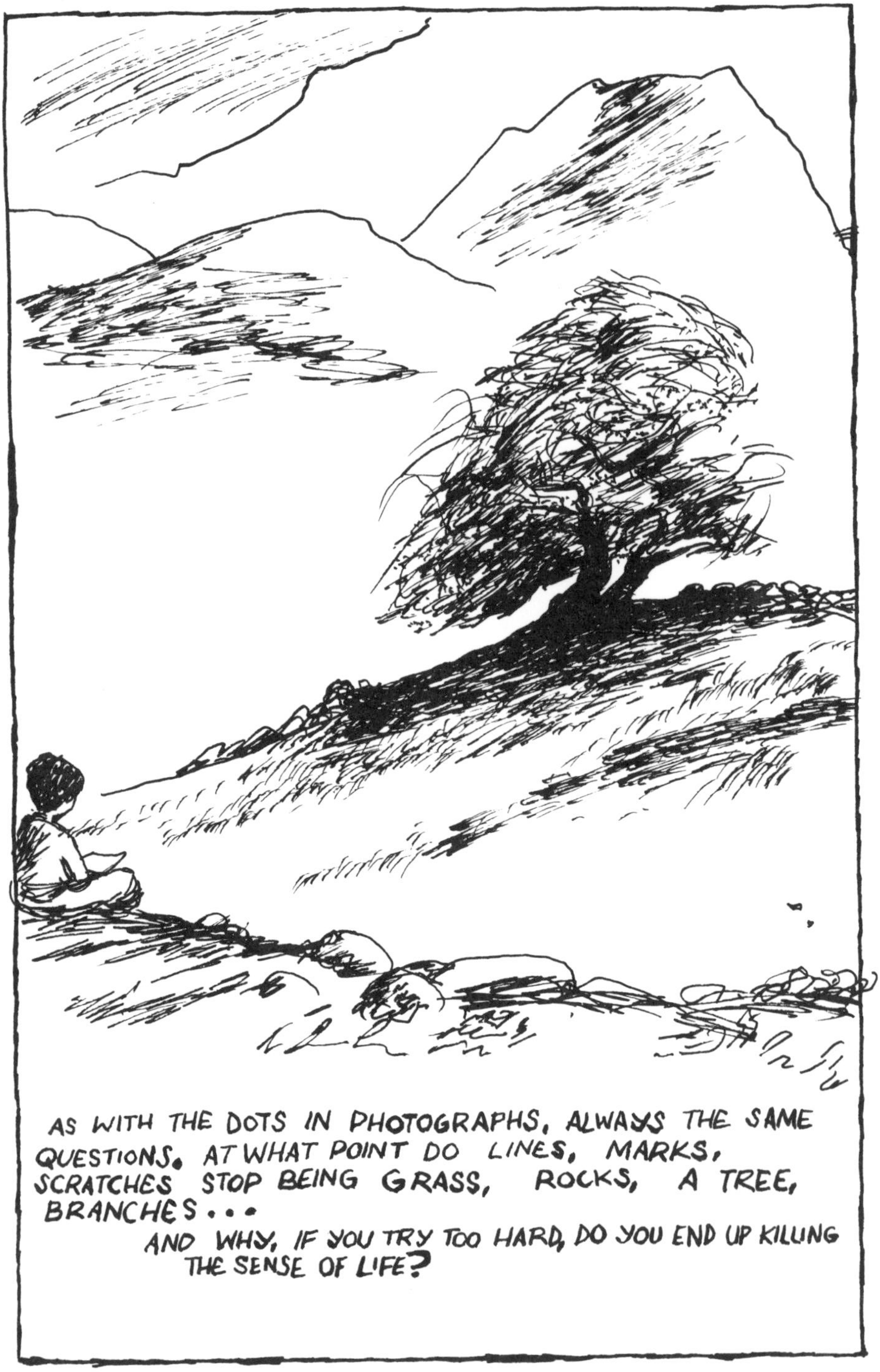
AS WITH THE DOTS IN PHOTOGRAPHS, ALWAYS THE SAME QUESTIONS. AT WHAT POINT DO LINES, MARKS, SCRATCHES STOP BEING GRASS, ROCKS, A TREE, BRANCHES...
AND WHY, IF YOU TRY TOO HARD, DO YOU END UP KILLING THE SENSE OF LIFE?

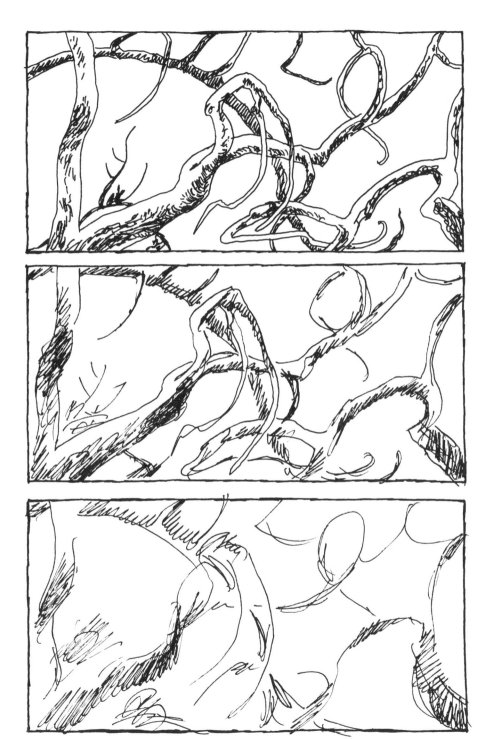

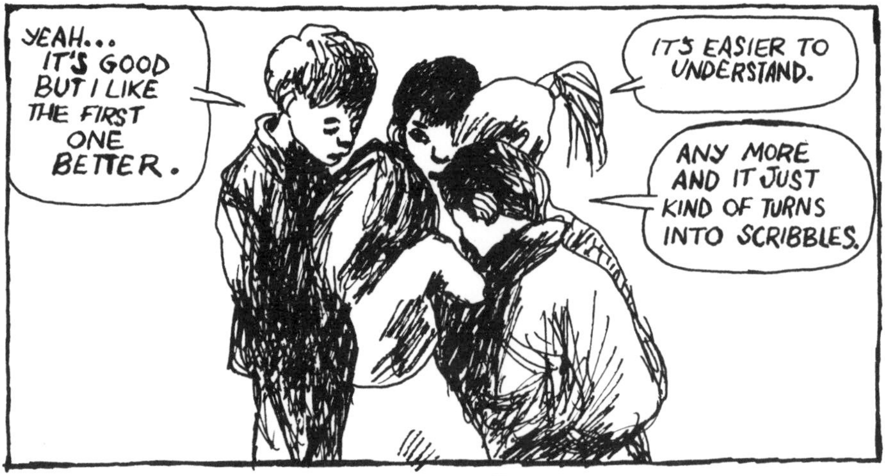
YEAH... IT'S GOOD BUT I LIKE THE FIRST ONE BETTER.
IT'S EASIER TO UNDERSTAND.
ANY MORE AND IT JUST KIND OF TURNS INTO SCRIBBLES.

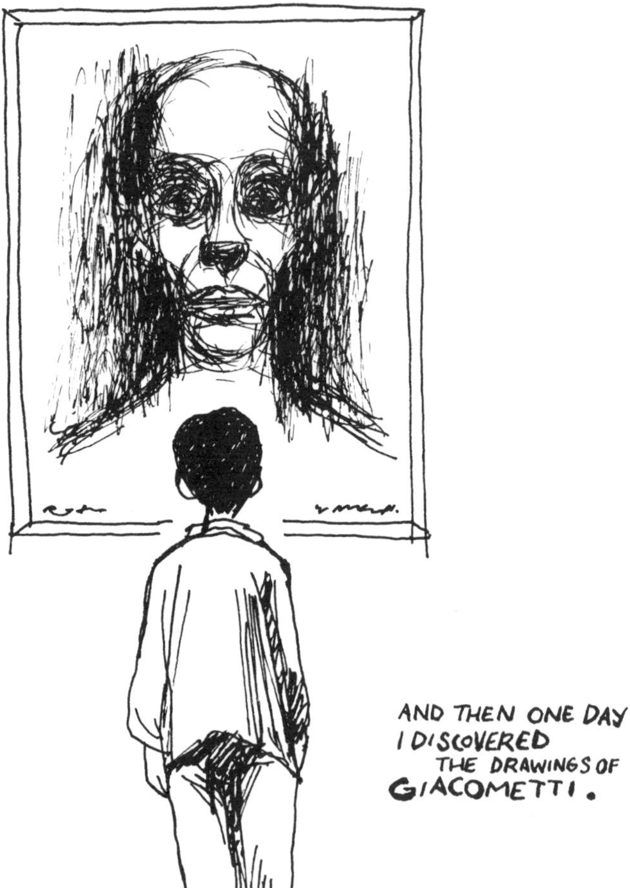
AND THEN ONE DAY I DISCOVERED THE DRAWINGS OF GIACOMETTI.

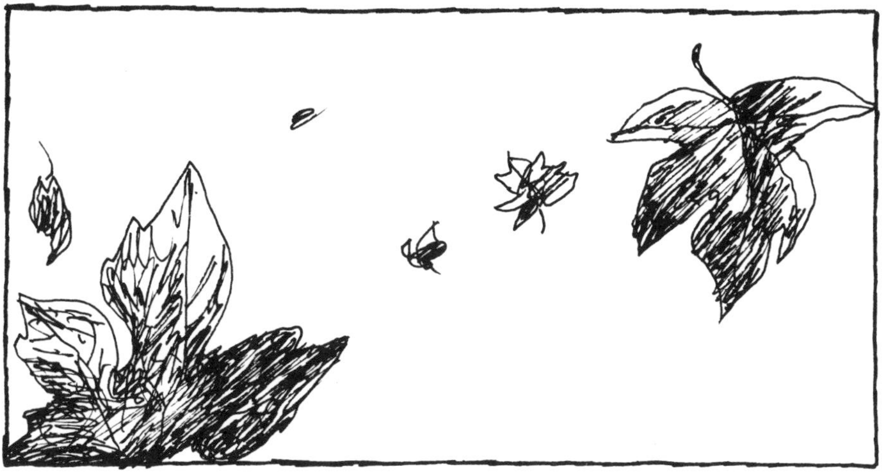

SO THERE WAS A MAN OUT THERE WHO DIDN'T JUST WONDER ABOUT WHAT THE EYE SEES, BUT ALSO ABOUT WHAT IS BEHIND THE EYES.

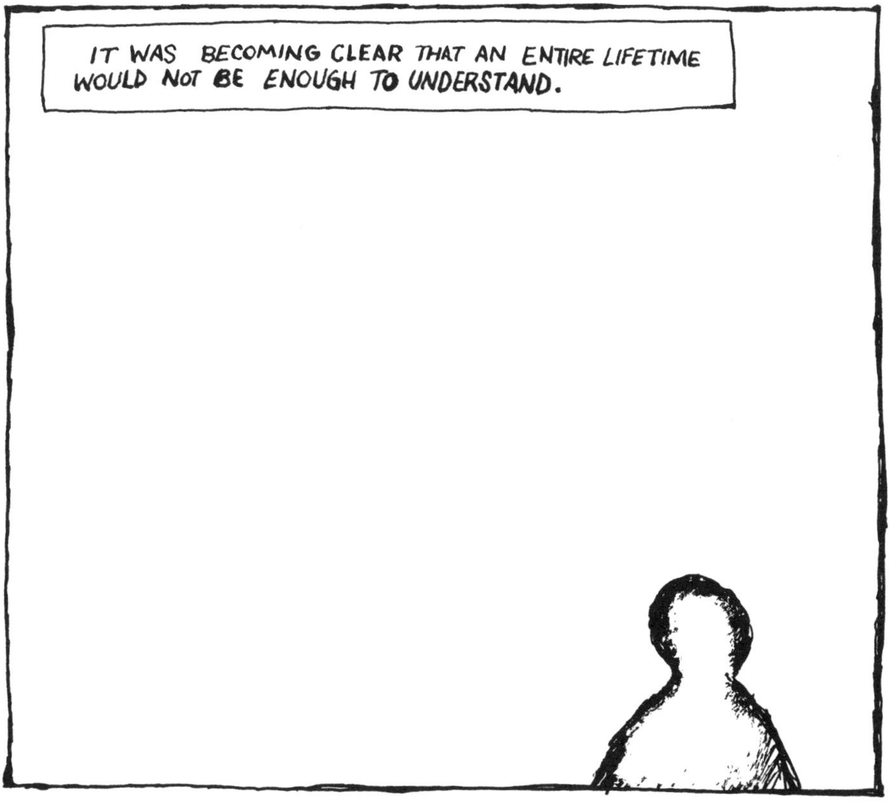
IT WAS BECOMING CLEAR THAT AN ENTIRE LIFETIME WOULD NOT BE ENOUGH TO UNDERSTAND.

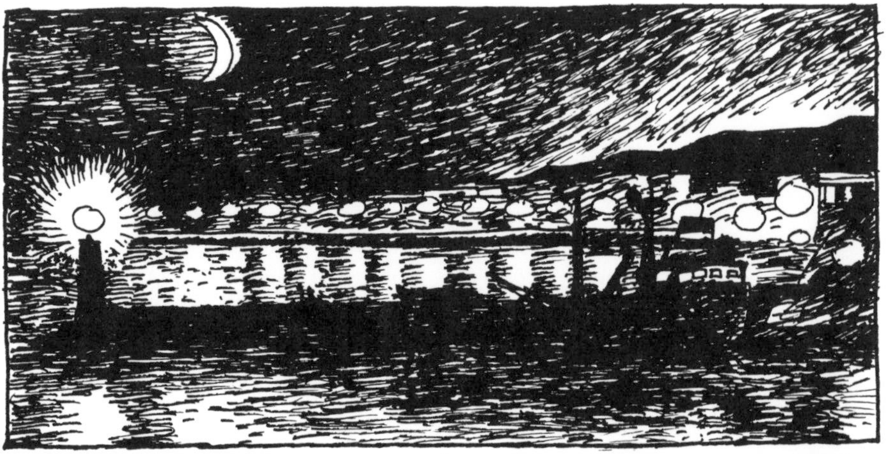

IT HAD BEEN A WHILE SINCE I SHARED A BED WITH PIERO. BUT WE STILL DREAMED OF FLYING HIGH OVER THE EARTH TOGETHER.

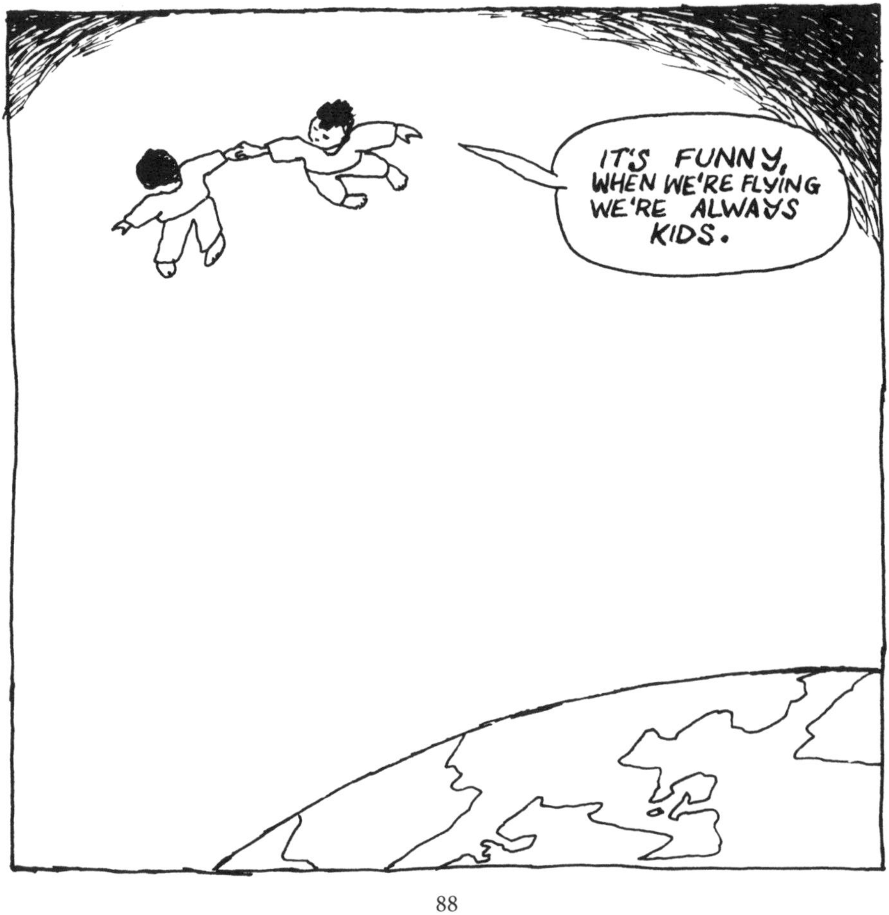
IT'S FUNNY, WHEN WE'RE FLYING WE'RE ALWAYS KIDS.

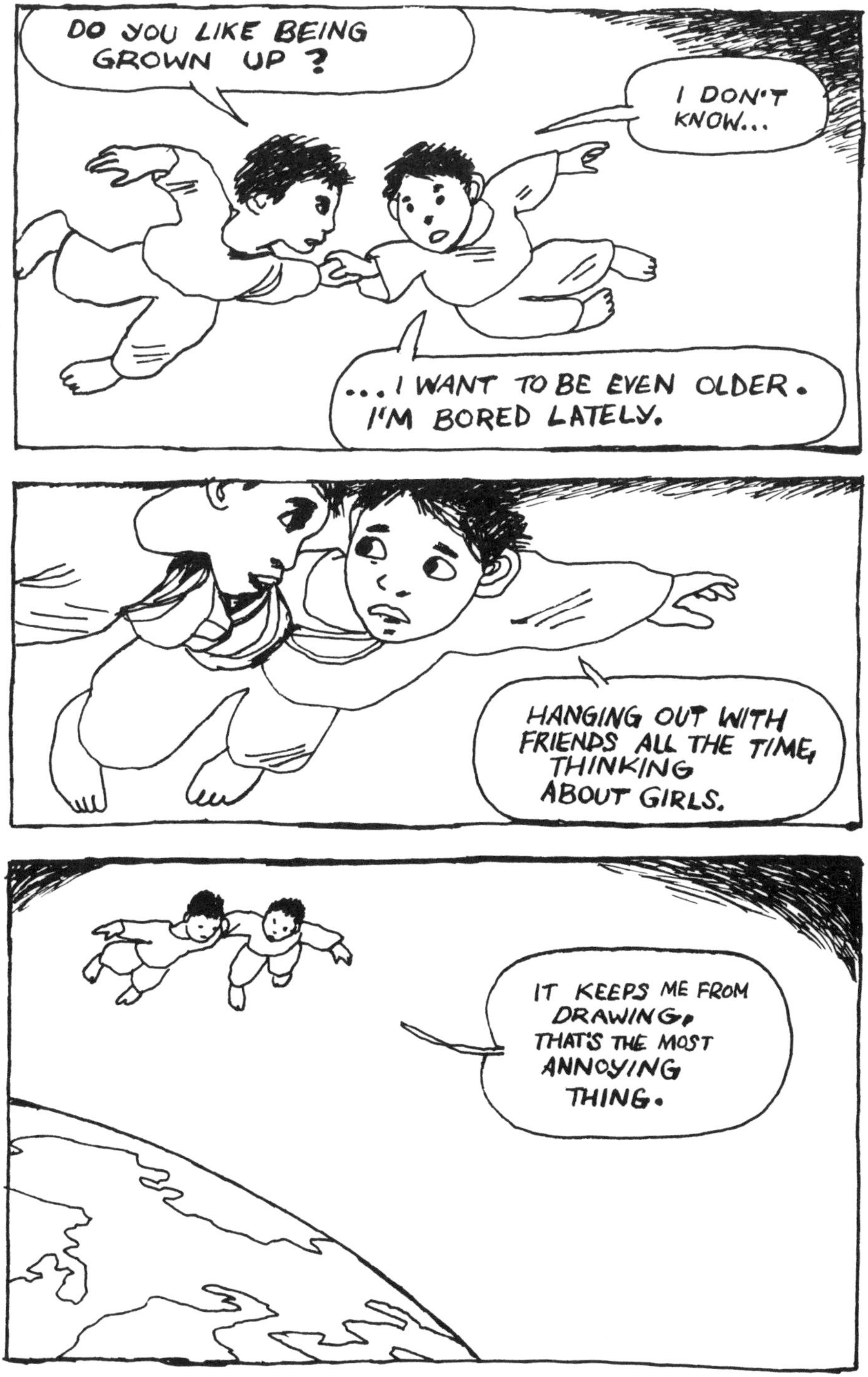
DO YOU LIKE BEING GROWN UP?
I DON'T KNOW...
...I WANT TO BE EVEN OLDER. I'M BORED LATELY.
HANGING OUT WITH FRIENDS ALL THE TIME, THINKING ABOUT GIRLS.
IT KEEPS ME FROM DRAWING, THAT'S THE MOST ANNOYING THING.

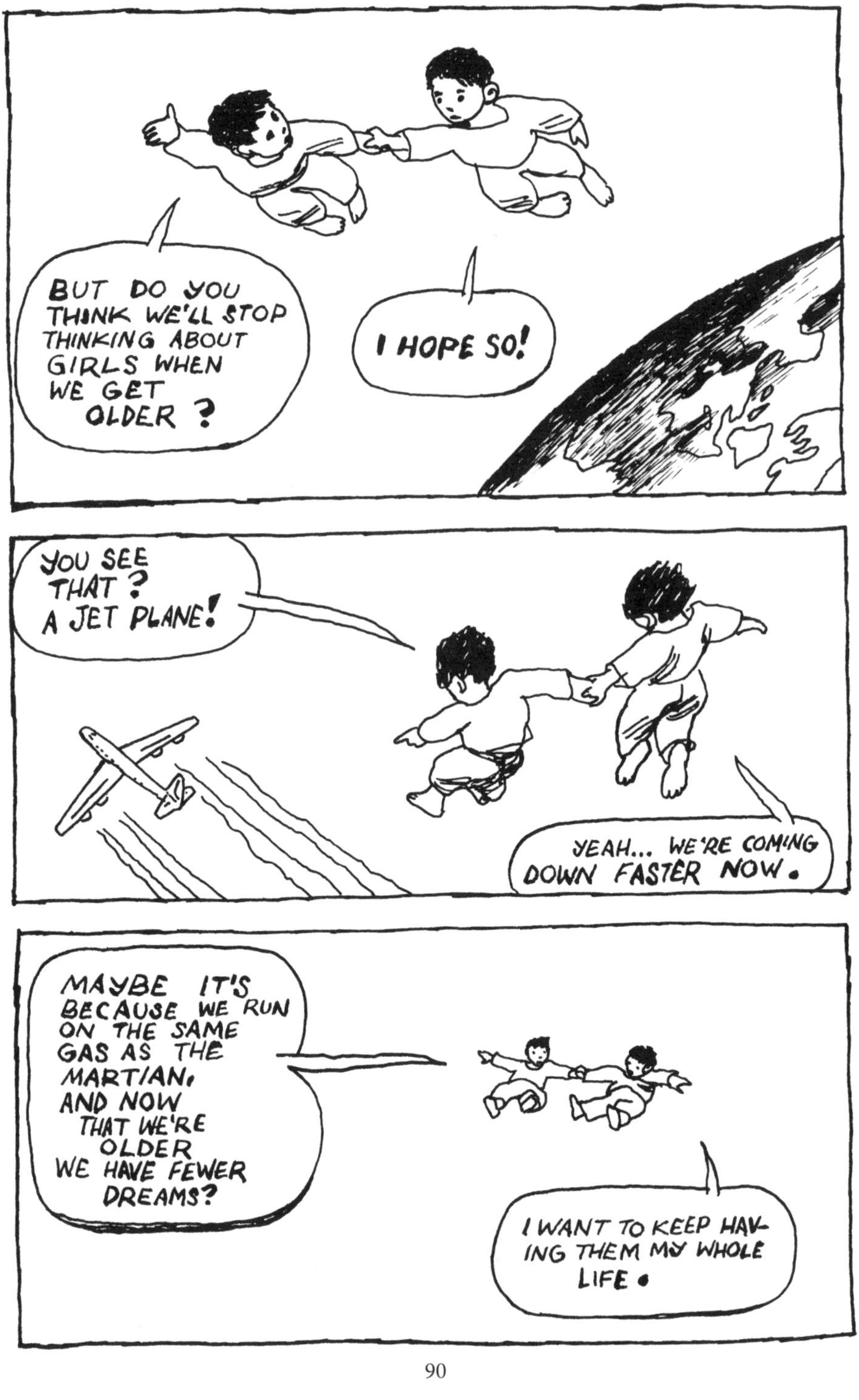
BUT DO YOU THINK WE'LL STOP THINKING ABOUT GIRLS WHEN WE GET OLDER ?
I HOPE SO!
YOU SEE THAT ? A JET PLANE!
YEAH... WE'RE COMING DOWN FASTER NOW.
MAYBE IT'S BECAUSE WE RUN ON THE SAME GAS AS THE MARTIAN, AND NOW THAT WE'RE OLDER WE HAVE FEWER DREAMS?
I WANT TO KEEP HAVING THEM MY WHOLE LIFE.

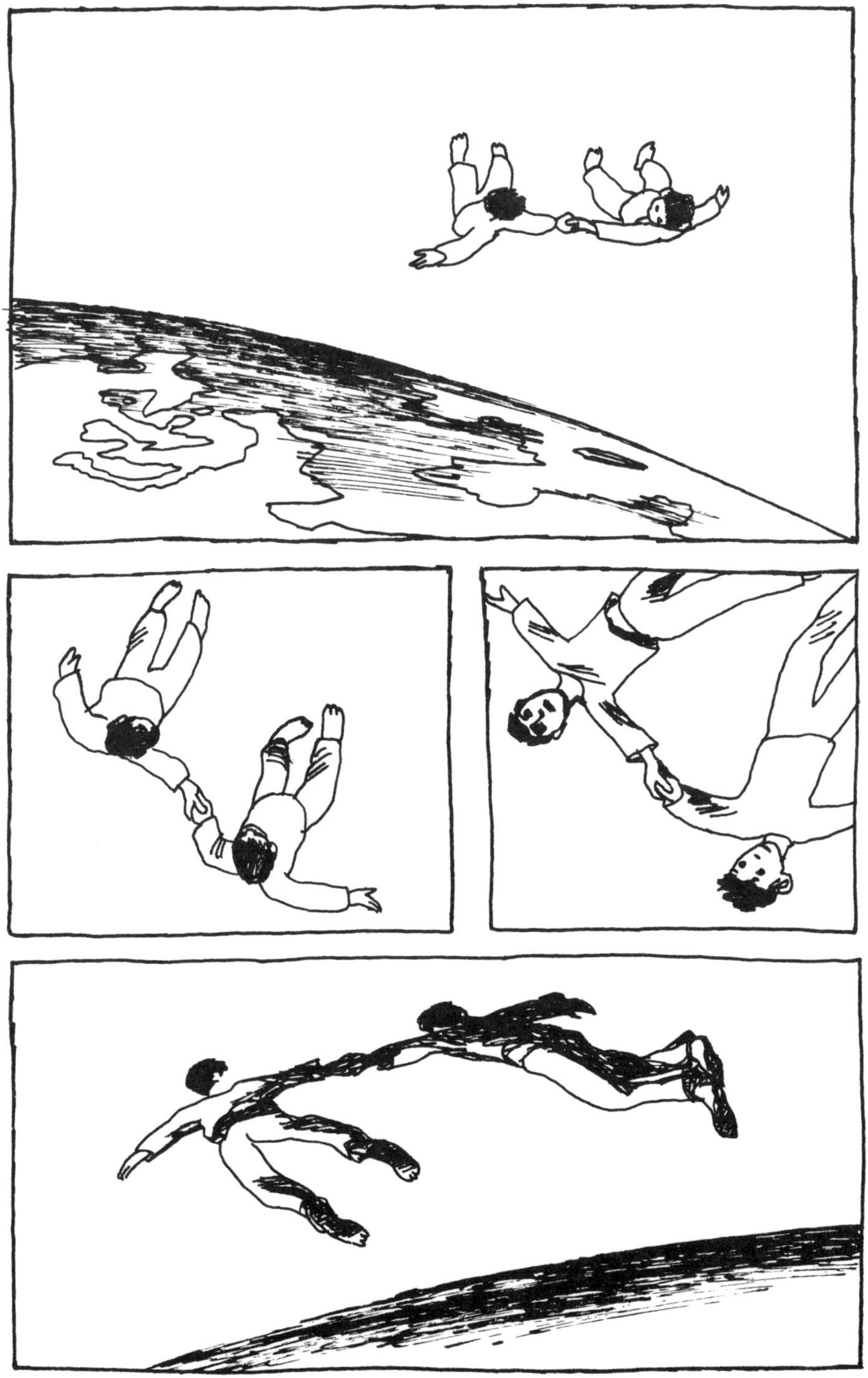

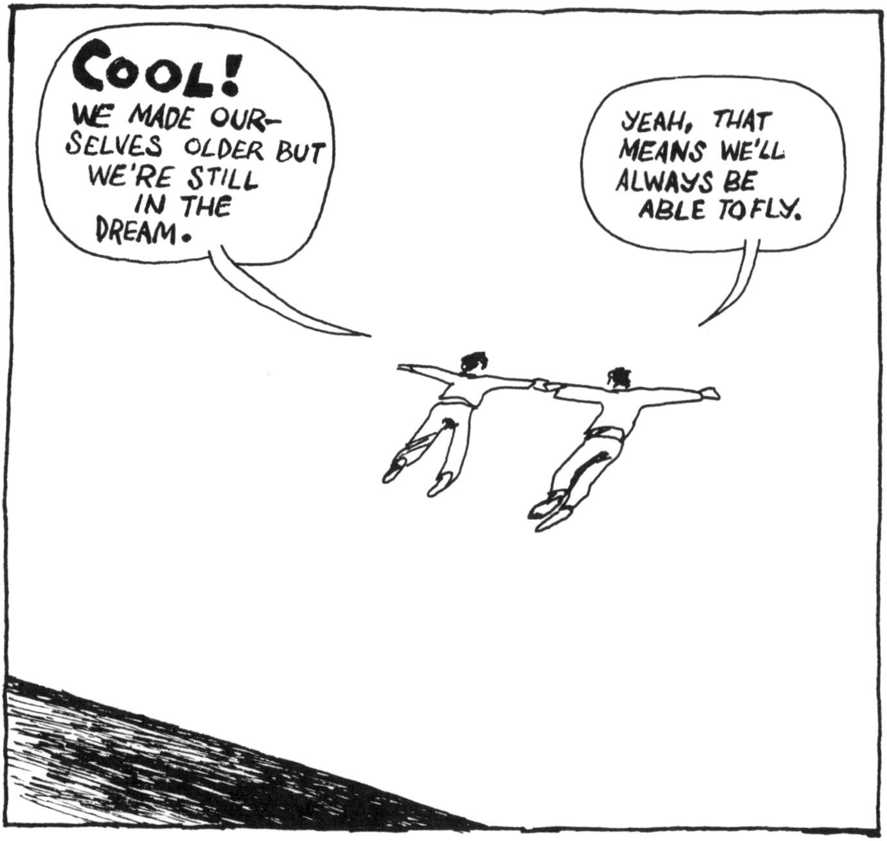
COOL! WE MADE OURSELVES OLDER BUT WE'RE STILL IN THE DREAM.
YEAH, THAT MEANS WE'LL ALWAYS BE ABLE TO FLY.

THE DAYS PILED UP. SUMMER IN THE VILLAGE, MIDDLE SCHOOL IN NICE.

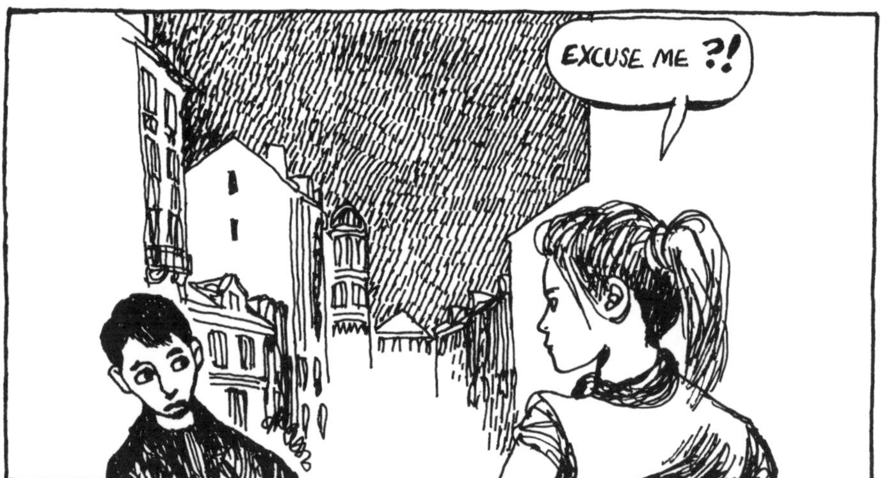
EXCUSE ME ?!

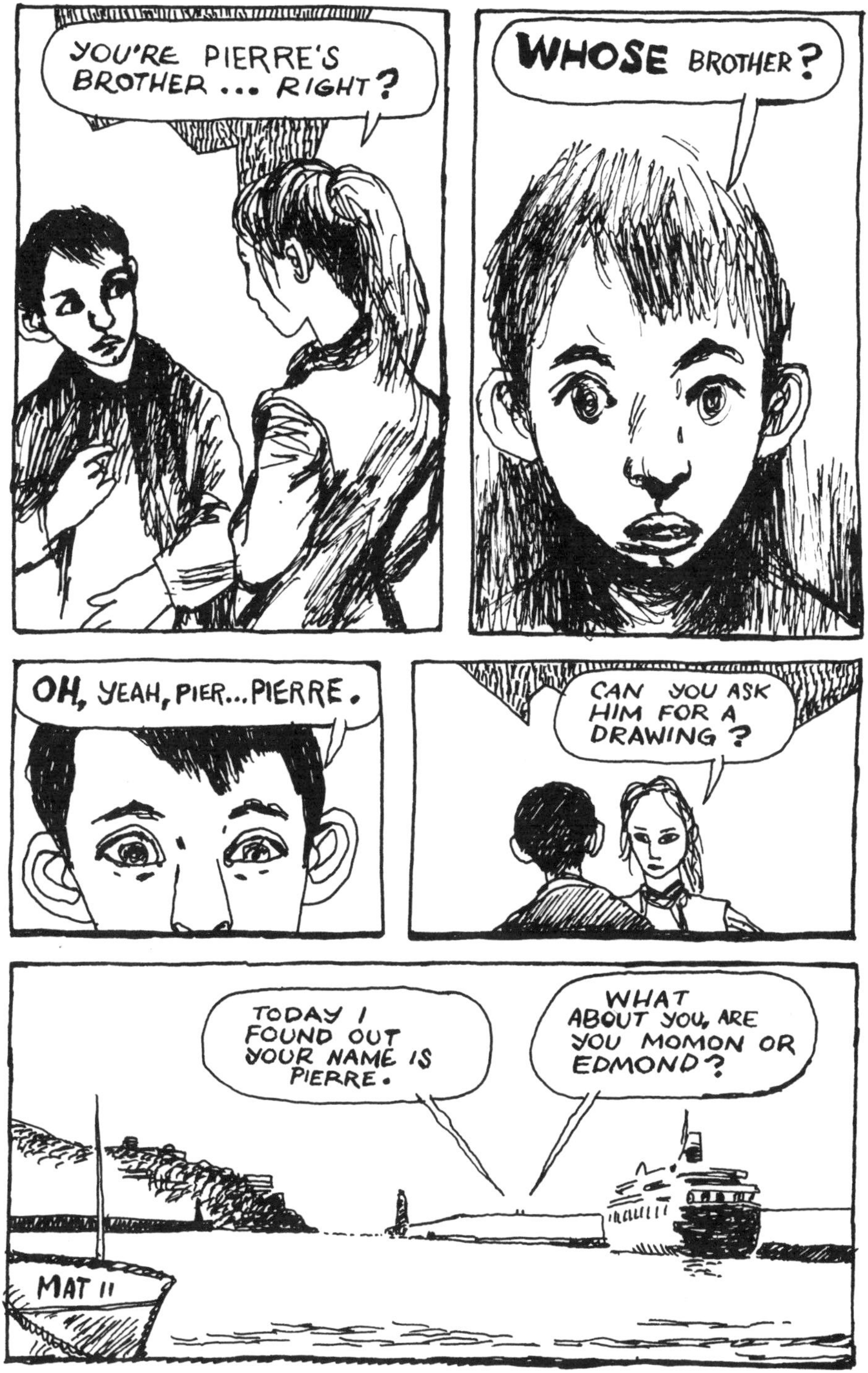
YOU'RE PIERRE'S BROTHER ... RIGHT?
WHOSE BROTHER?
OH, YEAH, PIER...PIERRE.
CAN YOU ASK HIM FOR A DRAWING?
TODAY I FOUND OUT YOUR NAME IS PIERRE.
WHAT ABOUT YOU, ARE YOU MOMON OR EDMOND?
MAT II

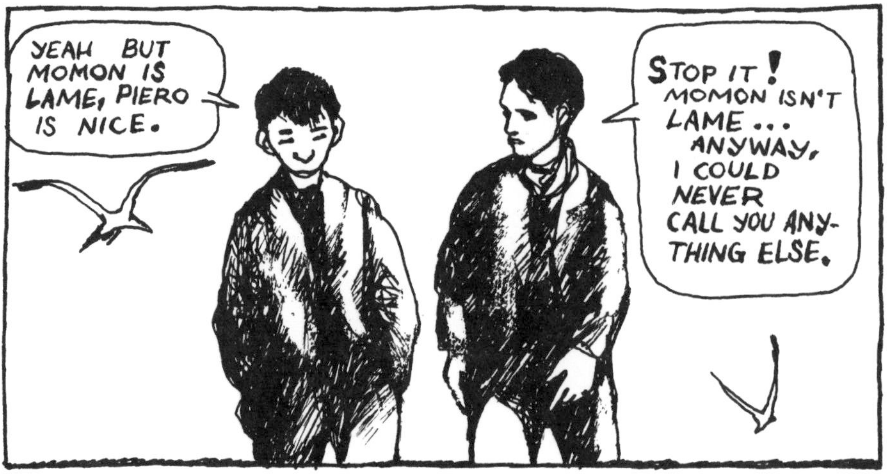
YEAH BUT MOMON IS LAME, PIERO IS NICE.
STOP IT! MOMON ISN'T LAME... ANYWAY, I COULD NEVER CALL YOU ANYTHING ELSE.

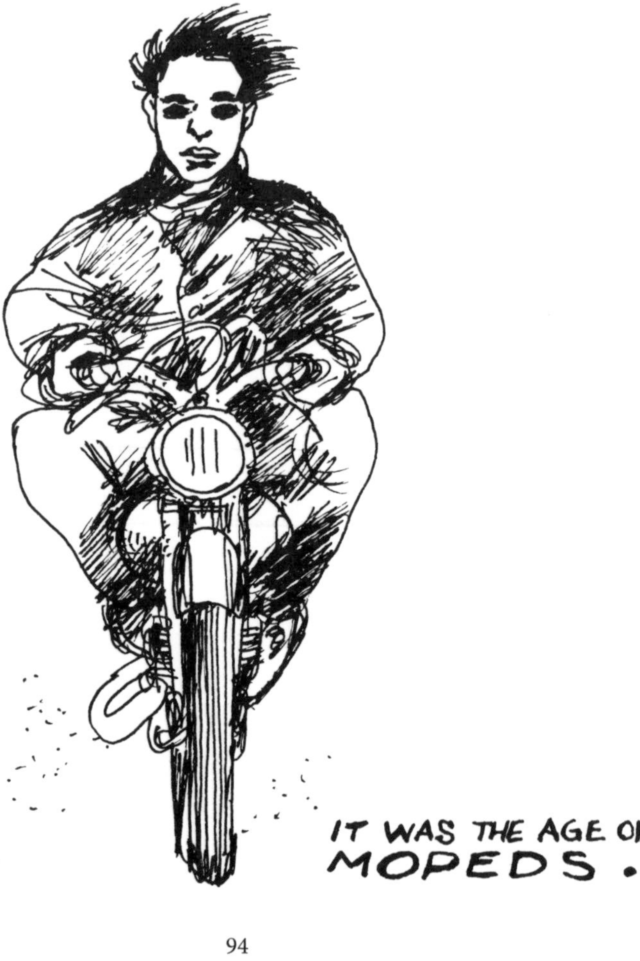
IT WAS THE AGE OF MOPEDS.

THE AGE OF DANCES.

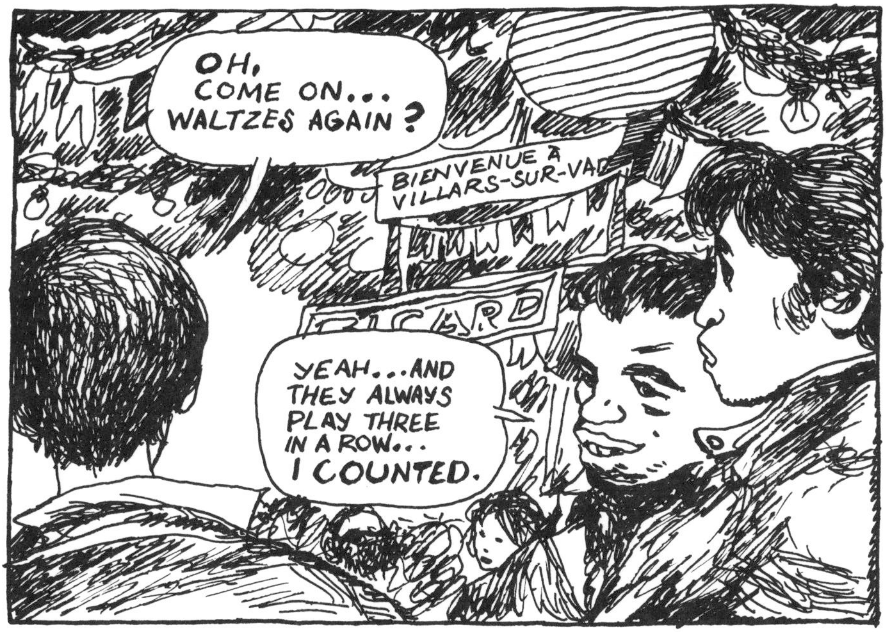
OH, COME ON... WALTZES AGAIN?
BIENVENUE À VILLARS-SUR-VAR
YEAH...AND THEY ALWAYS PLAY THREE IN A ROW... I COUNTED.

THE AGE OF ROCK.

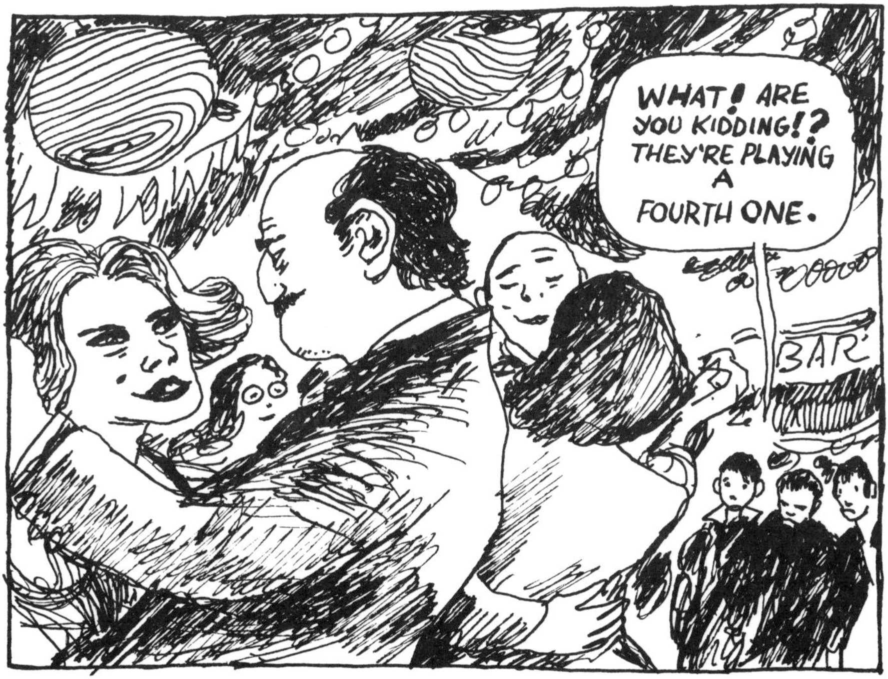
WHAT! ARE YOU KIDDING!? THEY'RE PLAYING A FOURTH ONE.
BAR

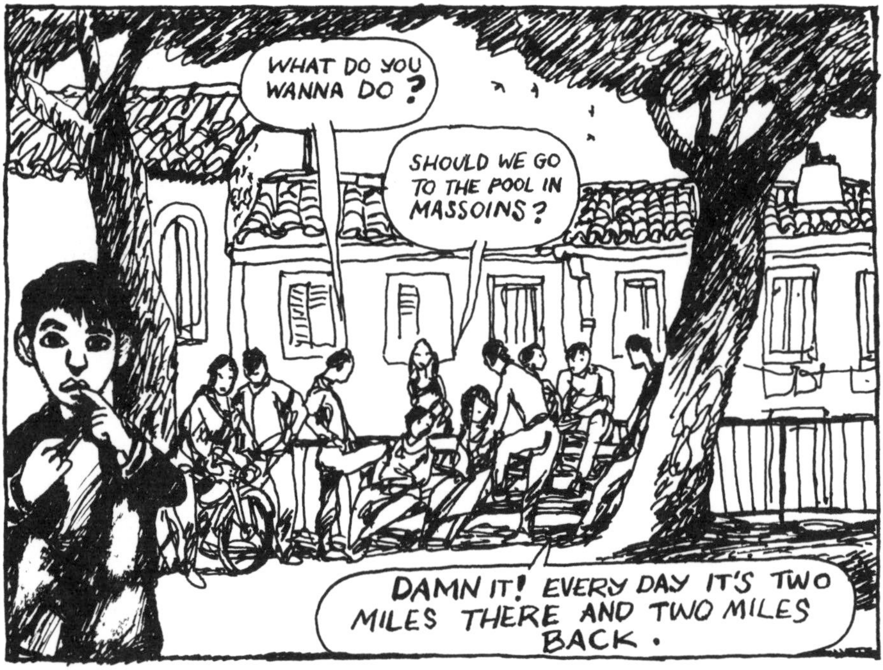
WHAT DO YOU WANNA DO?
SHOULD WE GO TO THE POOL IN MASSOINS?
DAMN IT! EVERY DAY IT'S TWO MILES THERE AND TWO MILES BACK.

WE WALKED A LOT... ALTHOUGH...

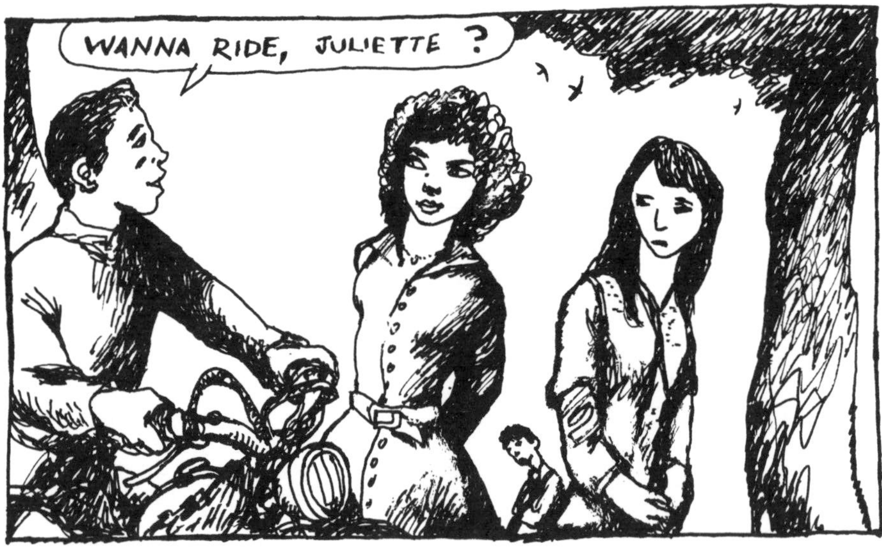
WANNA RIDE, JULIETTE?

...WHOEVER HAD A MOPED DIDN'T WALK, SAME FOR THE GIRLS WHO WERE GOING OUT WITH THE BOYS WHO HAD MOPEDS.

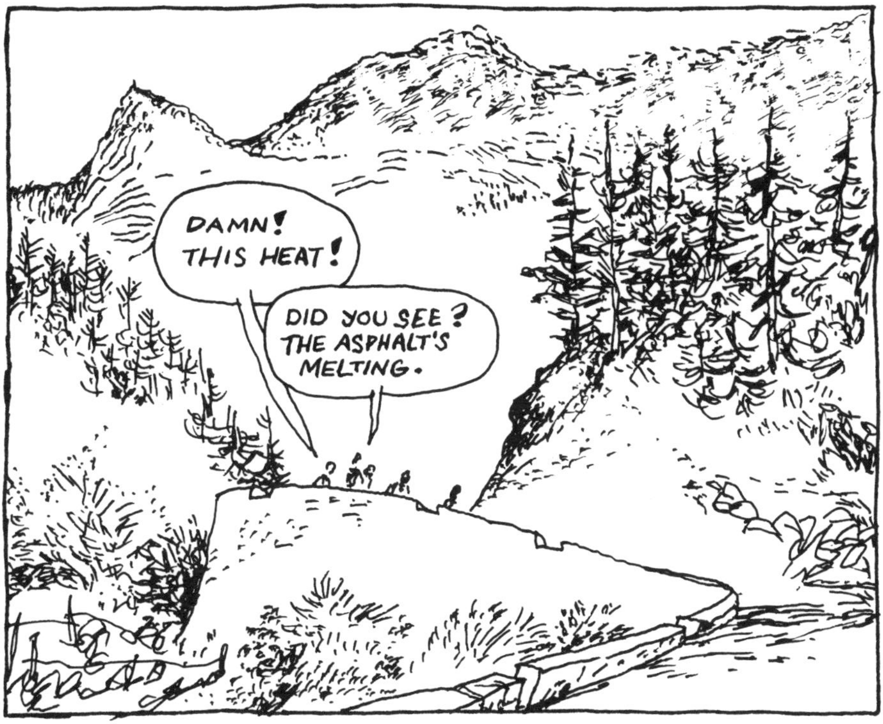
DAMN! THIS HEAT!
DID YOU SEE? THE ASPHALT'S MELTING.

BOYS WHO DIDN'T HAVE WHEELS HAD TO WALK. GIRLS WHO WERE GOING OUT WITH THE WALKING BOYS WALKED TOO.

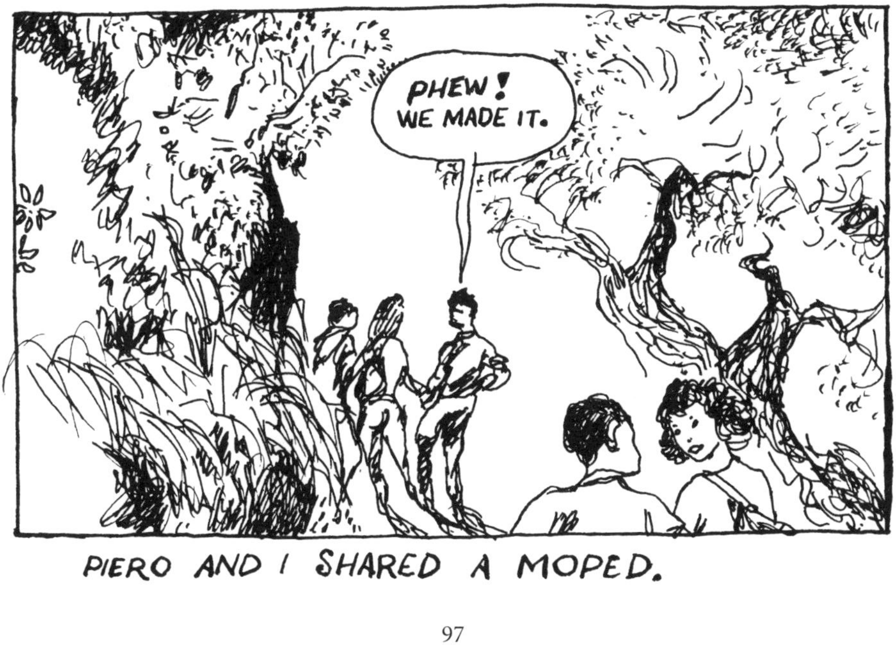
PHEW! WE MADE IT.

PIERO AND I SHARED A MOPED.

BUT PIERO WAS OFTEN TIRED BECAUSE OF HIS ONGOING ILLNESS, SO THE MOPED WAS FOR THE MOST PART HIS.

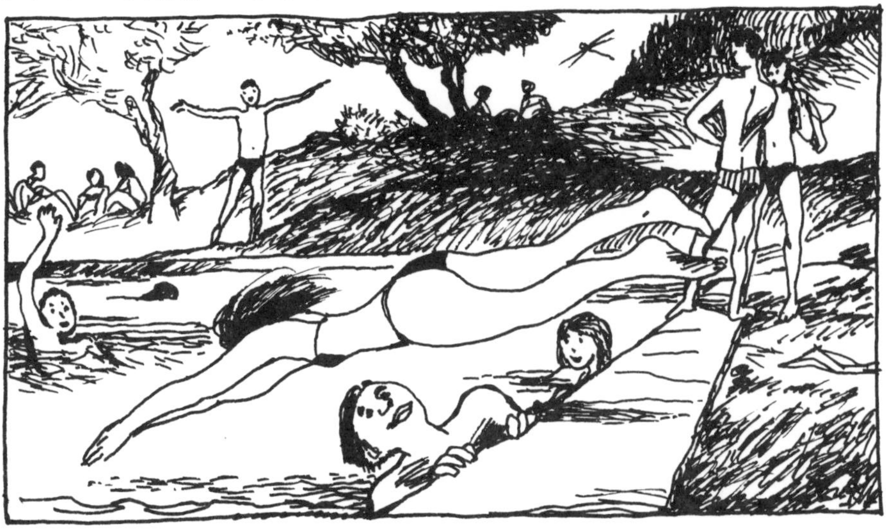

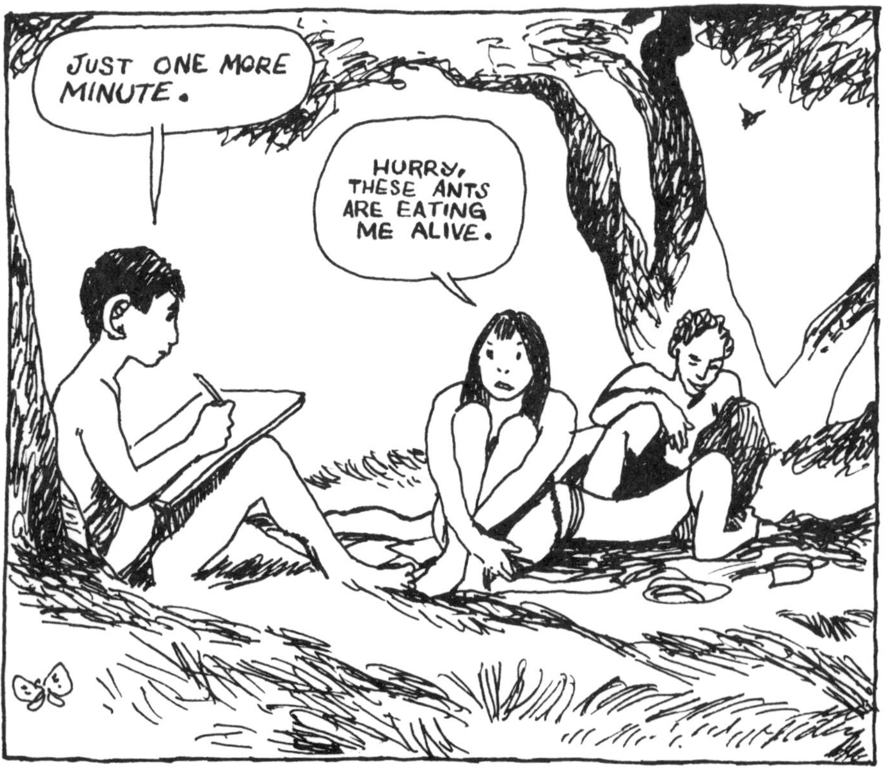
JUST ONE MORE MINUTE.
HURRY, THESE ANTS ARE EATING ME ALIVE.

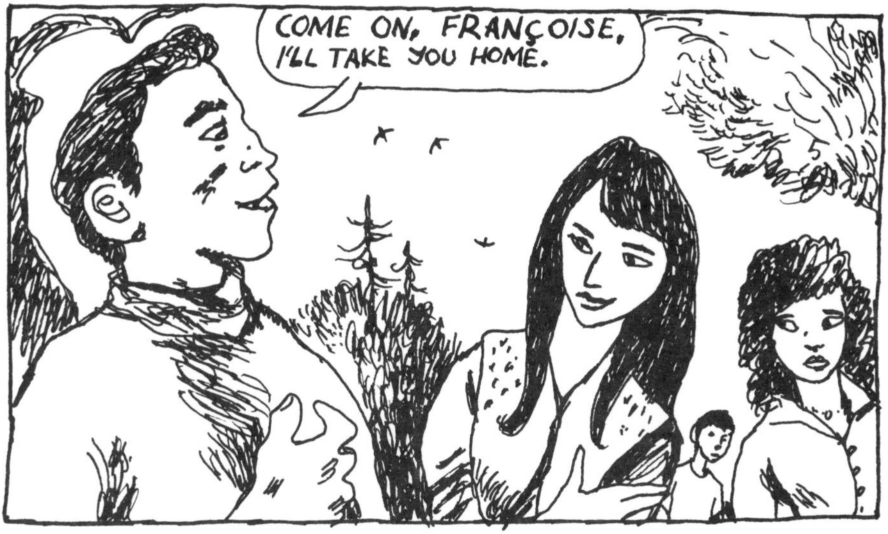
COME ON, FRANÇOISE, I'LL TAKE YOU HOME.

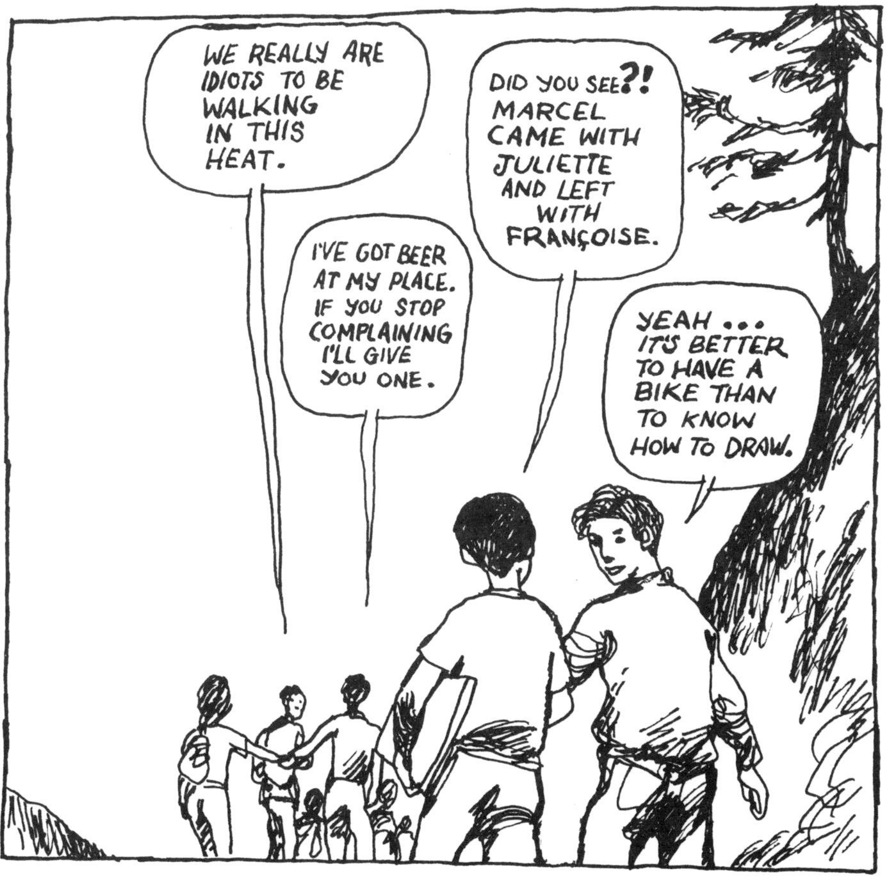
WE REALLY ARE IDIOTS TO BE WALKING IN THIS HEAT.
I'VE GOT BEER AT MY PLACE. IF YOU STOP COMPLAINING I'LL GIVE YOU ONE.
DID YOU SEE?! MARCEL CAME WITH JULIETTE AND LEFT WITH FRANÇOISE.
YEAH ... IT'S BETTER TO HAVE A BIKE THAN TO KNOW HOW TO DRAW.

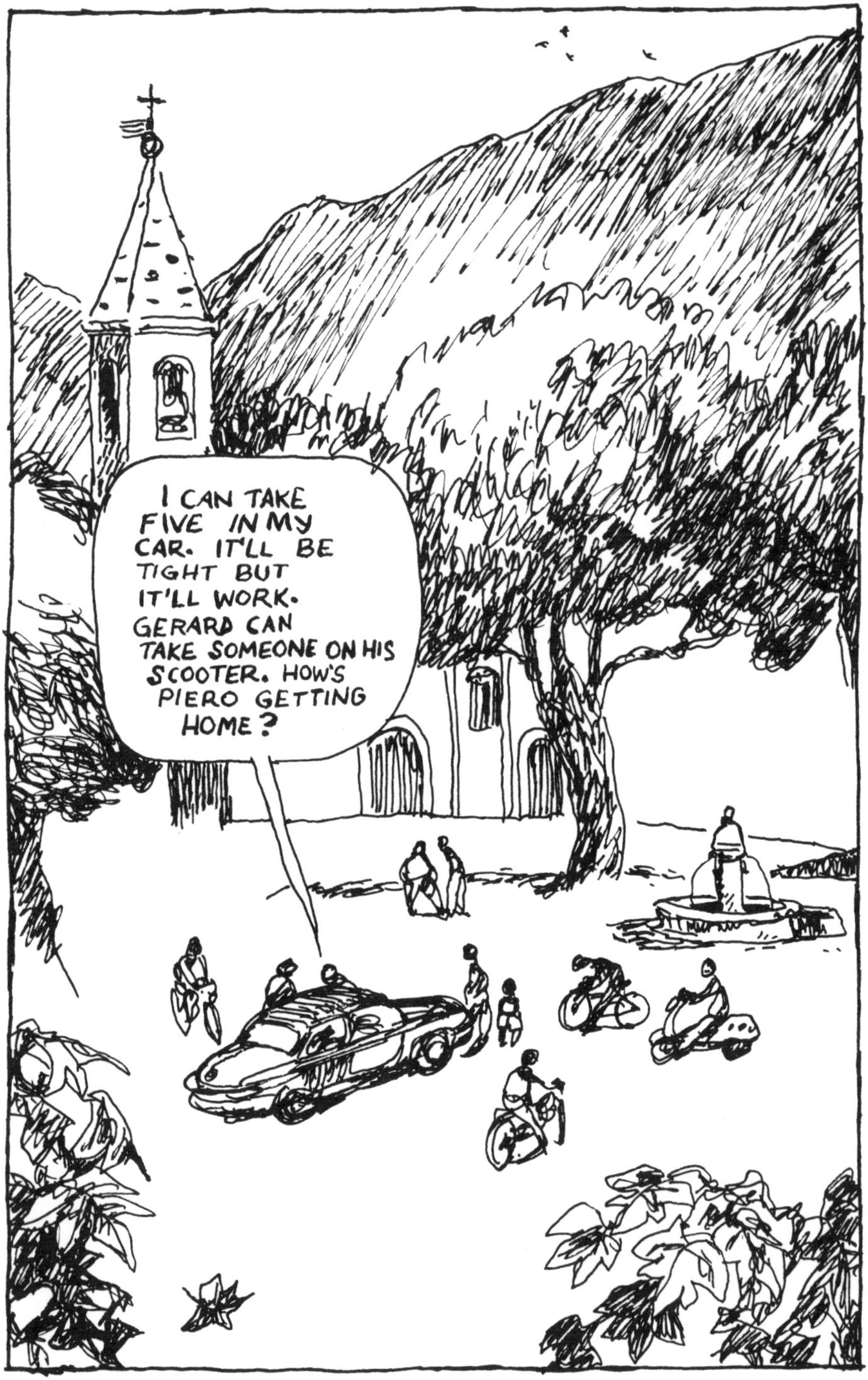
I CAN TAKE FIVE IN MY CAR. IT'LL BE TIGHT BUT IT'LL WORK. GERARD CAN TAKE SOMEONE ON HIS SCOOTER. HOW'S PIERO GETTING HOME?

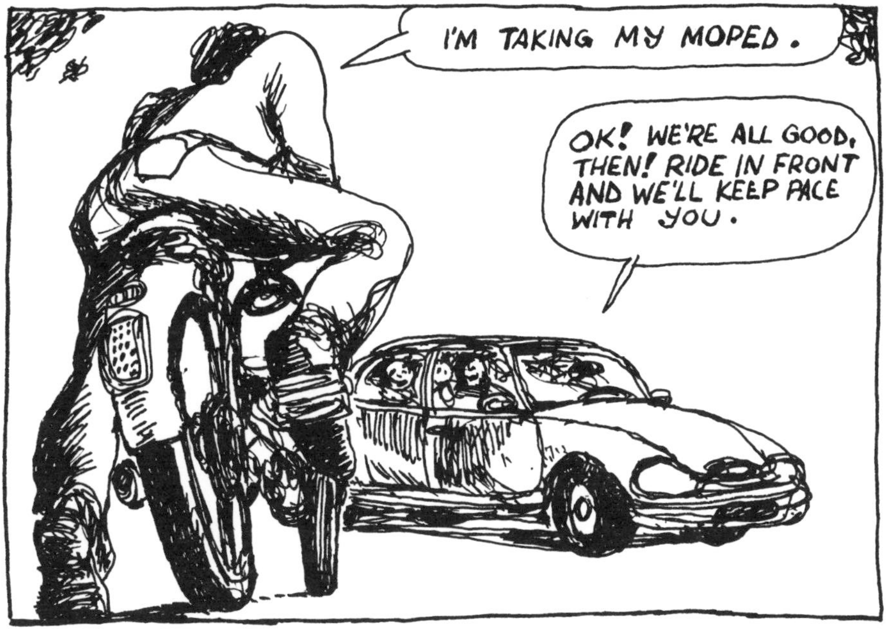
I'M TAKING MY MOPED.
OK! WE'RE ALL GOOD, THEN! RIDE IN FRONT AND WE'LL KEEP PACE WITH YOU.

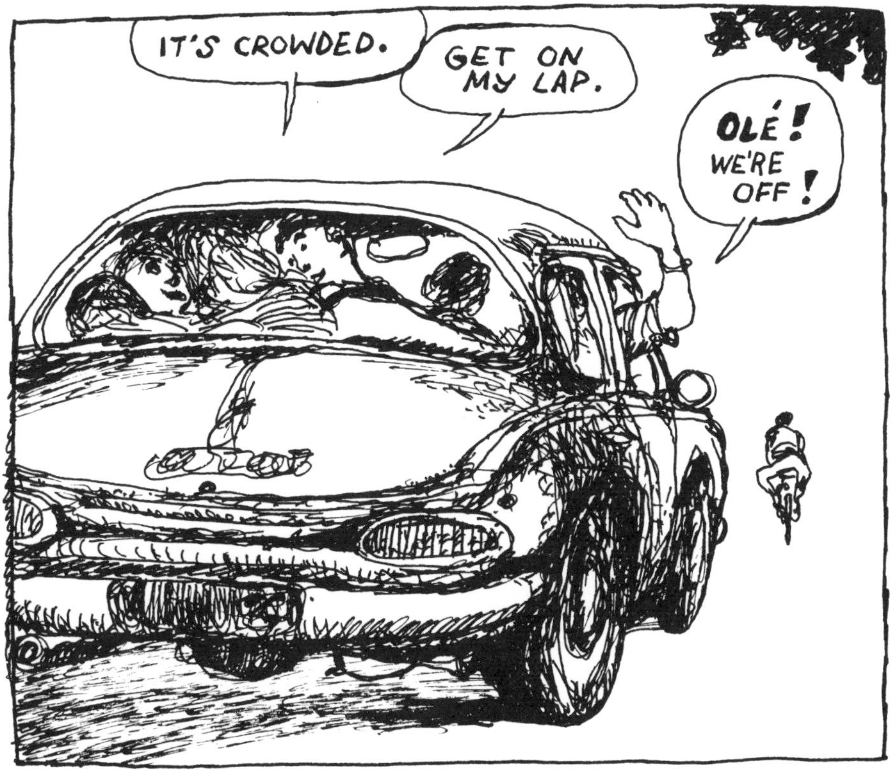
IT'S CROWDED.
GET ON MY LAP.
OLÉ! WE'RE OFF!

IT WAS VERY HOT. THE CICADAS WERE CHIRPING LIKE MAD.

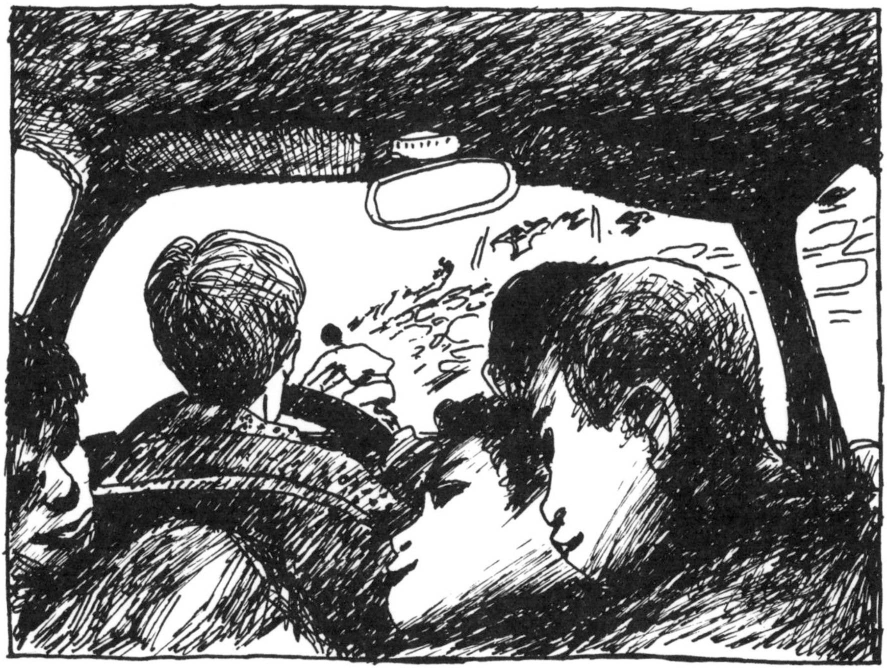

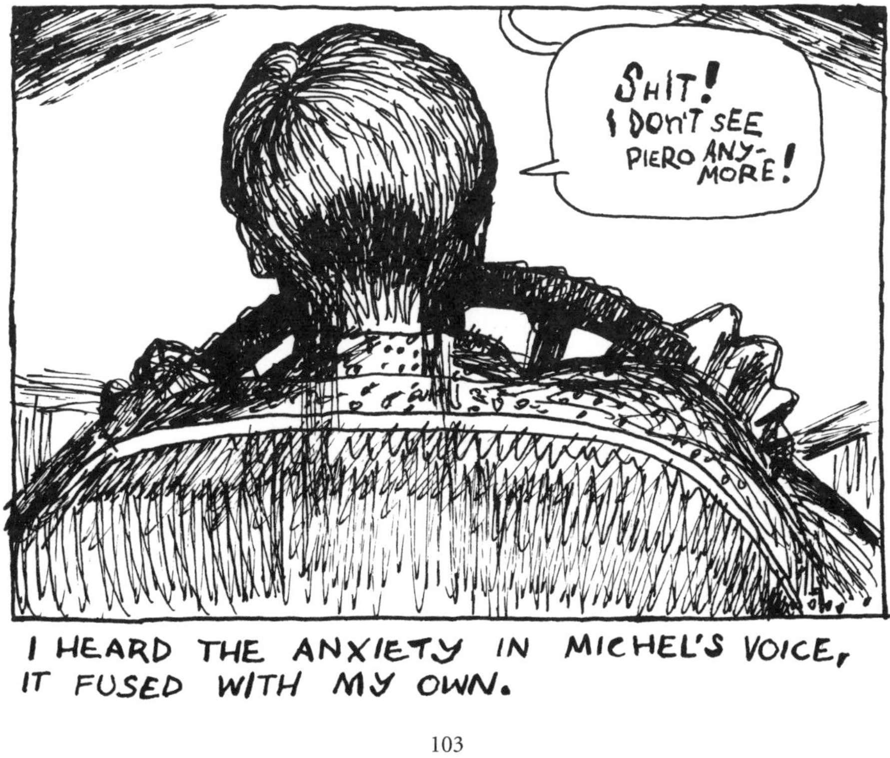
SHIT! I DON'T SEE PIERO ANY-MORE!

I HEARD THE ANXIETY IN MICHEL'S VOICE, IT FUSED WITH MY OWN.

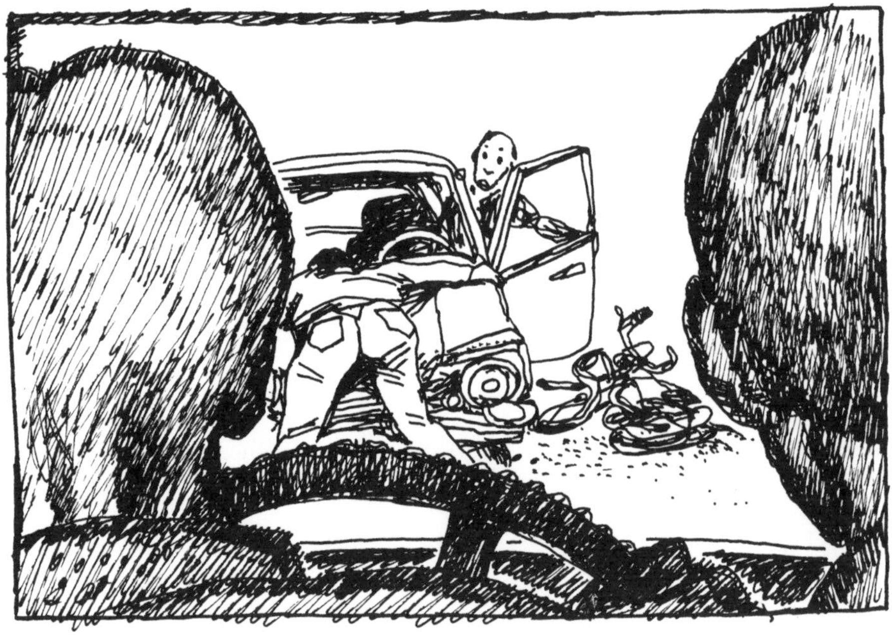

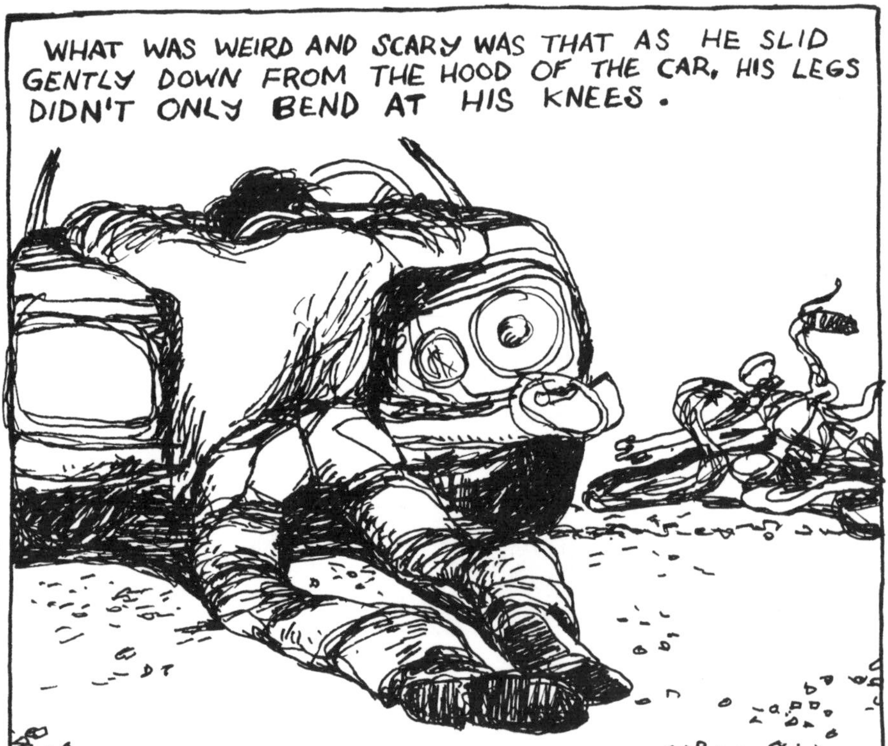
WHAT WAS WEIRD AND SCARY WAS THAT AS HE SLID GENTLY DOWN FROM THE HOOD OF THE CAR, HIS LEGS DIDN'T ONLY BEND AT HIS KNEES.

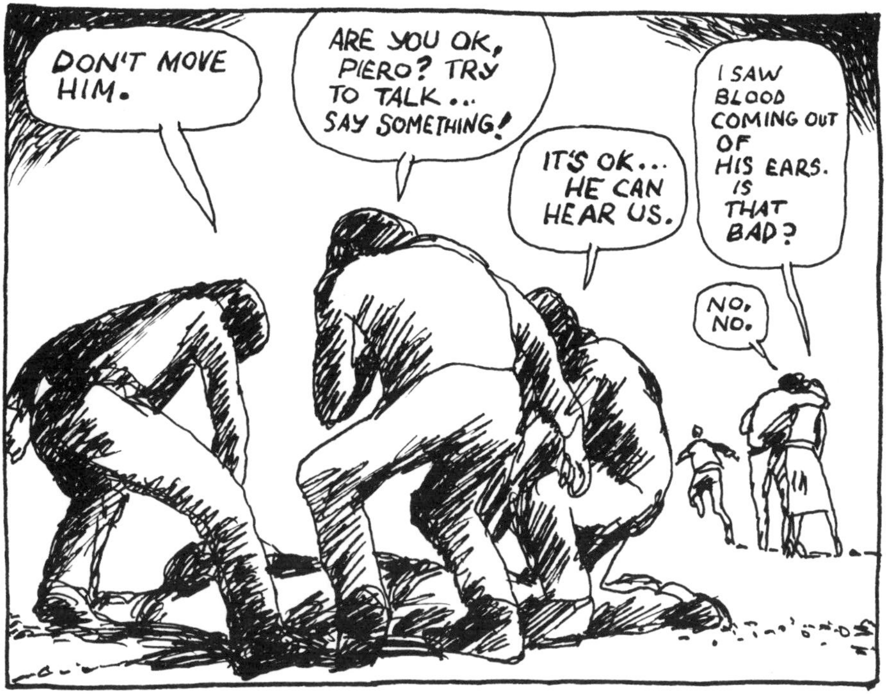
DON'T MOVE HIM.
ARE YOU OK, PIERO? TRY TO TALK... SAY SOMETHING!
IT'S OK... HE CAN HEAR US.
I SAW BLOOD COMING OUT OF HIS EARS. IS THAT BAD?
NO, NO.

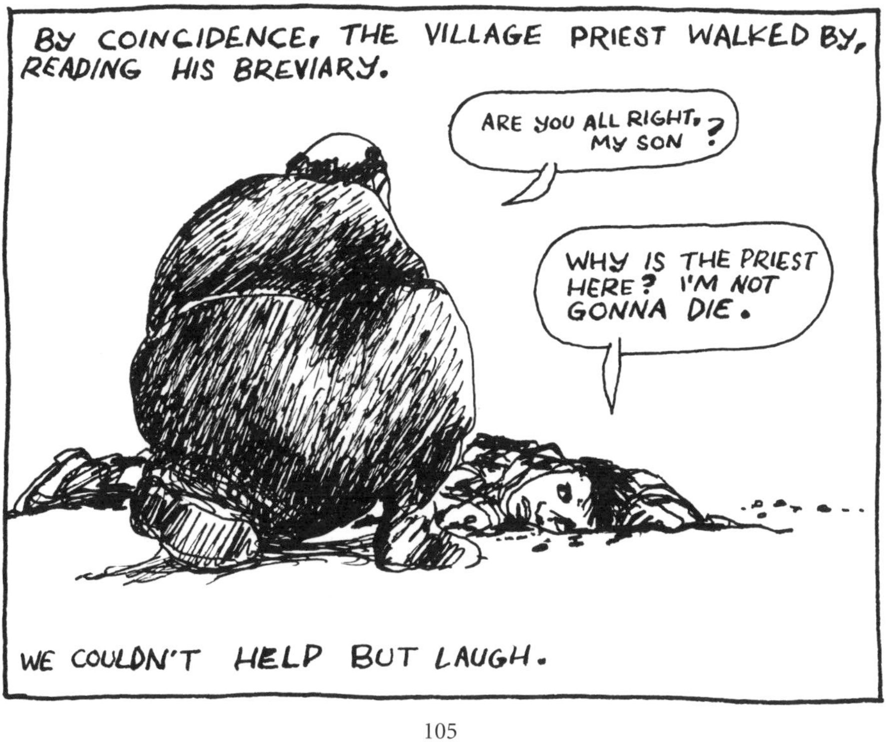
BY COINCIDENCE, THE VILLAGE PRIEST WALKED BY, READING HIS BREVIARY.
ARE YOU ALL RIGHT, MY SON?
WHY IS THE PRIEST HERE? I'M NOT GONNA DIE.
WE COULDN'T HELP BUT LAUGH.

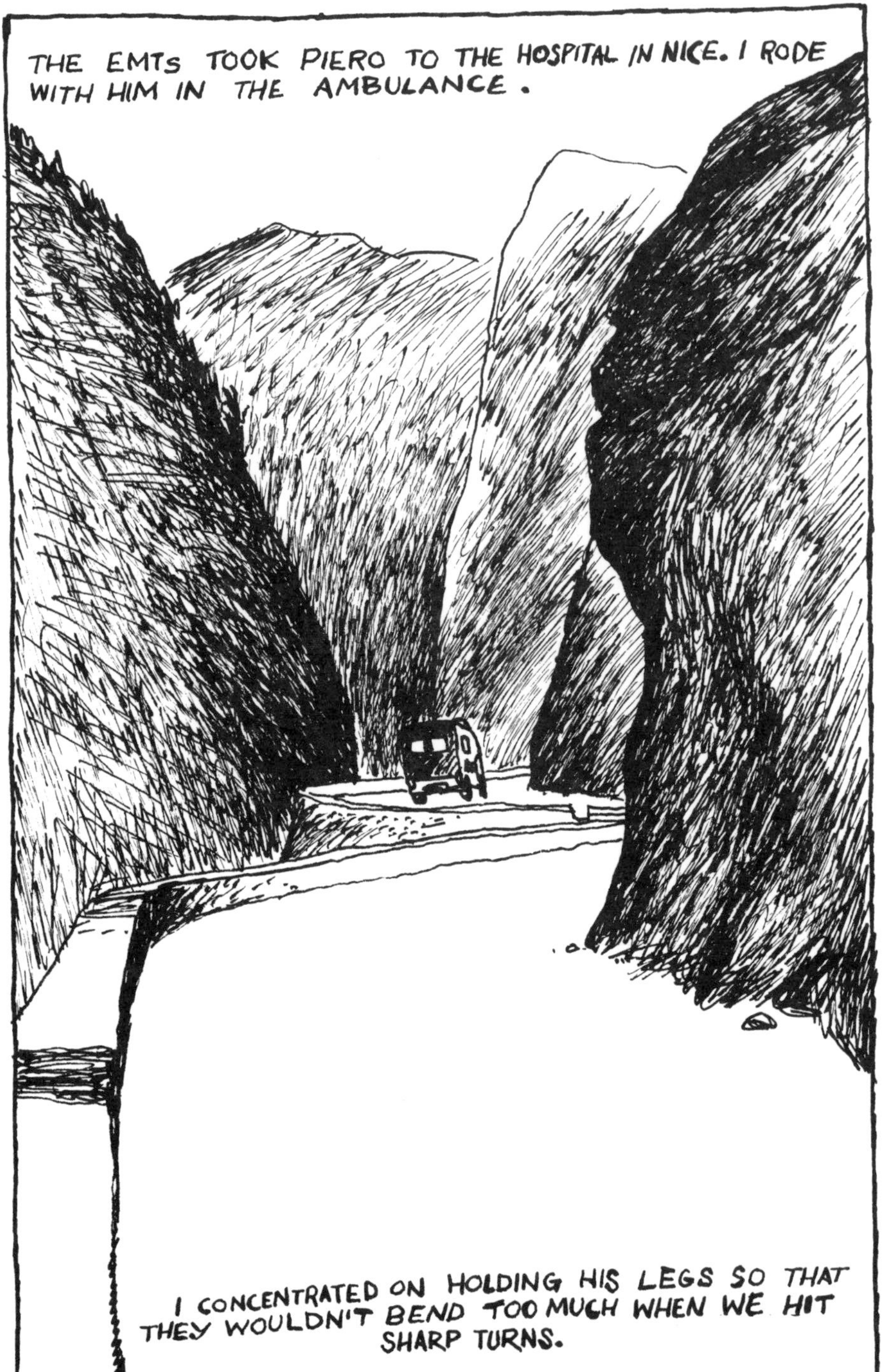
THE EMTs TOOK PIERO TO THE HOSPITAL IN NICE. I RODE WITH HIM IN THE AMBULANCE.
I CONCENTRATED ON HOLDING HIS LEGS SO THAT THEY WOULDN'T BEND TOO MUCH WHEN WE HIT SHARP TURNS.

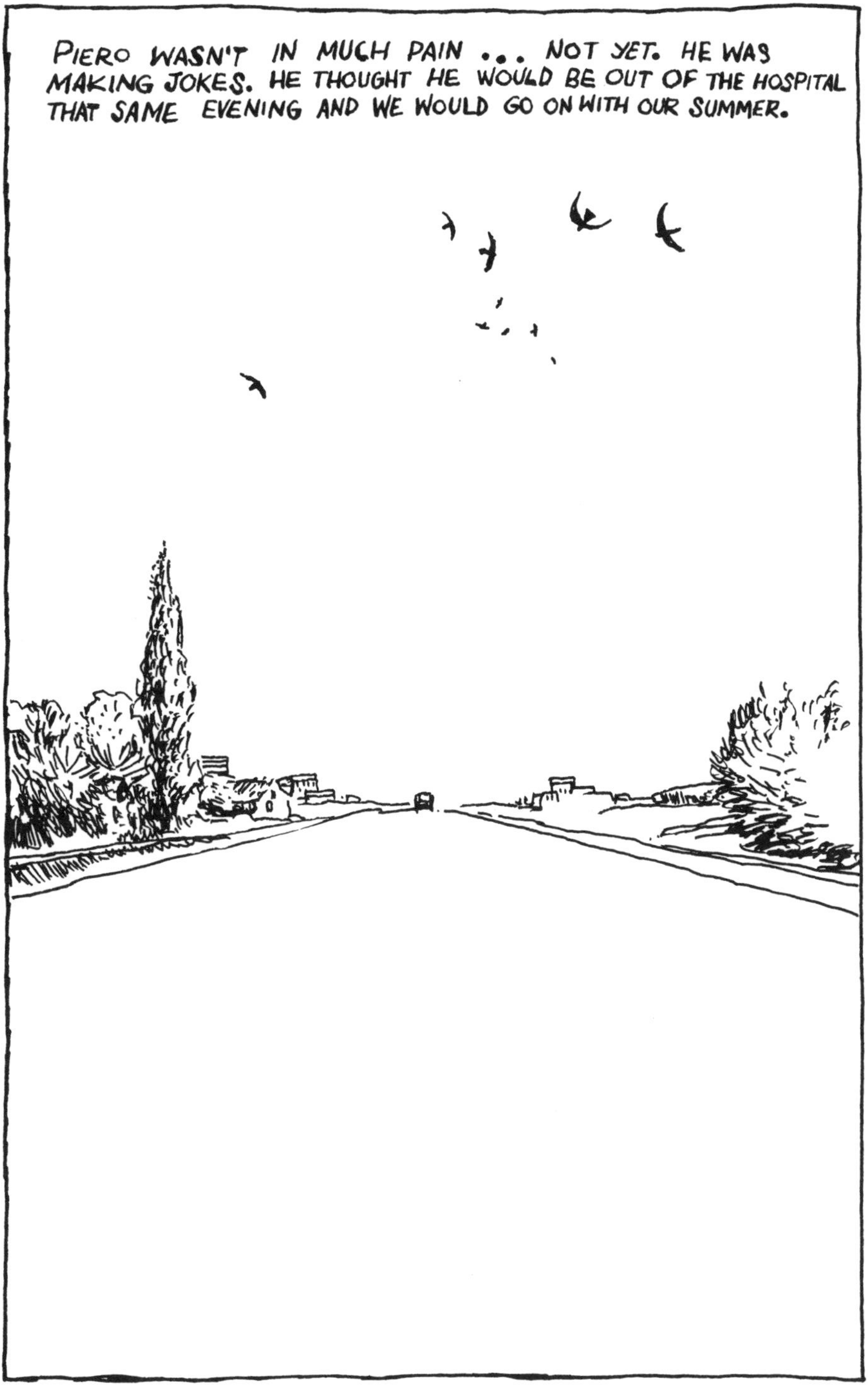
PIERO WASN'T IN MUCH PAIN ... NOT YET. HE WAS MAKING JOKES. HE THOUGHT HE WOULD BE OUT OF THE HOSPITAL THAT SAME EVENING AND WE WOULD GO ON WITH OUR SUMMER.

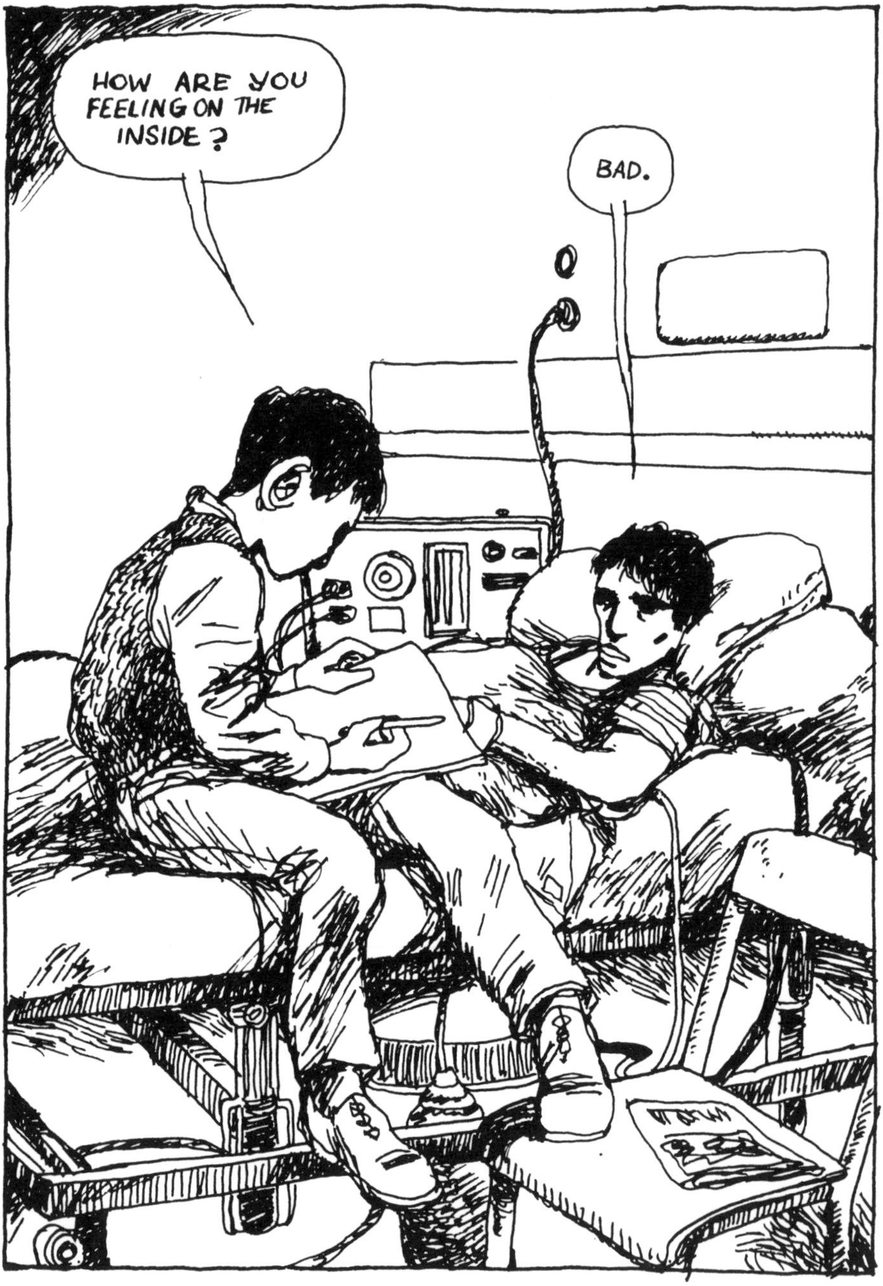
HOW ARE YOU FEELING ON THE INSIDE?
BAD.

HE WAS IN THE HOSPITAL FOR **SIX** MONTHS. SOMETIMES I ENVIED HIM... HE COULD DRAW ALL DAY LONG.

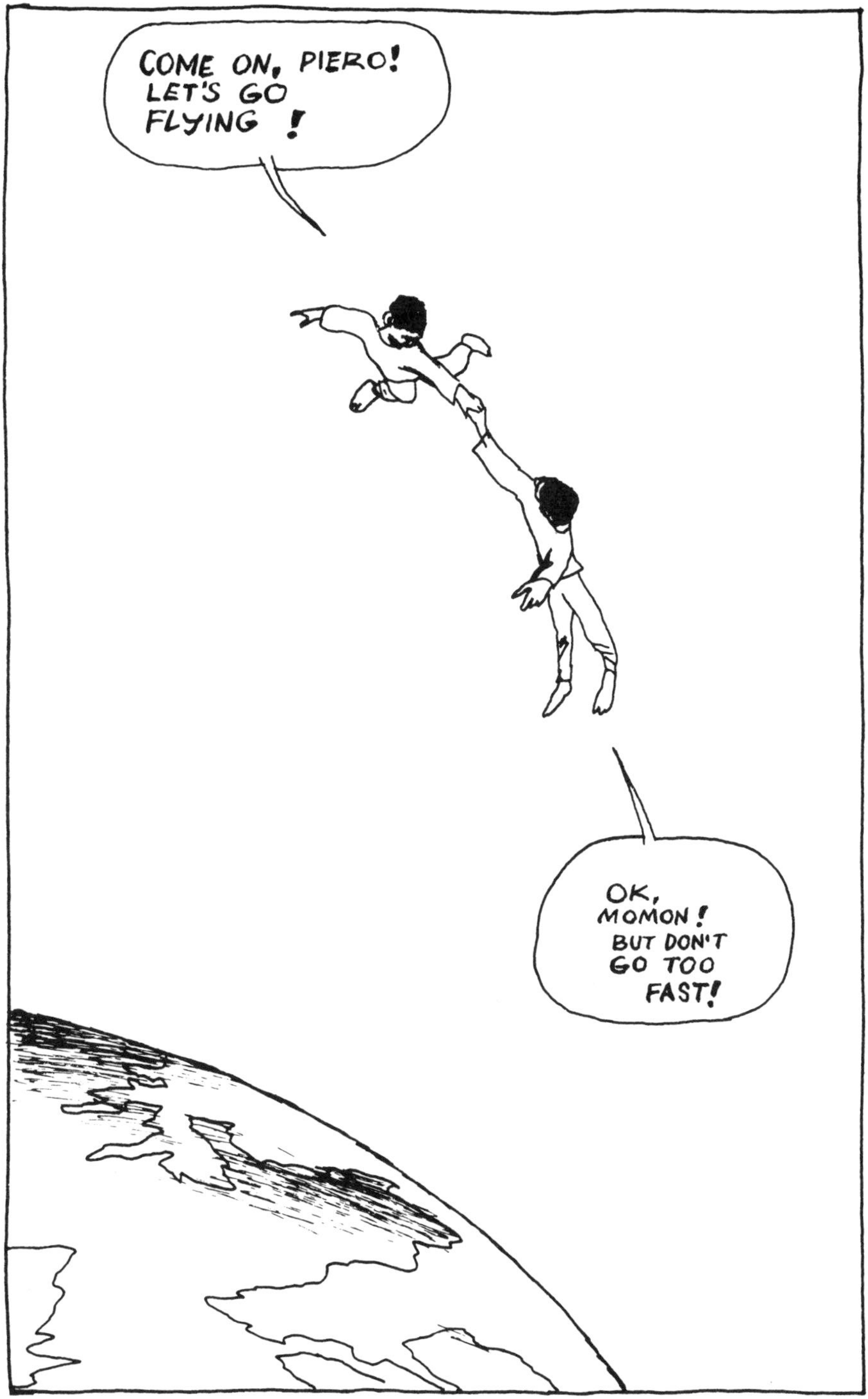
COME ON, PIERO! LET'S GO FLYING !
OK, MOMON! BUT DON'T GO TOO FAST!

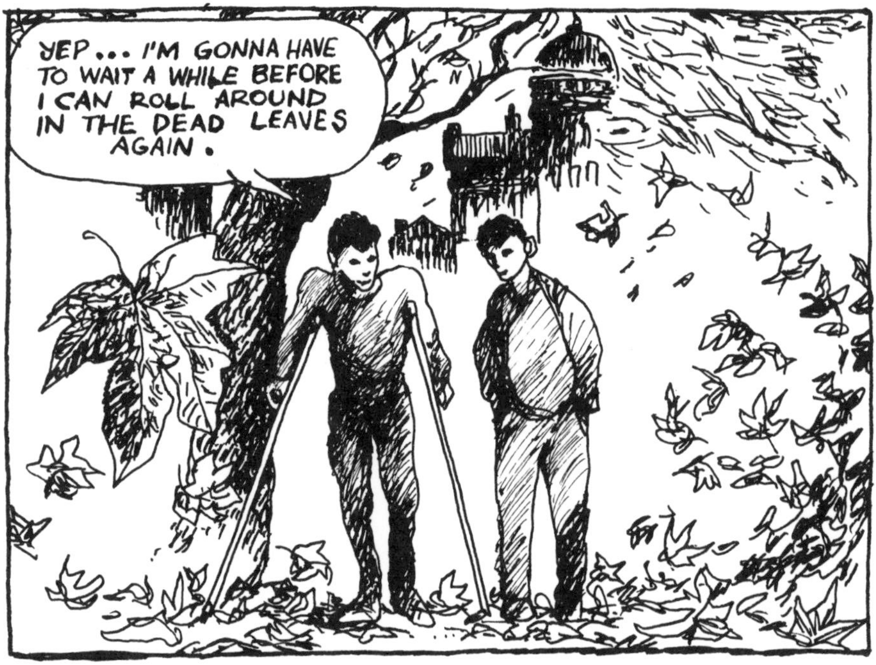
YEP... I'M GONNA HAVE TO WAIT A WHILE BEFORE I CAN ROLL AROUND IN THE DEAD LEAVES AGAIN.

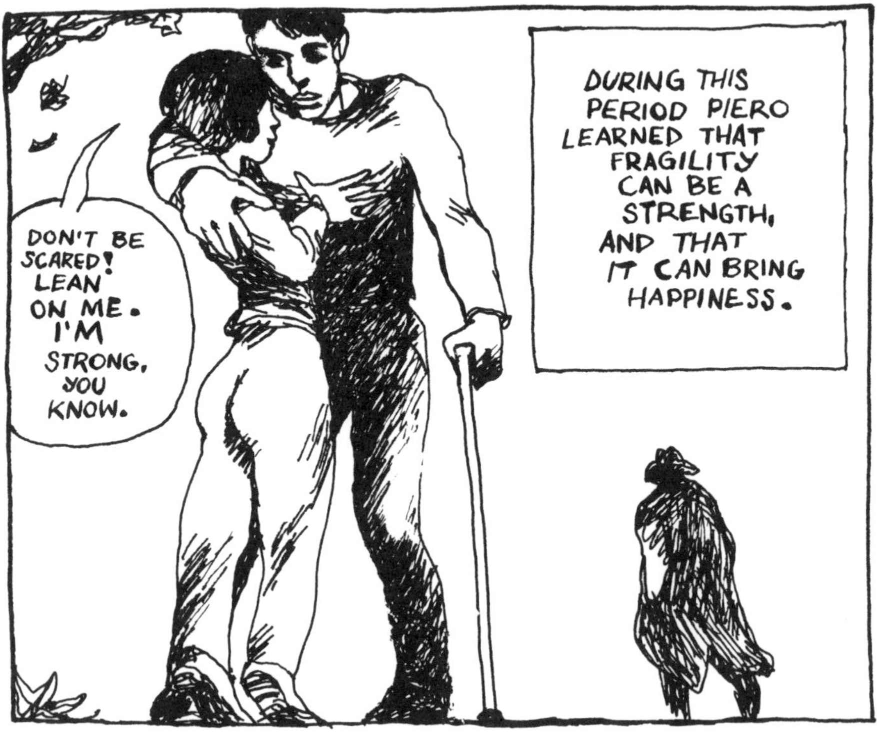
DURING THIS PERIOD PIERO LEARNED THAT FRAGILITY CAN BE A STRENGTH, AND THAT IT CAN BRING HAPPINESS.
DON'T BE SCARED! LEAN ON ME. I'M STRONG, YOU KNOW.

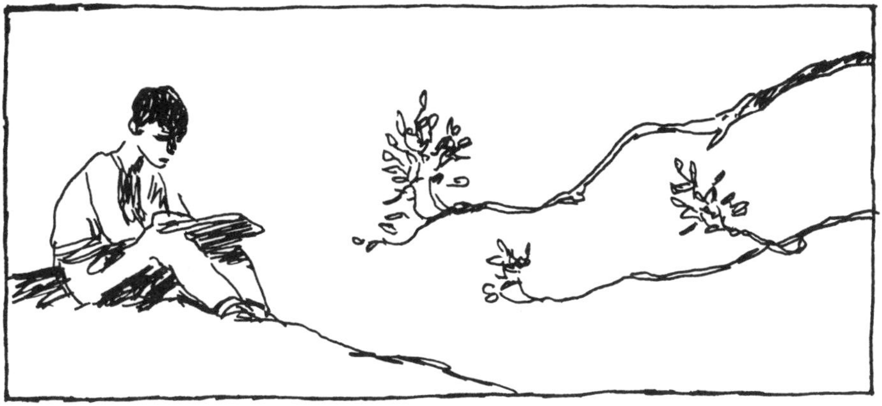

IS IT GOING TOO FAR TO WRITE THAT YOU LOVE SOMEONE MORE THAN YOURSELF?

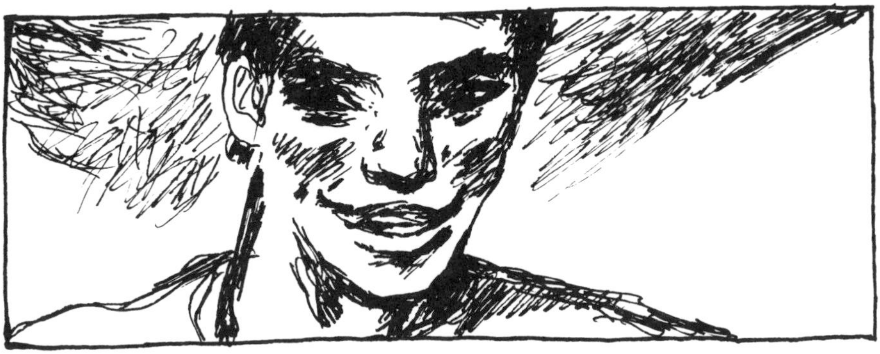

WHEN MY BROTHER SMILED, THE WHOLE WORLD SMILED.

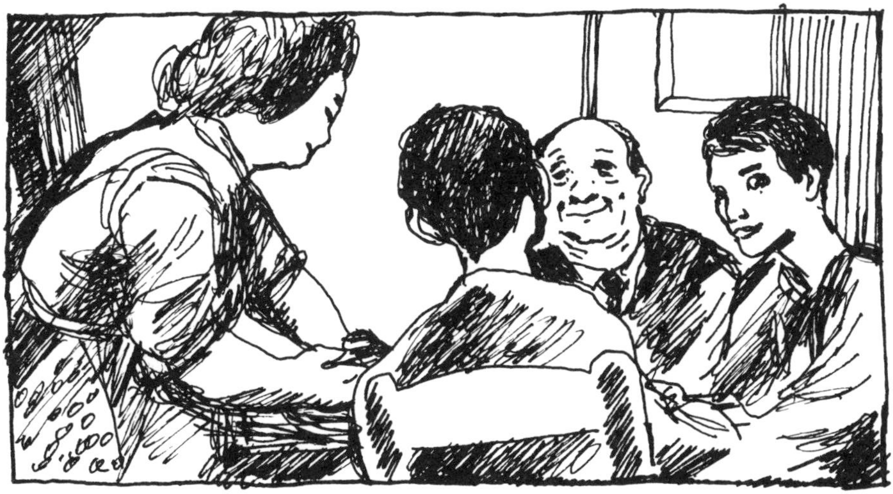

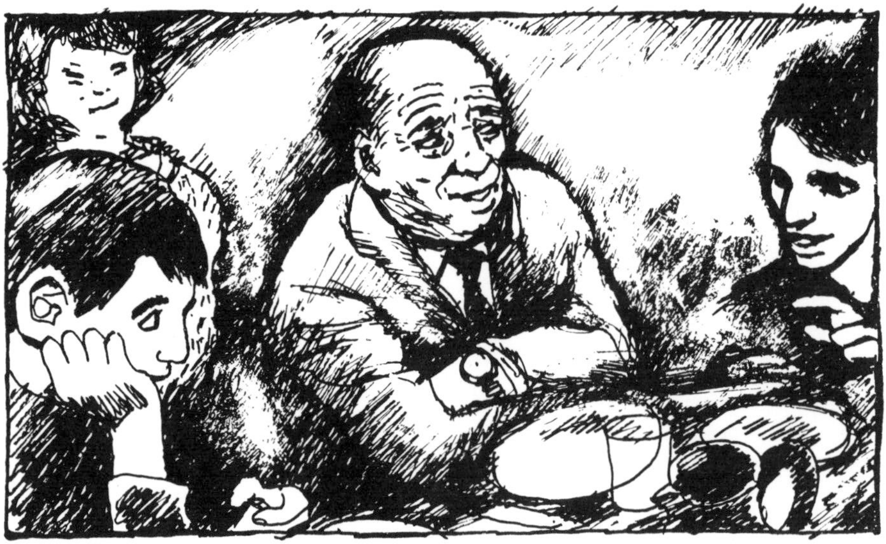

MAYBE WE DISCUSSED IT ONCE OVER DINNER? OR MAYBE AFTER A SUNDAY FEAST? BUT THEN AGAIN MAYBE WE NEVER DISCUSSED IT BECAUSE IT WAS OBVIOUS.

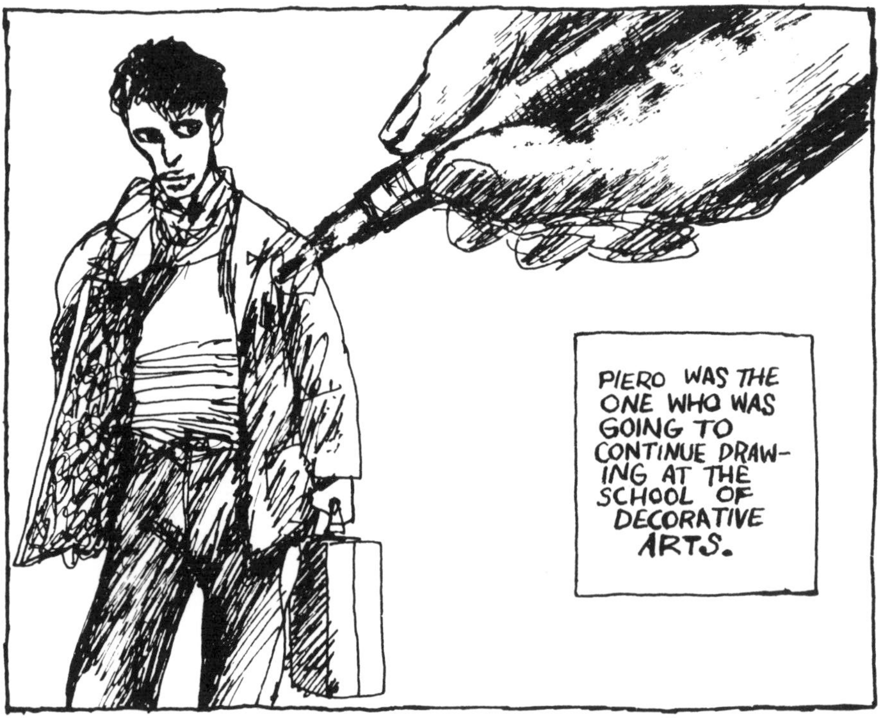
PIERO WAS THE ONE WHO WAS GOING TO CONTINUE DRAWING AT THE SCHOOL OF DECORATIVE ARTS.

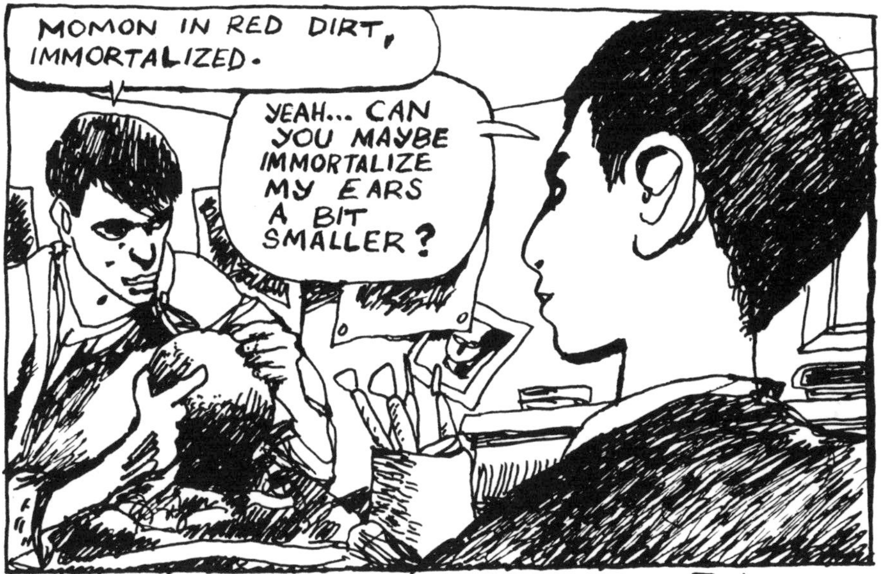
MOMON IN RED DIRT, IMMORTALIZED.
YEAH... CAN YOU MAYBE IMMORTALIZE MY EARS A BIT SMALLER?

ART SCHOOL ... I DREAMED ABOUT IT, OF COURSE. BUT WE COULDN'T BOTH GO TO A SCHOOL FOR "RICH KIDS." ONE OF US WOULD HAVE TO GET A SERIOUS CAREER. I WOULD BECOME AN ACCOUNTANT. PAPA WAS AN ACCOUNTANT.

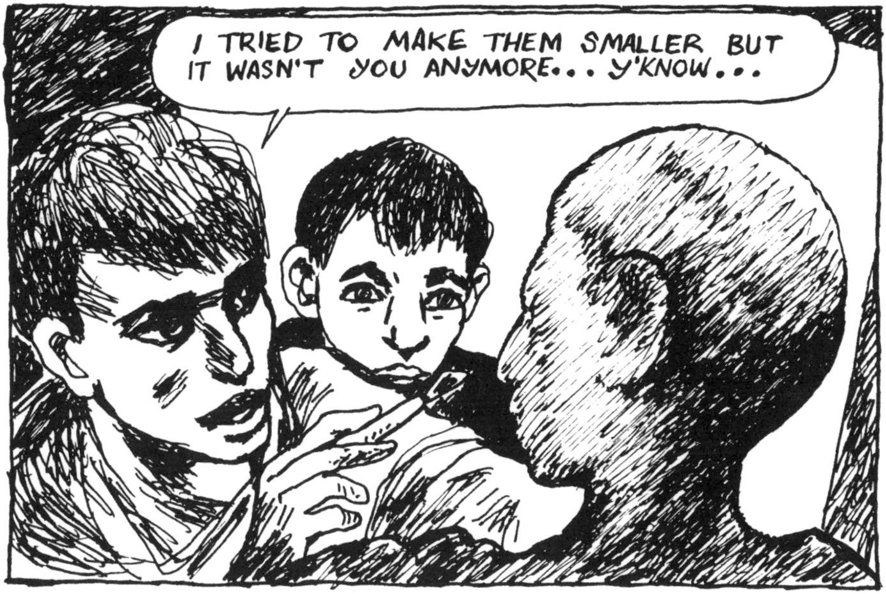
I TRIED TO MAKE THEM SMALLER BUT IT WASN'T YOU ANYMORE... Y'KNOW...

SO IT WAS PIERO WHO WAS TO BECOME AN ARTIST.

AND, IT STILL SEEMS TO ME TODAY, I WAS HAPPY IT WAS SO. SINCE MY BROTHER WAS JUST LIKE ME, I WOULD CONTINUE LIVING OUR DREAM THROUGH HIM.

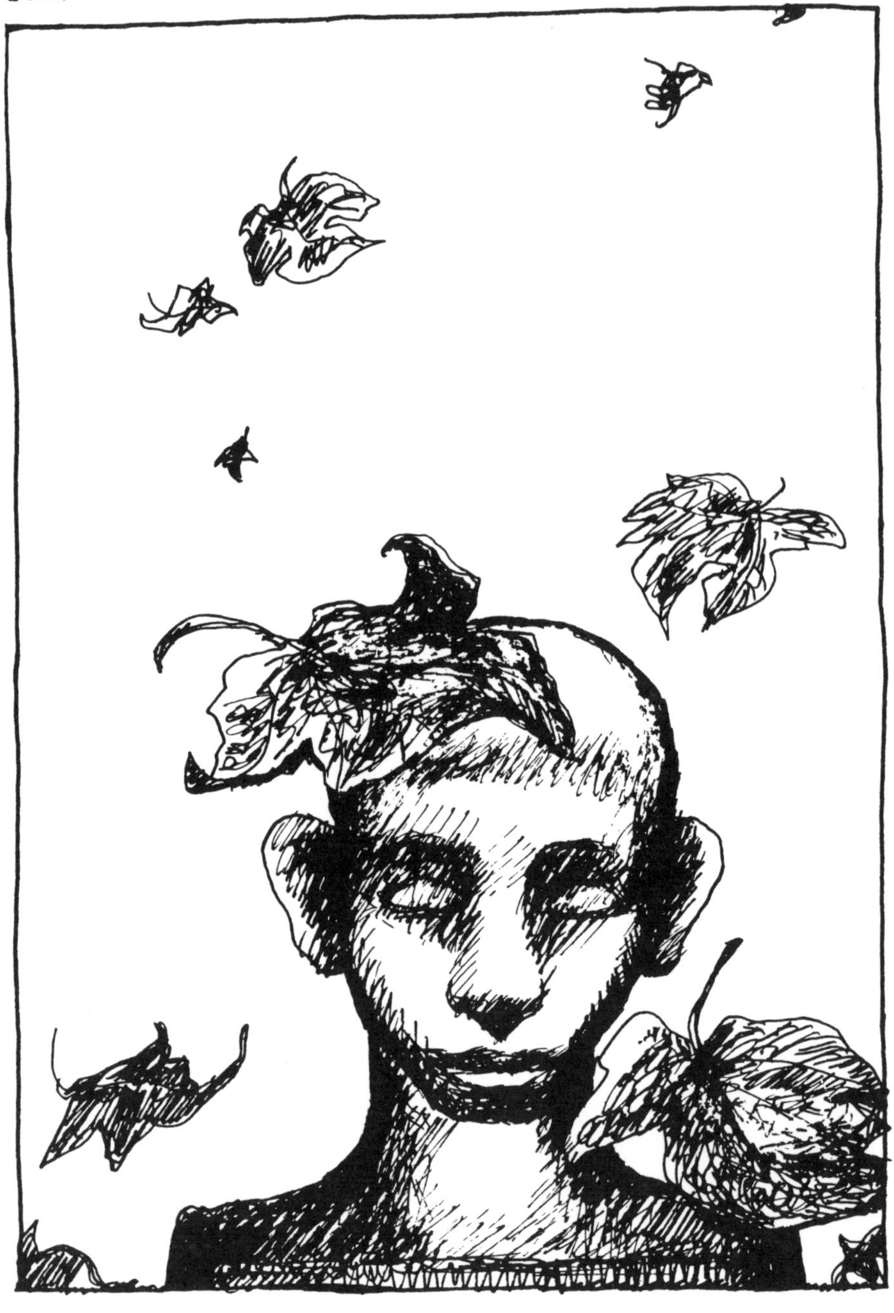

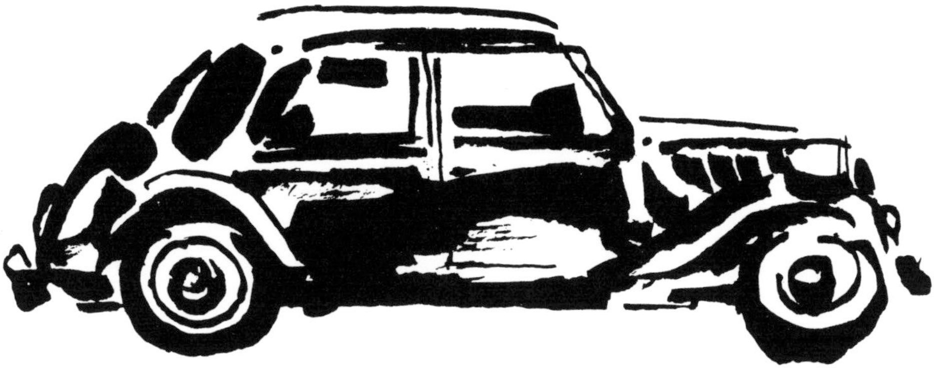

NATURALLY, PIERO WAS THE BEST STUDENT AT "ARTS DÉCO".

WHILE HE WAS AT SCHOOL, FRONT-WHEEL-DRIVE ENGINES BECAME COLLECTORS' ITEMS. THEY CALL THAT PROGRESS.

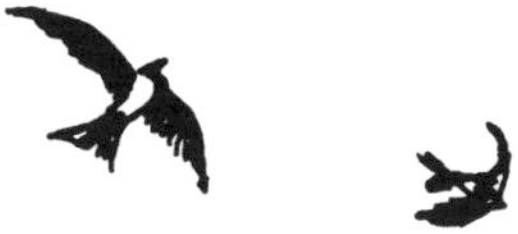

I STARTED WATCHING BIRDS AGAIN.

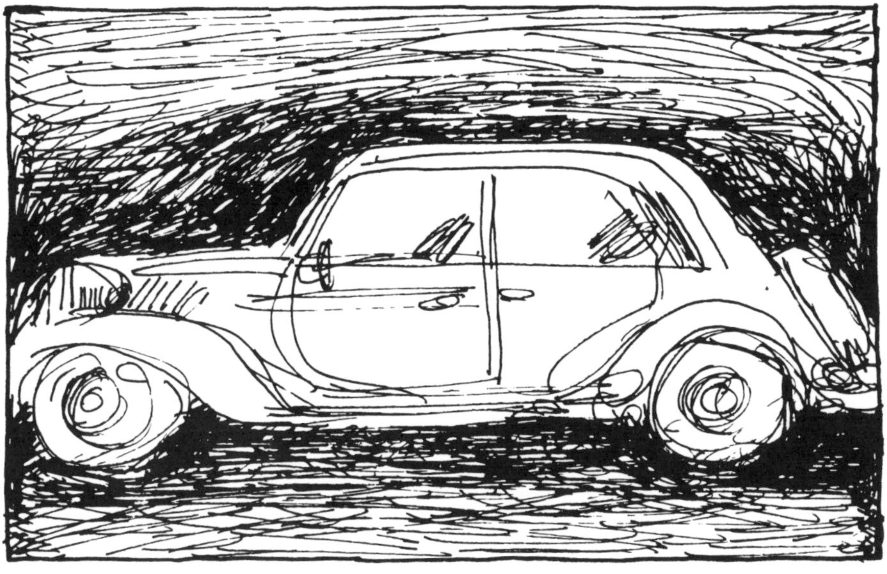

PIERO EARNED A DEGREE IN PRINTMAKING.

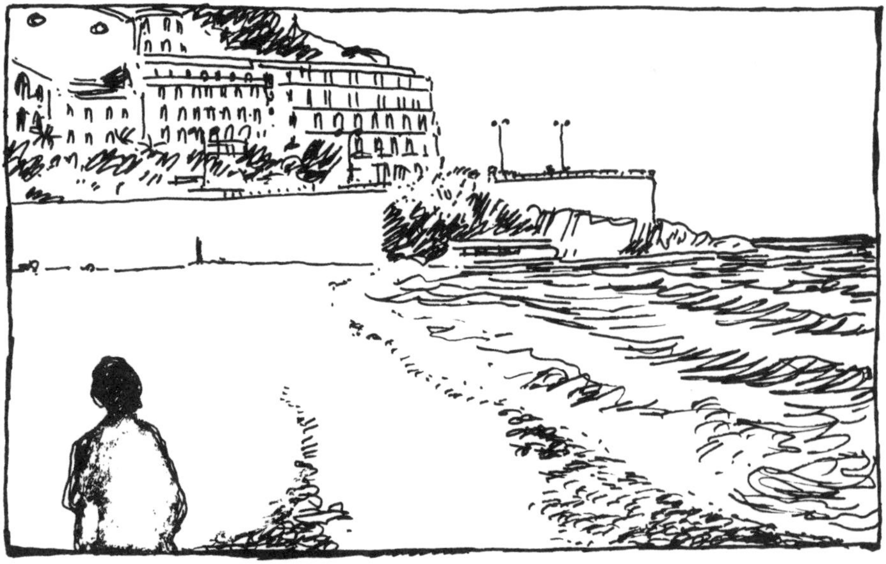

OF COURSE HE GRADUATED WITH FLYING COLORS. THE CITY OF NICE GAVE HIM A GRANT TO CONTINUE HIS STUDIES IN PARIS AT THE ACADÉMIE DES BEAUX-ARTS. HE GOT HIMSELF A ROOM AT AN ARTISTS' RESIDENCE. HE WAS WORKING TOWARDS A GRANT THAT WOULD TAKE HIM TO ROME. I WAS PROUD OF US.

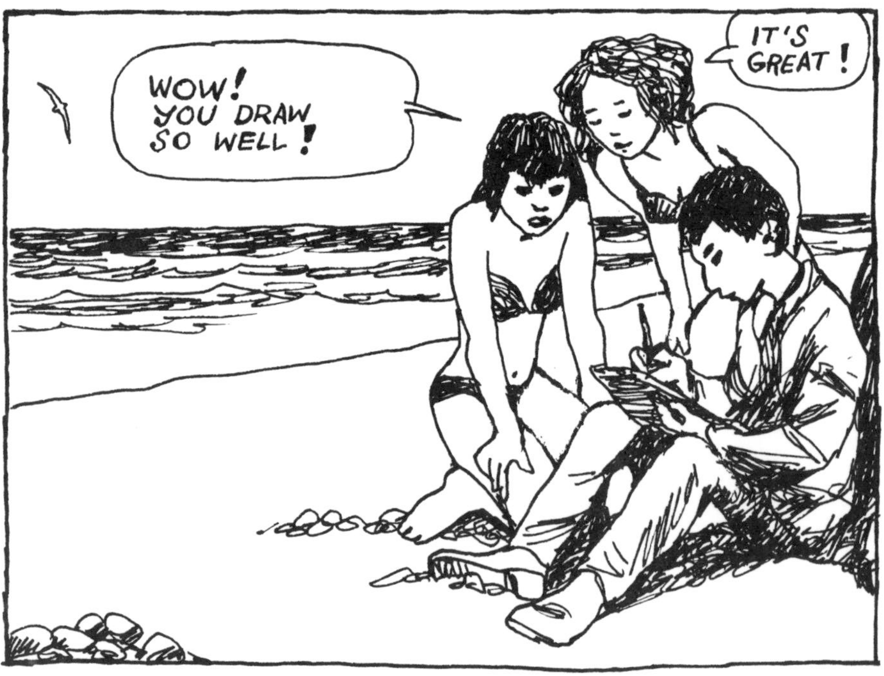
WOW! YOU DRAW SO WELL!
IT'S GREAT!

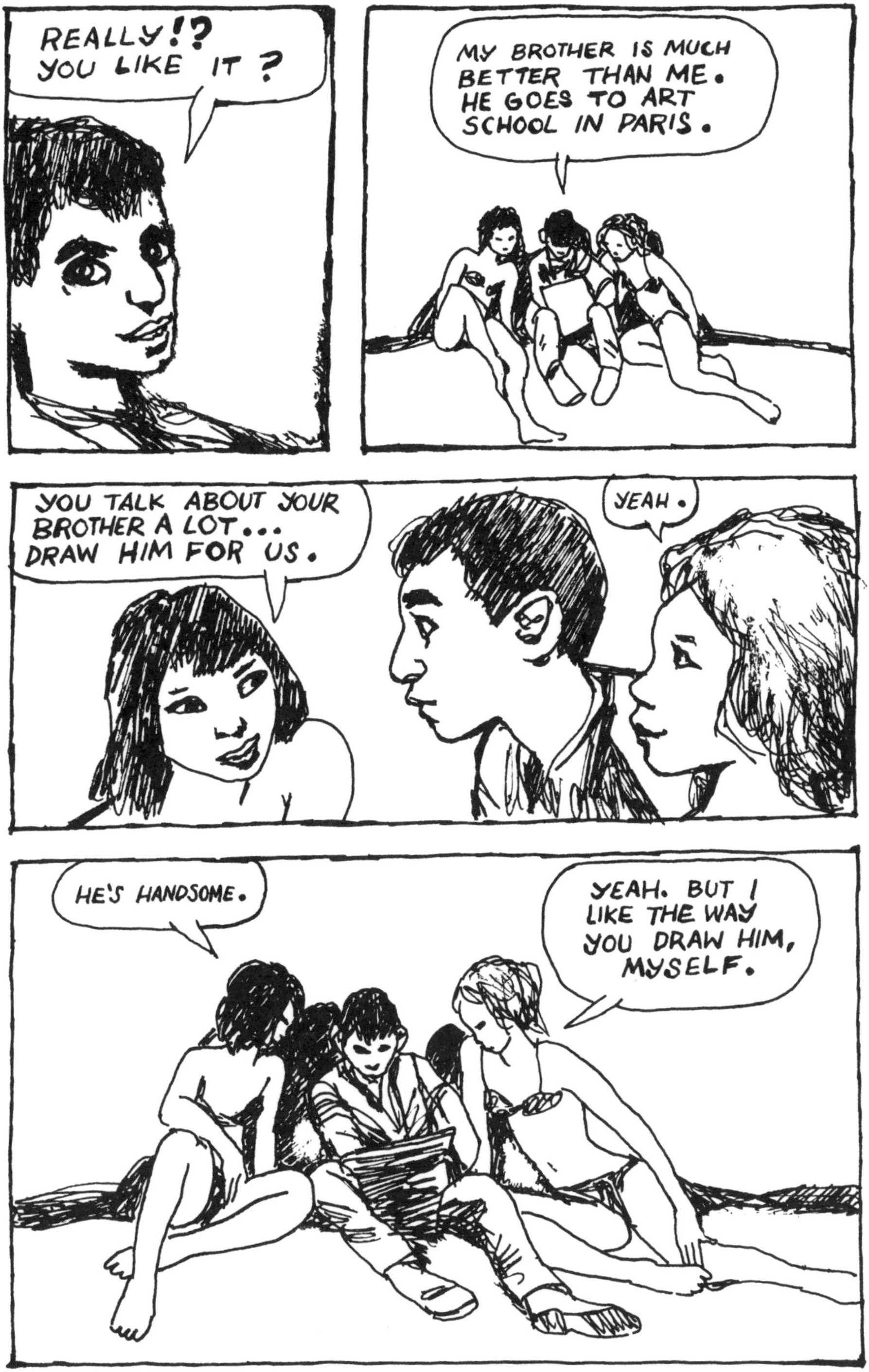
REALLY!? YOU LIKE IT?
MY BROTHER IS MUCH BETTER THAN ME. HE GOES TO ART SCHOOL IN PARIS.
YOU TALK ABOUT YOUR BROTHER A LOT... DRAW HIM FOR US.
YEAH.
HE'S HANDSOME.
YEAH. BUT I LIKE THE WAY YOU DRAW HIM, MYSELF.

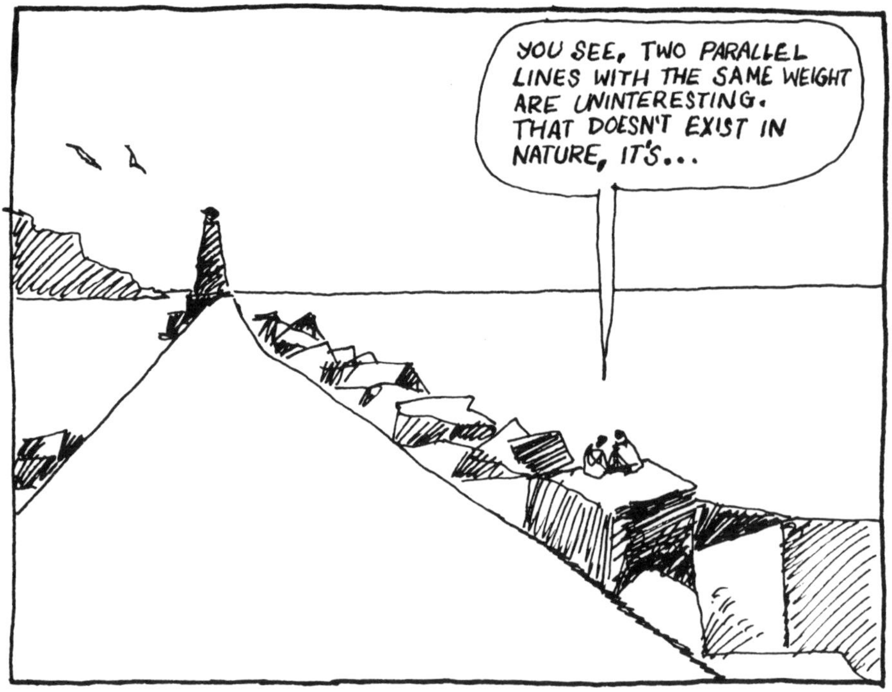
YOU SEE, TWO PARALLEL LINES WITH THE SAME WEIGHT ARE UNINTERESTING. THAT DOESN'T EXIST IN NATURE, IT'S...

WHEN PIERO CAME BACK TO NICE ON VACATION, HE WOULD TEACH ME EVERYTHING HE LEARNED AND I WOULD EAT IT UP.

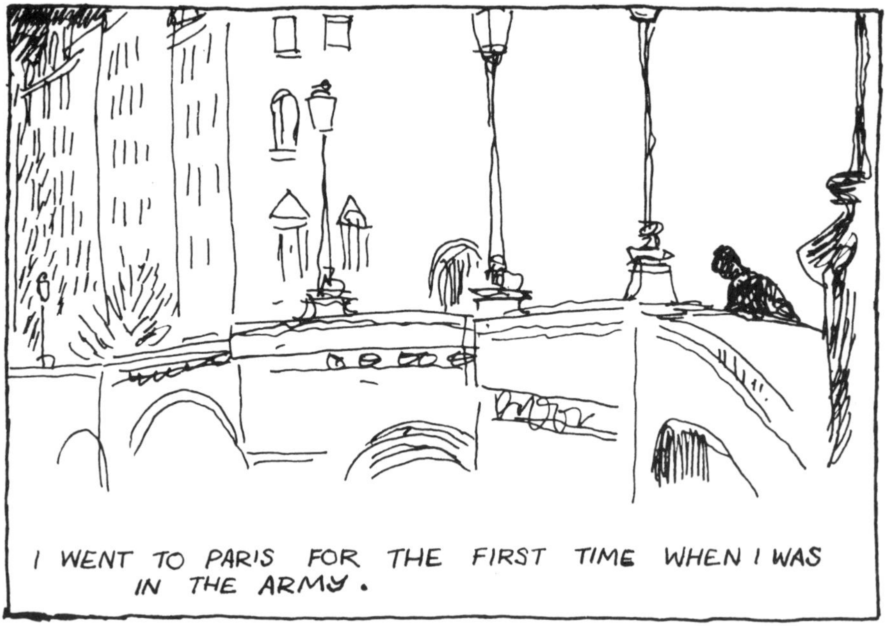
I WENT TO PARIS FOR THE FIRST TIME WHEN I WAS IN THE ARMY.

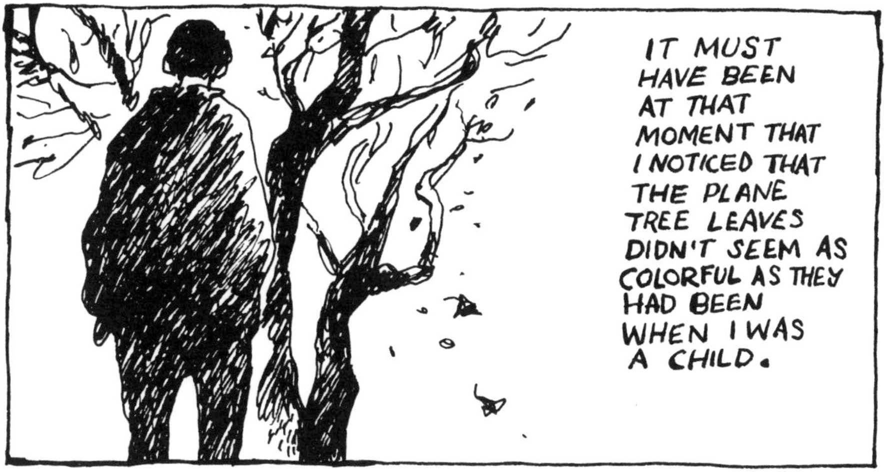
IT MUST HAVE BEEN AT THAT MOMENT THAT I NOTICED THAT THE PLANE TREE LEAVES DIDN'T SEEM AS COLORFUL AS THEY HAD BEEN WHEN I WAS A CHILD.

THEN ... I WAS AN ACCOUNTANT... THEN ...
ONE DAY PIERO CAME HOME FROM PARIS.

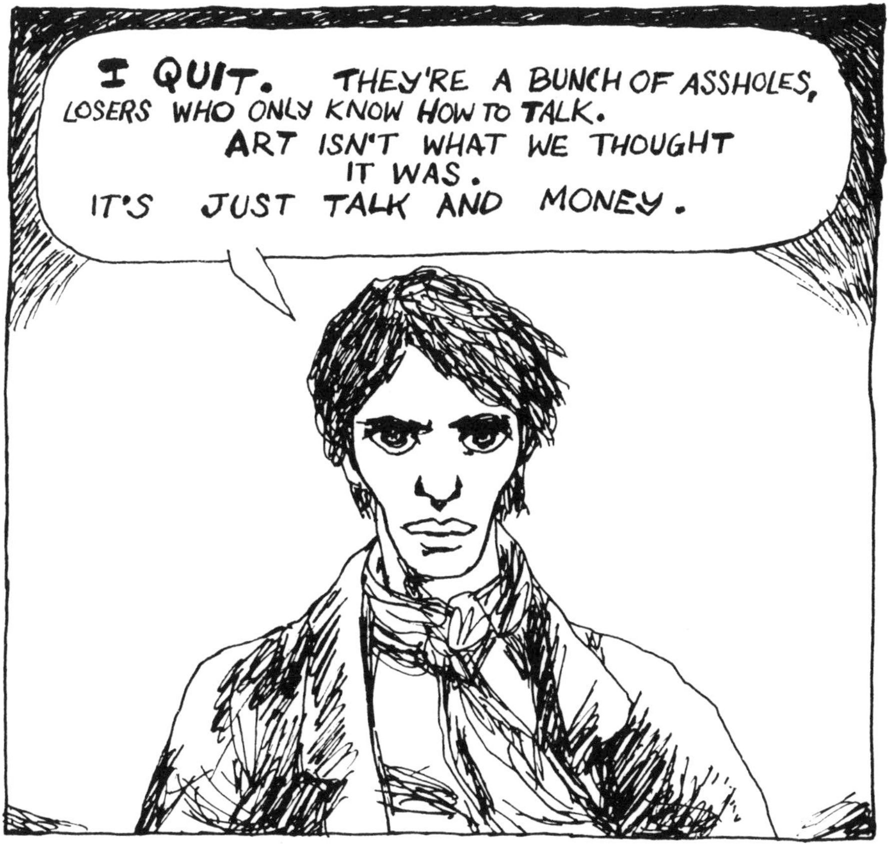
I QUIT. THEY'RE A BUNCH OF ASSHOLES, LOSERS WHO ONLY KNOW HOW TO TALK. ART ISN'T WHAT WE THOUGHT IT WAS. IT'S JUST TALK AND MONEY.

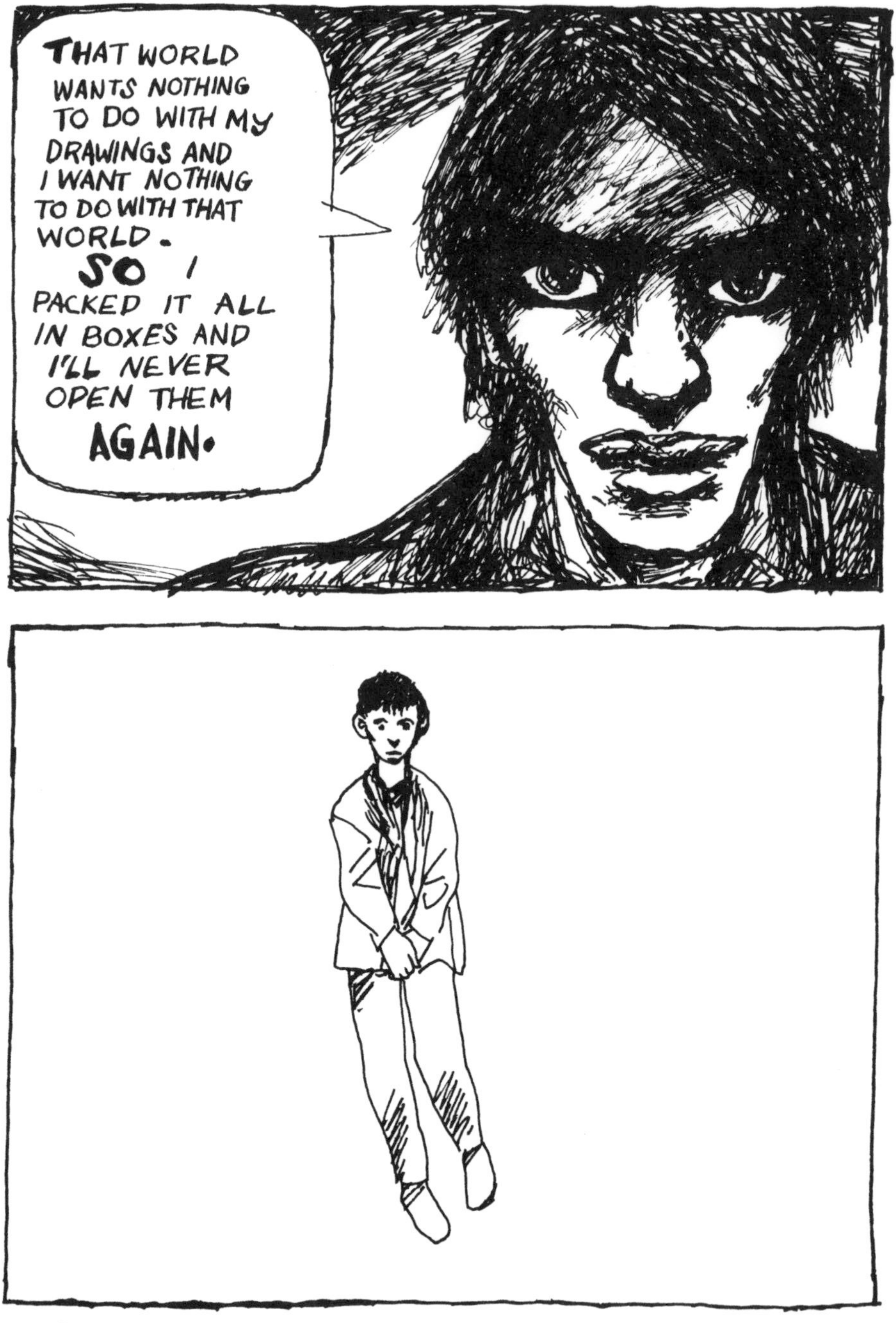
THAT WORLD WANTS NOTHING TO DO WITH MY DRAWINGS AND I WANT NOTHING TO DO WITH THAT WORLD. SO I PACKED IT ALL IN BOXES AND I'LL NEVER OPEN THEM AGAIN.
THEN... THEN ... THEN...

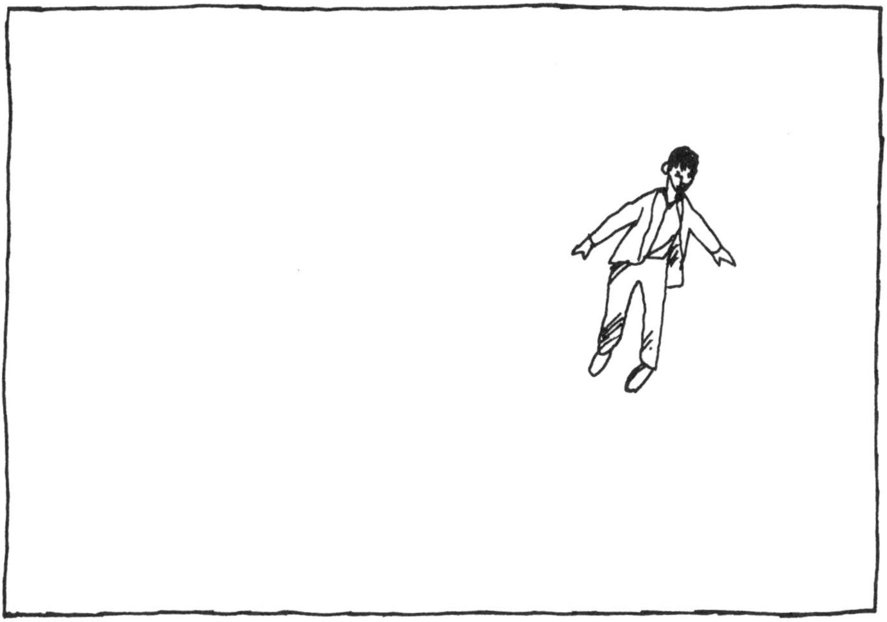

IF PIERO WAS QUITTING . . .

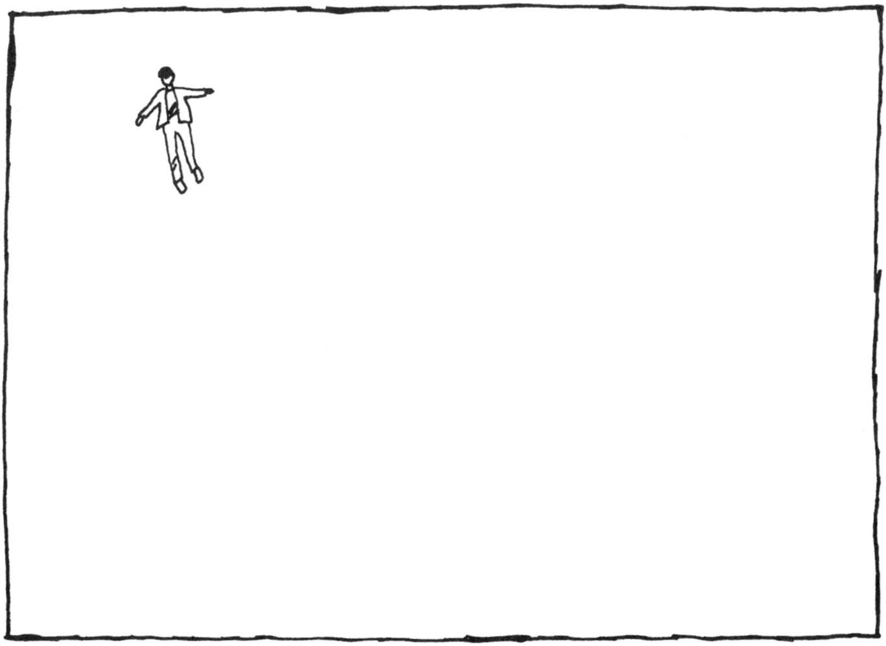

WHO WAS GOING TO KEEP DREAMING?

MAYBE PIERO MEANT IT TO HAPPEN THIS WAY...?

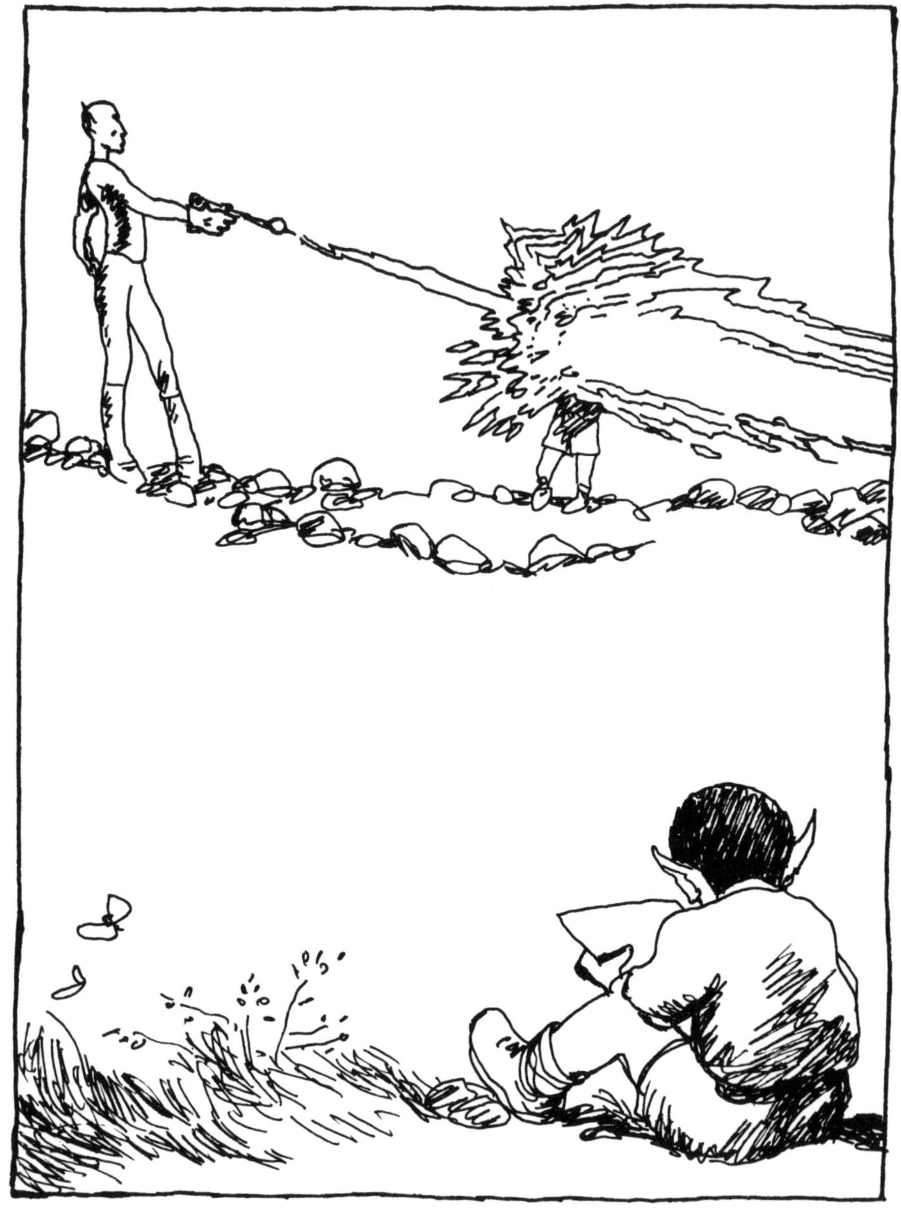

... MAYBE HE WANTED TO PASS SOMETHING ALONG TO ME, LIKE A RELAY? MY BROTHER'S EARS ARE A LITTLE POINTY, LIKE A MARTIAN'S.

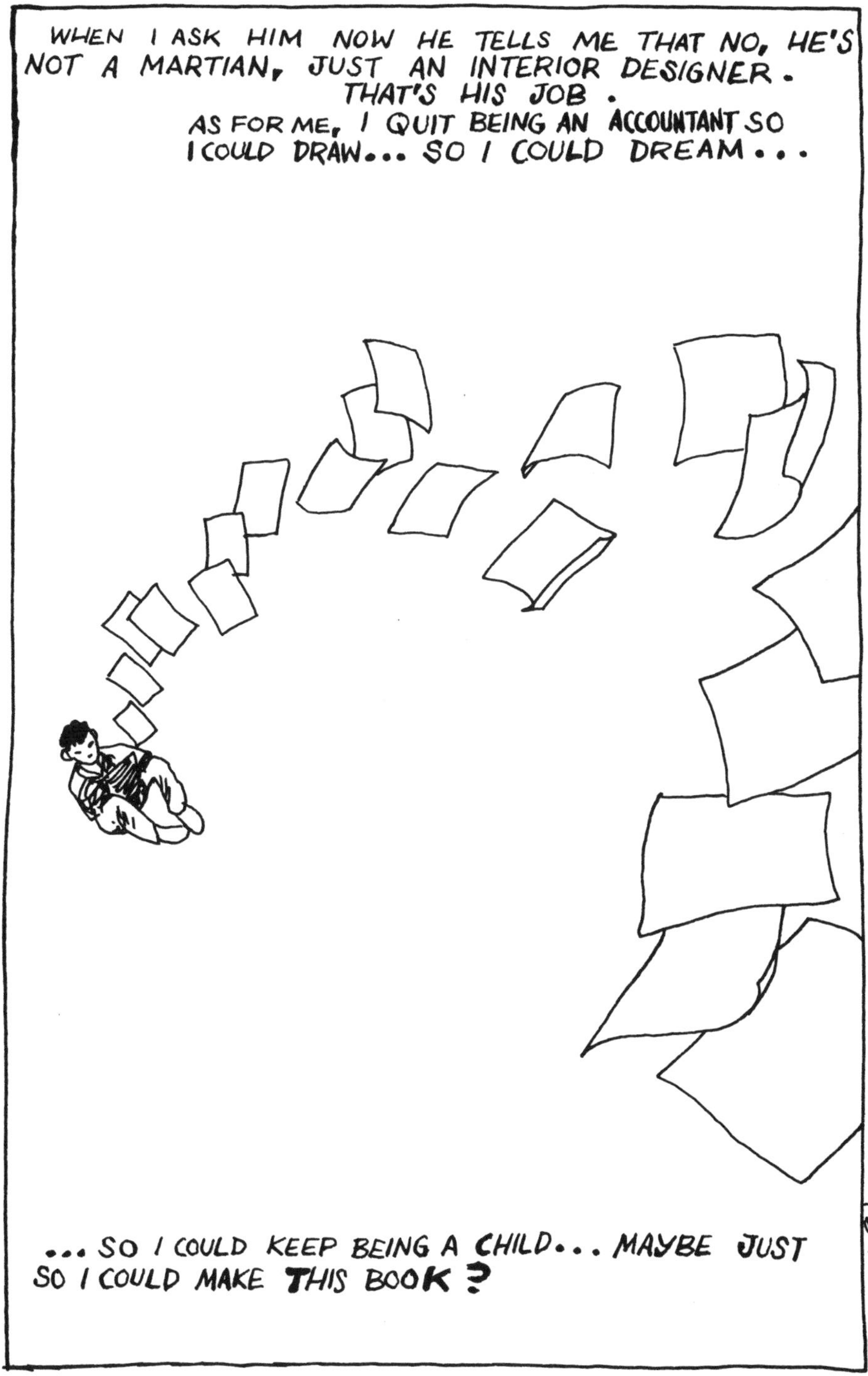
WHEN I ASK HIM NOW HE TELLS ME THAT NO, HE'S NOT A MARTIAN, JUST AN INTERIOR DESIGNER. THAT'S HIS JOB.
AS FOR ME, I QUIT BEING AN ACCOUNTANT SO I COULD DRAW... SO I COULD DREAM...
...SO I COULD KEEP BEING A CHILD... MAYBE JUST SO I COULD MAKE THIS BOOK?
BAUDOIN 97

C'est Piero
qui a
dessiné la
couverture.

Sur la photo il y avait aussi notre papa.

ALSO AVAILABLE
FROM NEW YORK REVIEW COMICS

YELLOW NEGROES AND OTHER IMAGINARY CREATURES
Yvan Alagbé

ALMOST COMPLETELY BAXTER
Glen Baxter

AGONY
Mark Beyer

PEPLUM
Blutch

THE GREEN HAND
Nicole Claveloux

WHAT AM I DOING HERE?
Abner Dean

PRETENDING IS LYING
Dominique Goblet

VOICES IN THE DARK
Ulli Lust

FATHER AND SON
E.O. Plauen

SOFT CITY
Pushwagner

THE NEW WORLD
Chris Reynolds

SLUM WOLF
Tadao Tsuge